ST JOHN'S CHAPEL

AND THE NEW TOWN

CHICHESTER

St John's Chapel, as built, with its architect, James Elmes, on the pavement outside. The elegant railings were later reduced in height and later still completely removed as part of the war effort. Picture painted in 2003 by Christopher Adams.

ST JOHN'S CHAPEL

AND THE NEW TOWN

CHICHESTER

Alan H.J. Green

PHILLIMORE

2005

Published by
PHILLIMORE & CO. LTD
Shopwyke Manor Barn, Chichester, West Sussex, England

© Alan H.J. Green, 2005

ISBN 1 86077 325 7

Printed and bound in Great Britain by
ANTONY ROWE LTD
Chippenham, Wiltshire

To my godson, Samuel

CONTENTS

List of Illustrations ix
Acknowledgements xi
Introduction xiii
List of Subscribers... xvii

1. New Town, New Church 1
2. John Marsh, a Founding Father 24
3. The Architect – James Elmes and his Chichester connections ... 27
4. Raising the Money – Raising the Chapel...................... 35
5. The Architecture of the Chapel............................. 49
6. Georgian St John's 1813-1830............................... 62
7. Victorian St John's 1831-1900.............................. 76
8. New Century at St John's 1901-1945 96
9. St John's: Struggle for Survival 1946-1973................. 106
10. Completing Newtown 1831-2000.............................. 120
11. Commercial Newtown.. 133
12. St John's – Recession and Restoration 149

Postscript I The St John's Trustees today 155
Postscript II The Churches Conservation Trust................. 156

APPENDICES
A The Act of Parliament – Summary of Provisions............... 157
B List of Incumbents 159
C Organ Specifications 160
D The Chapel Plate 162

Notes... 163
Index... 169

LIST OF ILLUSTRATIONS

Frontispiece: St John's Chapel 1813 by Christopher Adams, 2003

1. Chichester Town Plan, 1769 2
2. Garton Orme, aged 11. 3
3. Cover of 1808 sale particulars for Black Friars site 7
4. Sale lots for 1808 and 1811 sales 8
5. Title page of the St John's Act 1812 10
6. Extract from 1812 Chichester Town Plan 12
7. Dial of longcase clock by Henry Fogden. 13
8. Houses in New Town (the street) looking west 14
9. Friary Close, west front 16
10. Extract from 1820 Chichester Town Plan 18
11. 11 to 14 St John's Street. 22
12. James Elmes, portrait by James Lonsdale, 1820 28
13. Sussex Central Boys' School. 29
14. Oakwood, west front 30
15. Sennicotts, east front 31
16. Chichester Cathedral from the north, 1811. 32
17. Cheque from Trustees to James Elmes, 1811 36
18. Trowel used to lay the foundation stone 39
19. Notice advising forthcoming sale and rental of pews. .42
20. West front of the Chapel, 1910 50
21. East end of the Chapel in 1971. 51
22. Elmes' ground floor plan of Chapel 52
23. Interior of the Chapel in 1871 54
24. The painted panels over the Communion Table 56
25. Elmes' colour-washed transverse-section drawing of the Chapel. 57
26. The gallery as it is today 58
27. One of the gallery sliding doors in its undressed state. 59
28. Surviving pneumatic gas switch 61
29. Hogarth engraving – *The industrious 'prentice performing the duty of a Christian* 63
30. Floor plan of St Pancras, 1780. 67
31. Hogarth engraving – *The sleeping congregation* 69
32. The Rev. Stephen Barbut. 79
33. Tablet commemorating Douglas Henty's gift of new pews 86
34. Cover of *St John's Magazine*, 1880. 89

35. Cover of order of service commemorating rebuilding of the organ in 1898 94
36. Monument to Rev. J.H. Monti 97
37. The Trustees' Minute Book 1903 to 1985 98
38. St John's decorated for harvest festival in 1923 101
39. Interior of Chapel in 1943 looking east 103
40. The Communion table and rails in 1943 104
41. Interior of St John's in 1971 looking west 112
42. St John's Sunday School party 1955 114
43. A St John's choir list for October 1962 115
44. View from gallery in 1971 looking east 118
45. The Pastoral Scheme for redundancy, 1973 119
46. Newtown in 1896 from 1:2500 O.S. map 121
47. 8 St John's Street 122
48. Rear of 8 St John's Street in the 1930s 123
49. Exterior of St John's Chapel in 1871 126
50. Corner of East Street and St John's Street in 1919 127
51. 19 & 20 St John's Street 128
52. 7 St John's Street 129
53. 1 to 2 Friary Lane 131
54. Letter addressed to 1 Friary Lane Newtown 132
55. Invoice heading for William Johnson, builder of St John's Street. 133
56. View of East Street, c.1908 137
57. Advertisement for A.T. Humphrys' Chichester Motor Works. 138
58. Corn Exchange New Corn Store 139
59. Panoramic view of Moore & Tillyer's printing works, 1974. 139
60. Interior of Moore & Tillyer's printing works 140
61. Walter Stride in 1937 142
62. Advertisement for Clydesdale House School, 1894. 143
63. Maria Apedaile, dame school proprietor. 144
64. Advertisement for St John's School, 1936. 145
65. Dr Gough in the garden at 8 St John's Street 146
66. West front of St John's in 1971 148
67. Restoration work in progress, March 2003. 153
68. The interior of St John's following the 2003 restoration 154
69. The organ in 1910. 161
70. The two silver-gilt communion cups. 162

Endpiece: Portrait bust of Lt General Sir John Gustavus Crosbie

Acknowledgements

In many respects the writing of the acknowledgements is more difficult than scribing the whole of the text since, having been assisted by so many people, the risk of omitting someone is very high. So, if I *have* omitted anyone I crave their forgiveness and assure them that it is owing to oversight rather than ingratitude!

Thanks have to start with the ever-patient and helpful staff of the West Sussex Record Office, where the bulk of the research was carried out, and to the St John's Trustees for the loan of the second minute book and other archive material. The Churches Conservation Trust, who now own St John's, gave much encouragement and access to their archives as did Louise Bainbridge, the Conservation Architect who directed the 2003 restoration. The staff at Chichester District Museum were particularly helpful in granting me access to *Chichester Directories* and the bound copies of the *St John's Magazine* in their collections and I am particularly grateful to Simon Kitchin for sharing his knowledge of Chichester businesses and redirecting my researches when I became derailed. Chichester Freemasons kindly supplied the photograph of the trowel used in laying the foundation stone of St John's and gave other information regarding the early links between their Lodge and the Chapel. Victor Hoare and Rev. John McKechnie kindly supplied shared recollections of their respective associations with St John's and The Dean and Chapter gave permission to photograph the chapel plate; I am particularly grateful to Michael Moriarty who made access to it possible. Pat Dearling provided much useful information about the Georgian Dearlings and pointed out the family's Baptist roots. Noel Osborne provided information about the St John's Chapel Group and his St Richards Singers concerts which began the St John's revival.

For the domestic history of Newtown I have had assistance from an even wider audience and I am particularly grateful to those Newtown residents who granted me access to their houses and, where possible, allowed me to peruse the title deeds: the late Joy Woolley, Susan Stevenson-Hamilton, Bea and the late John Andrews, Keith and Deborah Michelson, Barbara Stride, Brian and Majella Taylor, Kathleen Read, Rod and Margaret Hurst and

Chichester Chiropractors. Personal recollections of Newtown were given by Christine Kimble and Ian Kimble (particularly regarding Miss Aipedale's and St John's Schools) Mary Hill (née Gough) and John Gough regarding their father's medical practice and for supplying the verbatim account of the crash of the Liberator bomber, Fred Atkey for details of the Atkey family and Kathleen Stephens and my mother, Kathleen Green, for their recollections. The manager of the Chichester Branch of the Red Cross Society kindly granted me access to the Gruggen memorial in All Saints Church and also supplied information about the other Gruggen memorials which have long been lost and the Headmaster of Oakwood School permitted photography of the school building, formerly William Dearling's house.

In researching the Newtown businesses I am indebted to Claire Holder, manager of Moore and Tillyer, and her father Derek Tillyer for information about and photographs of the Regnum Press and similarly to Nick Stride of Stride and Sons in respect of his family business. Ray Oliver of the St John Ambulance Brigade kindly supplied information about the discharge of the bequest of Dr Barford of 8 St John's Street to the Knights of St John and Dr Martin Collins filled in the gaps in my researches into the Langley House practice which was founded in St John's Street.

For the artworks included in the text I am grateful to Tom McHale of Chichester Gallery for procuring the painting of the Chapel by Christopher Adams which adorns the cover and to Chris himself who so faithfully interpreted my complicated specification for this commission; also to the Trustees of the Holburne Museum in Bath for permission to include the portrait of Garton Orme.

Finally my thanks to my friend Chris Bryan for his encouragement in reading some of the early drafts, discovering some important pieces of Chichester information with references to Newtown people and also for permitting me to photograph his Fogden clock.

ILLUSTRATION ACKNOWLEDGEMENTS

Author's collection, frontispiece, 7-9, 11, 14-16, 24, 26-9, 31, 33, 36-7, 51-3, 58, 67-8, 70; Chichester District Museum, 34, 50, 57, 62, 64; Chichester Freemasons: 18; Kathleen Green Collection, 42, 54; Mary Hill Collection, 47-8, 65; The Trustees of the Holburne Museum of Art, Bath, 2; Christine Kimble Collection, 63; Moore and Tillyer Archive, 56, 59, 60; OS, 46; RCHM, 21, 39, 40-1, 44, 66; RIBA, 12; St John's Trustees, 35, 43; Stride and Sons, 61; West Sussex Record Office, 1, 3-6, 10, 13, 17, 19-20, 22-3, 25, 30, 32, 38, 45, 49, 55.

INTRODUCTION

Chichester is a quintessentially Georgian city much visited by architectural historians and occupying no fewer than 58 pages in the Sussex volume of *The Buildings of England* by Ian Nairn and Nikolaus Pevsner. One building which is a 'must' for any visit to Chichester is the Grade 1-listed Chapel of St John the Evangelist. Opened in 1813, to the designs of James Elmes, it was built as an Anglican proprietary chapel in order to overcome the acute shortage of accommodation within the city's churches. A proprietary chapel, unlike a parish church, had to be run by its Trustees as a commercial enterprise, paying dividends to the shareholders, raising the necessary monies to pay the minister's and organist's salaries and maintaining the building. It closed in 1973 and is now in the care of the Churches Conservation Trust.

Newtown was the last area within the city walls to be newly developed in Georgian times on the site of the former Dominican Friary (the Black Friars). Intended to be a *New Town* of grand houses for the professional classes it was a classic example of a Georgian development, involving curious (and probably shady) deals between Chichester's main entrepreneurs as they vied with each other to make the most from their investments. The *New Town* provided the ideal site for the new Chapel and many of Chichester's wealthy names were associated with both projects but, unlike Somerstown to the north of the city, it failed to meet the developers' expectations in Georgian times. This book sets out to tell the story of St John's, its architect James Elmes and his Chichester connections, and the development of Newtown. It also tells of the vicissitudes which beset the Trustees in their strivings to make the Chapel a viable commercial concern.

So why should *I* be writing this book? Well, at the end of the Second World War my parents moved to Chichester from Eartham, renting a tiny cottage in Newtown at No 1 Friary Lane, and it was into this family home that I was born in 1950. When my maternal grandmother came from Wales to live with us a move to a larger house was necessitated, so we 'upped sticks' to Orchard Street in 1952. However, the family connection which had been made with St John's Chapel continued.

In the 1950s my two elder sisters and I would be packed off to St John's twice a Sunday; Morning Prayer and Sunday School, then Sunday School again in the afternoon. Whether this double dose was entirely in the interests of our spiritual well-being or partly to ensure that peace reigned in the house (father liked his Sunday afternoon nap) I remain uncertain, but go twice we did. As I sat there in the pews in my short-trousered, Sunday-best suit gazing up at that curious three-decker pulpit, little did I think that one day I would be speaking from the top of it, not as a preacher but telling the Chapel's history. Even less did I think that I would be writing a book about it. The fact was at that time I did not really *like* St John's as a building. I was already a compulsive reader and from encyclopaedias I had deduced that churches should be built of stone, have soaring columns and pointed arches, be lit by stained glass windows and be dark and mysterious – a view which was confirmed by visits to the Cathedral. St John's, in all its Georgian simplicity, was none of this – it was built of brick, devoid of arches and its round-headed, clear windows flooded the interior with light.

Around 1961 we changed our allegiances to St Peter the Great in West Street, a Victorian pile by R.C. Carpenter which had a robed choir, musical tradition, an even better Sunday School and, to my ten-year-old mind, was a *proper* church having all the features that I found so lacking at St John's. It is strange how tastes change for in adulthood I turned to despise the Victorians and virtually all they stood for and developed a passion for the Georgian era and its elegant understatement in matters architectural and artistic. By that time St John's had closed its doors, apparently for good, and the lack of access was frustrating since I was now in a position to appreciate it for what it was – and *why* it was.

Since St John's reopened to the public I have made it the centrepiece of my annual *Georgian Chichester* walk during the Chichester Festivities and, becoming acquainted with Nigel Bowers the custodian and the work of the Churches Conservation Trust, my interest in it deepened. In 2002 I volunteered to open the chapel for Heritage Open Days on behalf of the Trust and give hourly guided tours. Prior to this I needed to do some historical research; a day in the West Sussex Record Office not only provided more than enough material to fill a 45-minute tour but also showed just how vast the amount of material held there both on St John's and on Newtown. Francis Steer, the then County Archivist, had written a booklet in the *Chichester Papers* series[*] in 1963, to mark the 150th anniversary of St John's, which remained the seminal work on the subject. Well researched, it was all-too brief, did not benefit from the first-hand recording of events contained in the John Marsh diaries (of which he was apparently unaware) and, of course, only went down to 1963 at which time the chapel was still in use.

In writing this history I have started from scratch but have relied on Francis Steer's scholarship for the biographical details of the ministers. The starting point is the two volumes of the Minutes of the Trustees' meetings. Written by hand in bound books, these tell the story of the Trustees'

---

[*] CP 35 *The Church of St John the Evangelist Chichester, 1813-1963.*

struggles, or rather part of the story, for up to the 1950s the entries are tantalisingly brief and selective. The fact that they closed the Chapel in 1871 is not recorded, nor is the fact that the windows were blown out – or rather in – when an American Liberator bomber crashed nearby in 1944! Fortunately most of the missing parts of the story could be fleshed out from the multitudinous other sources available and from the recollections of people I interviewed.

I hope that I have been able to provide the reader with a complete history of St John's and also to give for the first time the history of Newtown, that overlooked corner of the city in which the Chapel is situated. Both have fascinating stories to tell.

Chichester, January 2005

LIST OF SUBSCRIBERS

Clare Apel
Louise Bainbridge, RIBA
Mrs J.F.T. Banks
Caroline Beauvois
Peter James Belcher
Walter Benzie
Andrew Berriman
Nigel Bowers, Chapel Custodian
Paul Bradley
Nigel C. Brown
Dr Ronnie Brown
Roy Brundle
Christopher and Rosemary Bryan
Jane Burnell
Pat and Rodney Chambers
Henry Chetwynd-Stapylton,
    B. Arch, ARIBA, FRSA
The Churches Conservation Trust
David Coles
Patrick D. Combes
Martin Cooke
Pat Cowan
Monica Cowell
Joy Crawshaw
M.G.F. Darby
Mrs M.H.L. Davey
Rosemary Dawe
Patricia Dearling
Pete Dennis - DTM Consulting
Mr and Mrs M. Eades
Mrs Jill A. Farrance

Stephen Fawcett
Barry and Rachel Fletcher
Peter David Fogden
Anthony Freeman
Mr Charles J. Gauntlett
Harry W. Gillespie
Mr M. Goodchild of Chichester
Mr and Mrs John Goss
John Gostling
Cllr Mrs Valerie Gostling
Allan Roy Gough
Ian Graham-Jones
Mrs K.J. Green
Ken and Sheila Green
Michael Harlock
June Hawkins
Mrs Ian Henderson
Tim Heymann
Michael M. Heywood
Mr and Mrs Adrian Higham
Peter Hiley
Ione Hill
I.H. Hodgson
Mr and Mrs J.E. Hooker
Andrew Housden
Mr R.P.F. Hughes
John Hurd
Rodney and Margaret Hurst
Joan and Roy Jackson
Roger Keyworth
Patrick Lacey

Garry Long
Dr Philip MacDougall
John Morrish
Ronald F. Norman
Noel Osborne
Joan Peerman
David J. Pilbeam
Nicholas M. Plumley
John Rank
Colin E. Reid
Adge Roberts
Sarah A. Russell
John Sainsbury
Jack Saunders
Barbara Scott
Patricia Sharp
Godfrey Shirt
David J. Siggs
A.M. Elizabeth Sinclair

Brian and Sarah Skilling
Greg and Katherine Slay
John R. Smith
Mrs Pamela Smith
Martin Snow
Susan Casher Soffe
Angela Softley
Dr John J.G. Springard
Mrs Susan Stevenson-Hamilton
David Stuckey
Alan Thurlow
Jim and Ann Tice
Brian K. Turbefield
Dr M. Turner
John E. Vigar
John and Diana Welland
West Sussex Record Office
Captain P.H. Wright

One

New Town – New Church

Although the New Town and St John's Chapel date from the early 19th century their story begins at the Dissolution of the Monasteries by Henry VIII. There were two friaries in Chichester, the Grey Friars in the north-east quadrant, the site now occupied by Priory Park, and the Black Friars in the south-east. It is with the latter establishment that we are concerned. Blackfriars was seized by the King, sold to one Edward Mylett in 1539 and the whole site became the estate of a large mansion house on the corner of East Street and Baffins Lane – and was to remain so for 270 years.

From an abstract of title for a plot of land in St John's Street[1] the complicated account of ownership in the 17th and 18th centuries, which sets the scene for the creation of the New Town, can be derived. In 1646 ownership of the site was split into moieties* and sold by Edward Hanchett of Westminster, Judith Elyott taking one part and Roger Heath and William Ellis of Gray's Inn jointly taking the other. The abstract of title describes the estate, sold for £180, as including:

> the backsides, gardens, orchards, barns, stables, malthouses, brew-houses, pigeon houses and other edifices, buildings, gates, lands.

On 3 August 1649 Judith Fish (as Judith Elyott had become) signed an indenture making over her moiety to John Bannister and received a covenant from Messrs Heath and Ellis, the other moiety holders, to allow for Bannister's *peaceful enjoyment* of his investment. Twenty-four years later, on 13 October 1673, an indenture was drawn up between Mary Bannister (presumably John Bannister's widow) and Francis Page for one fourth of the premises for which Page paid £200. However Francis Page died intestate and the moiety passed to his eldest son Edward, who also (rather carelessly) died intestate and so it passed in turn to his eldest son John. By 1739 ownership of the Heath-Ellis moiety had passed to one Garton Orme of Woolavington near Midhurst. Orme (1689-1745) was a doubtful character reputed to have killed his first wife and who incurred considerable debts which necessitated his selling half his property.[2] A portrait of him aged 11,

---

* A now-archaic legal term for 'halves' – but rarely exact 'halves'.

1

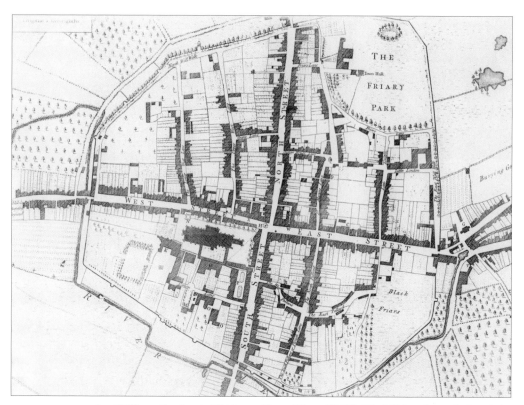

1   *William Gardner's Chichester Town Plan of 1769. Black Friars is marked and the area of the former friary can be clearly seen along with the first mansion house in the north-west corner of the site. The Grey Friars site has now become 'The Friary Park'.*

sitting at a spinet, was painted by Jonathan Richardson Snr (see Fig 2) in which he looks the picture of charm and innocence with no hint as to how he would turn out in later life!

Orme sold his moiety interest for £200 in October 1739 to one Sarah Tutte and, typically perhaps, persuaded her to lend him £100 at the same time to which she agreed, the arrangement being acknowledged in an endorsement to the indenture. As the deposited documents are property deeds we do not know whether Orme repaid his loan but with his reputation we can probably guess the answer. The description of the property now also includes – hop grounds, meadows, pastures and feedings. In November 1739 this moiety was made over to John Page who paid £300 12s. 9d. to Sarah Tutte and £59 7s. 3d. to Orme. John Page, who was MP for Chichester, now owned the lease on the whole of the Blackfriars estate. John Page was a wealthy man, lord of the manor of Donnington, and in 1756 he also acquired Barnham Manor,[3] a fine early 17th-century red-brick house built in the Dutch manner and closely resembling Kew Palace.

In January 1779 John Page died and was buried in Donnington Church where, in the Trinity Chapel, he is commemorated by a fine neo-classical

2 *Garton Orme, aged 11, pictured at the spinet by Jonathan Richardson.*

marble sarcophagus. An inscription on the end of the sarcophagus records
that it had been provided in 1780 by his daughters, Catherine and Frances
Page, to whom the Page estate had jointly passed. Katherina[*] died in 1788
leaving her interest in the Page estate to her sister Frances[4] with the proviso

---

[*] Although given as 'Catherine' on the sarcophagus, the indentures for the estate give the elder sister's
(official) name as 'Katherina' – perhaps she found it too exotic for everyday use!

that when she in turn died it would pass on to her daughter – i.e. Katherina's niece. Frances Page had now become Frances White-Thomas by virtue of her marriage to George White-Thomas, an MP and the then lord of the manor of Donnington, and they lived at Donnington Manor. George had inherited Donnington Manor from his father John White[5] who made his fortune as a plantation owner on the island of St Christopher in the West Indies and thus part of the White-Thomas fortune derives from the slave trade. Frances White-Thomas's daughter was also (confusingly) called Frances and in 1802 she, Frances White-Thomas the younger, married the splendidly-named Col. John Gustavus Crosbie of Funtington, an act which was to sow the seeds for the beginning of the New Town venture, as we shall see later.

Turning now to matters ecclesiastical we need to look at the state of the Anglican church in Chichester in the early 18th century. The city, as delineated by the Roman walls, was polygonal and roughly half a mile in diameter and was served by no fewer than six small parish churches as well as the Cathedral itself. These churches were St Peter the Great (which had been housed in the north transept of the cathedral since 1075), St Peter the Less, St Andrew's, St Olave's, St Martin's and All Saints.[*] Outside the walls there had been two more churches, St Bartholomew's in West Gate and St Pancras in East Gate, but both had been destroyed in the Civil War. Curiously none of these parish churches came under the direct control of the Bishop of Chichester, being instead peculiars of the Dean of Chichester, save that is for All Saints which was a peculiar of the Archbishop of Canterbury – a *peculiar* peculiar! This remained the case until 1845 when their status was changed.

The population of Chichester began to expand in the early 18th century and by 1720 was around 3,500 souls. The small churches could not provide the necessary accommodation for all those who wished to attend Divine Service, a problem which had been exacerbated by the aforementioned losses of St Bartholomew's and St Pancras. In 1723 Dean Sherlock put forward a proposal to abolish the city-centre churches under his jurisdiction and to combine them under one roof in a brand-new building and so drew up a petition for presentation to Parliament.[6] This petition required the prior approval of the Corporation of Chichester. Naturally the proposal to pull down their churches generated much heat when it was debated by the respective clergy and congregations and they all duly complained to the Corporation who decided to reject the petition. In the face of this resistance Dean Sherlock abandoned the idea but the problem did not go away – problems rarely do.

St Pancras Church, which was later to play a major part in the St John's story, is first recorded in 1291 in the taxation of Pope Nicholas.[7] It led a fairly quiet life adjacent to the East Gate until 1642 when the Civil War broke out. Chichester was divided in its loyalties, with the gentry and clergy

---

[*] All these churches have long-since closed. St Peter the Great transferred to a large new church across the road in 1852 known as the Sub-Deanery but this closed in 1979. St Martin's and St Peter the Less have been demolished but the others remain in alternative uses.

supporting the King whilst the remainder of the populace, led by the MP William Cawley, were for Parliament. In November 1642 Royalists had managed to gain local control of the city so in December troops under the command of William Waller were sent by Parliament to take the city back. The troops first captured the vulnerable parishes of St Bartholomew and St Pancras and at the latter besieged the church and used its tower as a battery from which to bombard the East Gate. After seven days of bombardment the Royalists surrendered and on 29 December Parliament gained control. As a token of his gratitude for the strategic advantage St Pancras Church had given him, Waller destroyed it and it was not to be rebuilt for over one hundred years, the congregation being dispersed to the other city churches although the Rector remained in office.

In 1750, spurred on by the growing shortage of church accommodation, a scheme was launched to rebuild St Pancras and generous benefactors included the Countess of Derby (£400), the Duke of Richmond (£105) and Elizabeth Prowlett (£100). Not to be outdone the Dean (Dean Ashburnham) contributed £25. The rest of the £804 11s. 2d. was raised by the parishioners.[8] The rebuilt St Pancras was, however, still a very small church seating only 196 and, whilst it would have gone some way to easing the accommodation crisis, it did not solve it, especially as St Bartholomew's still remained derelict and was not to be rebuilt for a further 82 years.

Throughout the 18th century the population of Chichester continued to expand. The new prosperity which had swept the land from the end of the 17th century, largely as a result of improved trading links and later the Industrial Revolution which gave rise to the middle classes after 1750, all led to a demand for more and better housing. The city had already spilt outside the gates and there was pressure to develop available areas within the city walls.

As we have seen, an interest in the former Blackfriars site had been acquired by John Gustavus Crosbie by virtue of his marrying Frances White-Thomas the younger. Major-General Crosbie (as he had now become, making his name even more resplendent) was born of a military family whose seat was at Northlands* in Funtington.[9] By his fortuitous marriage he acquired both the Page and White-Thomas estates, which included both Donnington and Barnham Manors as well as other land to the south of the city. In 1807 his father, Major-General Charles Crosbie, died leaving him Northlands and the land-holdings around Funtington and Fishbourne so his empire spread still further. By 1823, now of the rank of Lt General, John Gustavus Crosbie had moved to Watergate House at Up Marden (another part of the former Page estate) and his son Charles then occupied Northlands.[10] John Gustavus Crosbie was not a promoter of the Portsmouth and Arundel Canal which crossed so much of his land but despite this the new road bridge across it in Donnington was named after him.

---

* Northlands is situated at the top end of Salthill Road and is thus in the parish, rather than the village, of Funtington.

In 1807 John Gustavus Crosbie wanted to settle the reversionary White-Thomas estate upon his wife but could not do so as Frances White-Thomas Senior was still alive. However on 25 August 1807 he entered into an indenture[11] to covenant the sale ('for a proper cost') of the whole estate, upon the death of Frances Senior, to William Dearling, the man who was to become the second, and rather colourful, major figure in the founding of the New Town and St John's. William Dearling, born in 1767, came from a family much involved in the life of Georgian Chichester. His grandfather was James Dearling who had been a much-respected deacon of the Baptist Chapel in Eastgate Square[12] and his father was John Dearling, a merchant and brewer, who was mayor of the city in 1782. Although of Baptist birth there is strangely no mention of William in the membership list of the General Baptist Church Book for the Eastgate Chapel. William became an entrepreneur and acquired much land in Chichester, Funtington and the Ashlings as well as inheriting Kingsham Farm.[13] Deeds relating to his property dealings describe him variously as 'wine merchant' and 'common brewer' and he is recorded as being the brewer at the *Unicorn Inn* in Eastgate Square in 1802, a position which his father had held before him.[14] William Dearling also achieved public office having been High Sheriff of Sussex. Quite how John Gustavus Crosbie and William Dearling came to enter into the business arrangement over the New Town development is not certain but prior to it Crosbie had leased his newly acquired Donnington Manor to Dearling* who then assumed the mantle of lord of the manor of Donnington[15] and lived there until his new house, Oakwood,† was built in 1811.

Frances White-Thomas senior died in November 1807[16] which finally put things in motion for settling her estate. On 14 June 1808‡ Crosbie and his wife put up the whole site for sale by public auction at the *Swan Inn*§ and the earlier covenant with Dearling was honoured by his having a moiety of all the lease agreements.[17] Unfortunately, although a consortium of Messrs William Ridge, Richard Murray, James Hack, William Hack and Richard Dally had bought two lots for £705 and three other lots were also sold, the remaining six acres and the mansion house were not. Accordingly Crosbie tried again with another auction, dividing the site into 60 lots (See Fig 4), which was held at the *Swan Inn* on 24 October 1808. The site was described as 'Situate in the most airy and pleasant part of the City of Chichester'.[18] In actual fact there were 61 lots, since there were two plots numbered 1, and it will be noted that the north-east corner of the site does not feature, this is probably because that area comprised the lots which had been sold at the June sale. This time he was more successful and William Ridge and his

---

* The date is not certain but it was probably 1802, the year of Crosbie's marriage when Frances moved into her new husband's home at Northlands.
† See page 28.
‡ Francis Steer erroneously gives the year as 1809 in CP35.
§ The *Swan Inn* was in East Street near the Cross and was much used for public meetings. It closed after the arrival of the railway had deprived it of its coaching business.

cohorts bought Lots 8 to 15 inclusive for £1,050 later agreeing amongst themselves to make over the title simply to Richard Dally as trustee who paid the Crosbies and Dearling 10s. each for their 'consideration' of the deal.[19] Dearling was duly named in the lease agreements and undoubtedly did very well out of it; he was also directly involved in the onward sale of other plots to those who were to build the houses.

Major-General Crosbie's aim had been to create a New Town of fine townhouses aimed at the professional classes and the fact that each auction lot was 30 feet wide reflects this. A condition of the sale of the lots was a restrictive covenant preventing the trades of slaughtering, butchery, tallow or soap manufacture and metal working thus ensuring that the New Town was kept as a high-class area whose residents did not have to suffer olfactory or noisy assaults from industry. All this was in sharp contrast to the development which was just getting underway in Somerstown outside the North Gate by Richard Dally which was to be of small cottages between only 12 and 16 feet wide and aimed at the rapidly-expanding artisan market.[20] Curiously Dally had bought and extended a farmhouse, called Ellerslie, for himself on the edge of Somerstown rather than build a new

PARTICULARS

AND

CONDITIONS OF **SALE**

OF

AN EXCELLENT FREEHOLD

RESIDENCE,

REPLETE WITH

DOMESTIC OFFICES,

STABLES, AND CARRIAGE-HOUSE,

ALSO

FIFTY-NINE LOTS

OF VERY ELIGIBLE

SCITES FOR BUILDING ON,

THE WHOLE

Situate in the most airy and pleasant part

OF THE

CITY OF **CHICHESTER,**

WHICH WILL BE

SOLD BY AUCTION,

By MR. WELLER,

AT THE

SWAN INN CHICHESTER,

On MONDAY the 24th of OCTOBER, 1808,

AT TWELVE O'CLOCK.

PRINTED PARTICULARS, with a PLAN annexed, at 6d. each, may be had of Messrs. Winstanley and Son, and Chapter Coffee-House, Paternoster-Row, London ; Mr. Knight, Banker, Kingston ; at the Libraries Brighton, Worthing & Bognor ; of Messrs. Johnson, Price & Freeland, Solicitors, *And of Mr. WELLER, Chichester.*

3 *Cover of the particulars of the second sale of Black Friars. Note the description of the* Scite (sic).

house on one of his New Town plots. Many places had acquired New Towns in the Georgian era and one thinks of that in Edinburgh as being the supreme example. In Chichester everything was on a small scale and hence its New Town would be microscopic; the size of the site was to see to that. As the site had been occupied by the friary and its only dwelling had been the mansion house in East Street it was, and continued to be, extra-parochial. By January 1809 the street pattern had been set out and the first plots were being assigned to their new owners, the two main streets were *culs-de-sac* entered only from the north from East Street and Baffins Lane.

Richard Dally obviously had difficulty in selling Lots 8 to 15 on the east side of St John Street for on 14 and 15 July 1811 another auction took

4 *The 1808 sale lots for the New Town. Lots 8-15 were the subject of a second sale in 1811, the whole being split into ten new lots only 24 feet wide, numbered 5-14 from south to north. Those lots have been added by the author using dotted lines and the new lot numbers shown in square brackets.*

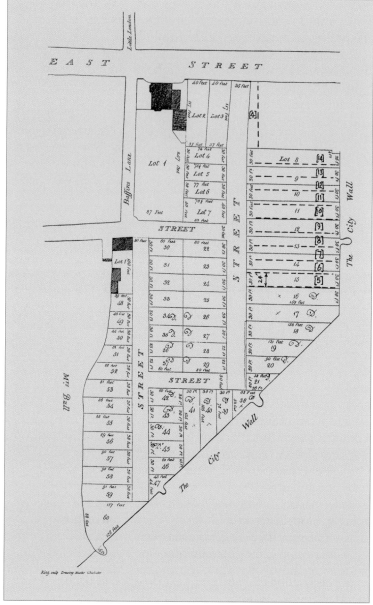

place[21] which included all these and also the four adjacent plots facing onto East Street which must have been bought at the June 1808 sale. A release,[22] dated 3 September 1811, for Lots 5 and 6 carries a plan which shows that the width of the plots had been reduced from 30 to 24 feet thus giving ten lots, numbered 5 to 14 south to north (see Fig 4), instead of the original eight, perhaps in the hope that there may be greater interest in building smaller houses. The release document shows that at the same auction the plot on the corner of East Street and St John's Street (lot 4) was sold to one Thomas Randall and that 'old' Lot 7 of the 1808 sale belonged to Mr Dearling. However, it also states that lots 9 to 14 were unsold – Dally's cunning plan had obviously not paid off.

Meanwhile the church accommodation crisis was getting worse and a solution, which would not offend the little churches, would be to build a proprietary chapel somewhere in the city. A meeting of potential shareholders was held on 23 September 1811 at which it was decided that,

> it would be expedient to obtain an Act of Parliament for the Erection of the new church in the place called the New Town as there is a reason to apprehend that a Deed of Trust cannot be so framed to embrace all the provisions which will be necessary in carrying the measure into effect.[23]

This last was certainly true. The Established Church required things to be done properly and at a further meeting on 22 October it was resolved to make an application. Chichester solicitors Johnson, Price and Freeland were engaged to carry out the legal drafting and the Bill was duly deposited before Parliament, becoming enacted on 5 May 1812. The Act[*] was in 52 sections, some very tedious. A summary of its provisions is given in Appendix 'A' but the ways in which some of them were implemented by the Trustees will be described in the text.

The preamble of the Act starts with the following words, which sum up the problem nicely:[†]

> Whereas the Inhabitants of the ancient City of Chichester, in the County of Sussex, having of late years considerably increased, and still increasing, the Cathedral Church and the six small parochial Churches within the same City, and the Liberties thereof, are altogether insufficient for the Accommodation of the several Inhabitants professing the Doctrine of the established Church of England, who are inclined to attend Divine Service therein: and divers persons are desirous that a chapel should be erected and built in some convenient Part of the same City, for the celebration of Divine Service therein, according to the Ceremonies of the Church of England ...

That this insufficiency of accommodation had occurred may seem strange in today's religious climate, especially seeing that all six of the little churches, as well as St John's Chapel itself, have closed, but those were more God-fearing times and for the majority weekly attendance at Divine Service was as much the norm as was getting up in the morning.

The preamble then goes on to petition His Majesty to enact the building of the chapel. Section X of the Act permits land to be bought for the Chapel in any part of the city save for within the parish of All Saints (which, as we

---

[*] 52 Geo III Cap 71.
[†] Although I have modernised the spelling I have retained the charming, typically Georgian, haphazard use of capital letters in mid-sentence.

5 *Title page of the*
St John's Chapel Act
1812.

ANNO QUINQUAGESIMO SECUNDO

GEORGII III. REGIS.

✱✱

Cap. 71.

An Act for building a Chapel in the City of *Chichester*,
in the County of *Suffex*.   [5th *May* 1812.]

WHEREAS the Inhabitants of the ancient City of *Chichester*, in
the County of *Suffex*, having of late Years confiderably in-
creafed, and being ftill increafing, the Cathedral Church, and
the Six fmall Parochial Churches within the fame City, and the Liberties
thereof, are together infufficient for the Accommodation of the feveral
Inhabitants profeffing the Doctrine of the eftablifhed Church of *England*,
who are inclined to attend Divine Service therein ; and divers Perfons are
defirous that a Chapel fhould be erected and built in fome convenient
Part of the fame City, for the Celebration of Divine Service therein, according to the Rites and Ceremonies of the Church of *England*, and have
already engaged to contribute thereto in the Manner herein-after mentioned ;
but as fuch Object cannot be accomplifhed without the Aid and Authority of Parliament ; May it therefore pleafe Your Majefty that it may be
enacted ; and be it enacted by the King's moft Excellent Majefty, by and
with the Advice and Confent of the Lords Spiritual and Temporal, and
Commons, in this prefent Parliament affembled, and by the Authority of
the fame, That the very Reverend the Dean of the Cathedral Church of the   Truftees.
Holy Trinity of *Chichefter*, the Canons Refidentiary of the faid Cathedral
Church, the Venerable the Archdeacon of *Chichefter*, the Reverend the
Chancellor of the Diocefe of *Chichefter*, and the Precentor of the faid
Cathedral Church, for the Time being refpectively, together with the
Mayor of the City of *Chichefter* for the Time being, *Charles Baker*
     [*Loc. & Per.*]   17 M   Efquire,

have seen, was a peculiar of the Archbishop of Canterbury and therefore out
of bounds) for a sum not exceeding £1,000. The Act sets out commercial
parameters for establishing and running the Chapel, for that is what is was
to be – a *commercial* venture. The first proprietary chapel* to be built was the
Mayfair Chapel in London in 1730 and the idea soon caught on; in Bath no
fewer than six were created.[24] The principle was simple. Enough speculators
would agree to put up money as shareholders and raise any other monies
to build the Chapel by borrowing, public subscription and advance sale of
pews. The Chapel would have no parish of its own (hence the term chapel

---

* The term 'proprietary chapel' derives from the fact that it was owned and run by proprietors.

rather than church) but be built, cuckoo-like, in somebody else's and the minister would have no parochial duties, these remaining with the parish priest. As such there was no need to carve out a new parish with all the difficulties that would entail. However, with no parish from which to derive income the revenue to pay for the minister's salary, the upkeep of services and maintenance of the building had to come from sale or rent of pews, investments, bequests and the generosity of the worshippers. A board of Trustees would be set up to administer the affairs of the Chapel and pay the dividends to the shareholders. Where pews were sold, the Trustees would have a right to levy a rate of so much in the pound upon the owners should income be insufficient to meet outgoings, and the pew-holders' rights and obligations in this respect were recorded in signed memoranda.

That a Church of England place of worship should be built and run on these lines may seem incredible today (although no doubt Margaret Thatcher would have lauded the premise had this been the 1980s) and indeed it could be a precarious path to follow as we shall see in the following chapters. For establishing St John's, though, the principle seemed sound and the Act allowed the Chapel to be built virtually anywhere in the city. As the shareholders had already observed, the ideal site was the New Town where, in addition to land being available, it could draw on the wealthy new inhabitants as potential 'customers'. The New Town also had the distinct advantage of being extra-parochial, so there would be no incumbent vicar's or rector's toes to tread on. New Town, then, it was to be.

In respect of the site chosen for the chapel there is an (as yet) unresolved mystery. Whilst the purchase and conveyance of the present site is well recorded that of a slightly earlier one is not. A claim arose from one of the contractors in respect of extras on foundation depths and in his completion report[*] the architect states that after the digging of the foundations had started the building was removed 'from Mr Dearling's spot of ground to the present'. We know no more, the minute book is silent on the matter, as is John Marsh. Did Dearling own the adjacent plots and 'donate' them to the Trustees, later withdrawing his offer perhaps over some dispute? If he did so, when did it occur? Anyway the lots finally bought for the Chapel were 9, 10 and 11 of the 1811 sale (which some held to be the site of the Black Friars' Chapel) and it was conveyed to the Trustees from Richard Dally. The street name was then changed from Friars' Street to St John's Street[†] to honour the new arrival. Raising the money and the building of the Chapel will be dealt with in Chapter Four but before that we will look at how the New Town developed up to 1830 – the utmost end of the Georgian era.

We can deduce the early development of Newtown[‡] from examination of the three town plans published between 1812 and 1822, the title deeds

---

[*] See Chapter Four where the outcome of this sorry saga is dealt with in some detail.
[†] We do not know how the dedication was chosen but it was to St John the Evangelist rather than St John the Baptist.
[‡] The development was known as The New Town at the outset but later this was changed to Newtown (see page 20). In this book both names have equal meaning when applied to the whole development.

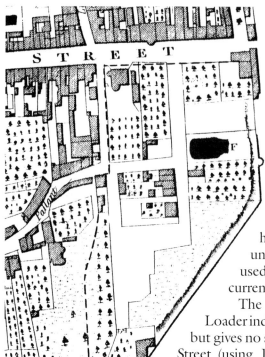

6 *Extract from the 1812 Chichester Street Plan by George Loader. The Chapel is marked* F *and it can be seen that little development of the site had taken place by that date. The Mansion House with its outbuildings is in the north-west corner of the site, facing onto East Street. The boundary of Newtown is indicated by the dotted line.*

to some of the properties and by measurement of the existing buildings and relating them to the original sale-lot dimensions. House numbering did not come into force until after 1847 and the houses in Newtown were not numbered until 1894 but, for ease of reference, I have used in the text the numbers and names currently carried by the individual houses.

The 1812 plan of Chichester by George Loader indicates the first buildings to be constructed but gives no street names. On the east side of St John's Street (using 1811 Lot numbers), in addition to the chapel on lots 9, 10 and 11, a house has been built on what appears to be lot 7. As this lot had been conveyed to William Gruggen,[25] a surgeon, in 1812 it may have been under construction when Loader carried out his survey. On the west side of the street Lot 22, on the corner, had been developed into two three-storey red-brick houses under a hipped, tiled roof (now No 1 New Town and 17 St John's Street) cunningly designed so that both appear to be double-fronted to their respective streets whereas in fact only one (the former) is. Half way along the linking street a house had been built at the east end of Lot 30, now No3 New Town. Lot 30 had been sold in 1808 to a usual consortium[*] of William Ridge, George Gatehouse and Richard Haslar but joined by a new investor, Henry Fogden.[26] Henry Fogden was described in the lease as 'a victualler' and in Pigot's 1839 *Directory* he is listed as being of the *Kings Head* in South Street and as also carrying out the trades of corn merchant and clock maker. We do not know whether he lived in his new investment and carried out clockmaking on the premises or whether, as with most of the Newtown houses, they were let.

The detached three-storey house was built of red brick with smart burnt headers at right angles to the street and occupied the full 30-foot width of the plot. As a result of this orientation it presented only one bay as its north elevation and its frontage faced west onto a garden. The house was given a matching[†] two-storey extension to its west front in 1970 which moved the

---

[*] The consortium also bought lots 41, 43, 44 and 45 which were not developed.
[†] Matching in all except the brickwork – being of modern construction the extension has cavity walls in plain stretcher bond, unfortunately without snapped burnt headers to replicate the original detail.

7   The dial of a long-case clock made by Henry Fogden c.1820.

entrance onto the street, reusing the doorstep and door case, and provided an ingenious roof garden instead of the third storey. At the west end of Lot 30, at the bottom of No 3's garden, there is a narrow building shown on the 1812 town plan which was its coach house and stables. This stable block was later extended northwards, curiously in rubble stone (Mixon rock from Selsey) and was, after 1950, to become a separate, commercial, property numbered 4 New Town, now occupied by estate agents.

Back in St John's Street lot 23 was used to provide two more 15-foot wide houses (now Nos 15 and 16) which were three-storey and contiguous with those to the north but of lower height. Next door Lot 24 and part of Lot 25 were developed as one large double-fronted three-storey house, now No14, with a frontage of 45 feet. The front is faced with white brick to complement the Chapel but the side and rear elevations are in cheaper red. Most Newtown houses had vaults under the pavement for fuel storage served by coal holes with cast-iron covers, a number of which have survived.

North of the Chapel, Lots 12 to 14 of the 1811 sale had been bought by Charles Cooper, described as a coal merchant, who used it for commercial purposes and by 1827 it was occupied by Charles Reynolds and in use as a timber yard.[27] Charles Cooper was in fact more than just a coal merchant* as in 1807 he had developed the eponymous Cooper Street, off South Street,[28] and owned several other properties in the city (his own house was 16 North Pallant) as well as being one of the contractors engaged to build St John's. In 1827 Cooper had got into debt to the tune of £1,100 with Charles Ridge the banker (how unwise!) so, in order to safeguard his

---

* In the many agreements involving Cooper he is also described variously as merchant and bricklayer.

8 *The houses in New Town (the street) looking west. 17 St John's Street and 1 New Town both appear to be double-fronted but only 1 New Town is. Beyond can be seen No 2 (with the blue stucco) and No3.*

interests, Ridge entered into an indenture with Cooper whereby the debt would be secured, plus five per cent per annum interest, by the sale of all Cooper's properties in Chichester. The St John's Street site is described in the Indenture as:

> All that piece or parcel of ground situate lying and being on the East Side of a certain street called Friar Street* ... containing in front of said street 72 feet of assize ... and in depth one hundred and sixty eight feet, together with a timber yard and the several messuages or tenements erected and found upon ... now in the occupation of Charles Reynolds.

In 1828 Charles Ridge, who was now Mayor of Chichester, and Cooper entered into an indenture to sell Cooper's property to one Edward Martin, whilst the following year another indenture provided for Martin to sell the property by public auction in order to pay off Cooper's debts.[29] The site eventually got developed but as this was after 1830 so we will come to it in Chapter Ten.

In Friary Lane,† which was intended to have been named Paternoster Row, Lot 31 provided two small, two-storey red-brick cottages under tiled roofs now Nos 1 & 2. The date of these cottages can be determined from the brick and flint boundary wall which was built to separate Lot 31 from the adjacent Lot 30 into which was built a stone inscribed on both faces (i.e., it can be read from either side of the wall) as follows:

---

* This was the name originally intended for St John's Street.
† The name Friary Lane was not introduced until 1918; prior to that it was treated as an extension of New Town (the street) and the three houses were so addressed.

> The whole of this wall was built at the joint expense of JOHN HUMPHREY and JAMES CARTER, 1810.

John Humphrey was a builder who had bought Lot 8 (in St John's Street) of the 1811 sale and we know that James Carter was a Newtown resident as he was a signatory to the 1825 agreement regarding the chaining-off of the development from East Street as we shall see later, but curiously neither was party to the original sale of Lot 31. The rebuilding of 1 Friary Lane will be dealt with in Chapter Ten.

On the west side of Friary Lane nothing had been developed, and never would be since William Brereton,[30] who owned East Pallant House, had bought lots 48 to 59 in order to enlarge his already enormous garden. That garden is now the Friary car park whilst East Pallant House has become part of, and swamped by later extensions to, the Chichester District Council offices.

The largest house in the whole Newtown development is at the south end of Friary Lane, now known as Friary Close. Plots 46, 47 and 60 were bought at the auction by George Gatehouse who then agreed to convey them to Henry Hobbs, a merchant, who developed them in the construction of his town house. Hobbs negotiated with William Brereton to exchange parts of his (Brereton's) Lots 58 and 59 for a part of his own Lot 60 in order to create the ideal site for his new house and grounds.[31] Hobbs' estate was further enlarged in June 1809 when the portion of land which was to have been the south end of Paternoster Row was released to him by Crosbie and Dearling for a consideration which involved his paying 10s. to each of the other Newtown landowners – this came to a total of £60.[32] In Hobbs' mortgage agreement dated 28 December 1814 (for £2,000 on a 1,000-year lease) it describes Lots 46, 47 and 60 as '... all of which are now thrown in together and inclosed [sic] by a newly erected wall. Also that dwelling house, lately erected – on that piece of land and in his own [i.e Hobbs'] occupation.'[33] The house was formerly known as St John's House and the 1812 plan shows it and its grounds apparently complete. Of flint with brick dressings this huge house was built adjacent to, and partly into, the city wall the top of the latter, providing a high-level garden. The builder, however, did not seem to be aware of how to use pattern books for there is no symmetry to any elevation with the windows occurring in a rather haphazard manner and, although he used a break in the frontage to provide a visual separation of the southern portion that was built into the city wall, he could not go so far as to make the northern part symmetrical about the front door! Inside, though, Hobbs spared no expense, having a stone-flagged entrance hall, a fine staircase, high ceilings and good quality joinery. We can quite see how he required a £2,000 mortgage to fund all this.

Hobbs obviously soon fell on hard times (or more probably had over-stretched himself on the mortgage) for on 1 June 1820 an indenture[34] was drawn up for Hobbs to sell his estate to the Rev. Stephen Barbut, who was

9   *Friary Close, west front, in 2003. The right-hand end of the house has been built up to and into the city wall.*

the first minister of St John's, for £2,000, but the money had to be paid to Hobbs' bankers Hack, Dendy and Hack[*] with a proviso that £500 would be paid to Hobbs in five years' time. It is likely that the name St John's House was coined at this time. The Land Tax Redemption Certificate for 1823 shows that Barbut lived in the house with one John Rogers who, one must assume, was a sub-tenant. Barbut was obviously a man of means (not uncommon for a Georgian cleric) for on 15 June 1820 he took on the lease of adjacent Lots 38 to 41 from Charles Ewens[35] for £330 and at the same time bought the lease on a portion of land outside the wall in order to create another garden and a tunnel was made through the city wall to access it.

[*] The Hacks were also investors in the New Town project.

The next town plan to be published was that of Edward Fuller of 1820 which gives street names, but all are different from those originally intended. The main street is now Saint John Street, Paternoster Row has become George Street and the northerly linking street, to have been Convent Street, is now Cross Street. The southerly linking street, which was to have been called Cross Street, was not to be built for another 150 years.

Fuller's plan shows that in the ensuing eight years lot 7 of the 1808 sale on the west side of St John Street (which was 40 feet wide rather than the normal 30) has been developed with a narrow two-bay, three-storey detached house (now No 18, Hasted House) built on the north edge of the plot, the remainder being laid out as a walled garden to south and west, whilst on the east side of the street, south of the Chapel (using the 1811 lot numbers again), it shows the Freemasons' Hall built on lot 8. This three-storey, two-bay building opened in 1814 but the Freemasons moved on in October 1824[36] after which it underwent several metamorphoses into a private residence. The former Masonic Hall was extended southwards, but only as two storeys, annexing the house which had been built on Lot 7. The extended building was unified under a stuccoed frontage, that to the extension being topped by a parapet to hide its roofline and make its lesser height less apparent. Unfortunately, the resulting distribution of the ground-floor windows either side of the main Doric doorcase is rather clumsy. Prior to 1894 the extended house was divided into two separate dwellings,[37] numbered 5 and 6, No 5 being the largest with six bedrooms whilst No 6 had two.* In 1989 both houses were put on the market, advertised as having the potential of re-unification but the estate agent's sale particulars over-optimistically dated the building as ... 'believed to be late 18th century'!

Next door Lots 5 and 6 (1811 sale again) had been leased from William Ridge to John Batcock on 3 September 1811[38] after which a complicated series of exchanges resulted in both lots ending up, by December 1818, with William Gruggen.[39] He now owned three adjacent lots and built a house†on Lot 6, leaving Lot 5 to the south as gardens. The lease documentation refers to this site as including a limehouse which is not mentioned in the descriptions of the buildings on the Black Friars estate in the abstract of particulars, but presumably was some relic of its long history. The Gruggen family had considerable influence in Chichester in the late 18th and 19th centuries and were involved with both Newtown and St John's Chapel. William Gruggen Senior (1765-1828), who lived in West Pallant[40] and bought the lands to build these houses, followed the strange joint professions of apothecary, surgeon and banker and his son, William Junior (1789-1867), followed in his footsteps.[41] Another, younger, son named John Price Gruggen, in order to help keep the family business going, entered a four-year apprenticeship with his father in 1823[42] but only as apothecary and surgeon – not as a

---

* By 1898 the two parts had been reunited as one house, the directories listing no No 6, but by 1970 they had been split up again – and still remain as two separate houses.
† This was on the site now occupied by the Victorian No 7 St John's Street which replaced the original Georgian house– See Chapter Ten.

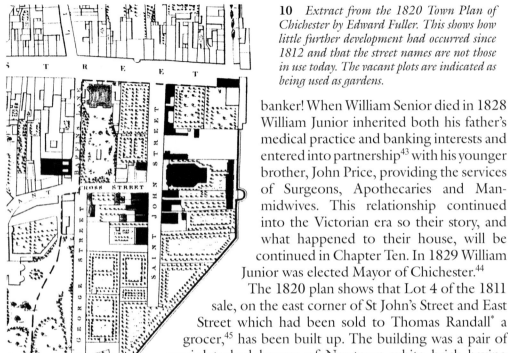

10   *Extract from the 1820 Town Plan of Chichester by Edward Fuller. This shows how little further development had occurred since 1812 and that the street names are not those in use today. The vacant plots are indicated as being used as gardens.*

banker! When William Senior died in 1828 William Junior inherited both his father's medical practice and banking interests and entered into partnership[43] with his younger brother, John Price, providing the services of Surgeons, Apothecaries and Man-midwives. This relationship continued into the Victorian era so their story, and what happened to their house, will be continued in Chapter Ten. In 1829 William Junior was elected Mayor of Chichester.[44]

The 1820 plan shows that Lot 4 of the 1811 sale, on the east corner of St John's Street and East Street which had been sold to Thomas Randall* a grocer,[45] has been built up. The building was a pair of semi-detached houses of Newtown white brick having three storeys under a hipped slate roof. One has a three-bay double frontage onto St John's Street with a curious single-storey side extension, whilst the other had a two-bay frontage onto East Street. Both were later converted to commercial use but when street numbering was adopted in 1847 both shops were given East Street addresses, as Nos 56a and 56 respectively, despite the former having a front door in St John's Street which remains unnumbered. At the southern end of Lot 4 three more three-storey, two-bay houses have been built each with two rooms per floor. These became numbers 1 to 3 St John's Street but they have since been demolished and replaced by Blackfriars House, a modern residential development.

The third Town Plan is that of James Bingley, dated 1822, which is more schematic than cartographic, and indicates no further development having taken place. The street names are as they were in 1820. At the south end of the east side of St John's Street no buildings are shown even though there had been much sale and resale of the lots, nearly always involving William Dearling. In the WSRO records are some incomplete particulars for a 42-lot sale of Chichester properties[46] but as the cover is missing we do not know the names of the vendors or the precise date. However, the conditions of sale require the purchasers to agree to pay their balance by 25 March 1817 which suggests the sale took place at the end of 1816 or early in 1817. Lots

---

* Thomas Randall was still listed in Pigot and Co's 1839 *Directory* as being a Grocer and Tea Dealer of East Street.

22 to 42 relate to plots in Newtown, the description of Lot 22 being as follows:

> A piece of Building Ground in the New Town, including a part of the Ramparts, with most substantial lofty flint stone walls, a most eligible scite [*sic*] to build on fronting Chapel Street – front 30ft and depth 168ft.

The use of the term Chapel Street[*] is at first misleading as it is a name never applied to St John's Street but close examination of the plan of the 1808 sale particulars (Fig 4) reveals this to be 'old' Lot 16. Similarly, all the other lots can be identified as those of the 1808 sale: 17-21, 27-29 and 35-45, since the dimensions tie up and two of the lot-descriptions refer to existing owners, namely adjoining Mr Hobbs' wall and fronting Col Brereton's garden wall. Interestingly, all these plots had been endorsed by hand with a 'D' on the 1808 plan in the WSRO collection as again can be seen in Figure 4. This suggests that the 1816/1817 sale, or at least a substantial part of it, had been on behalf of William Dearling who owned them; the other lots are lands in Funtington and East Ashling including Mount Noddy[47] which is known to be part of Dearling's portfolio. Dearling had been getting into financial difficulties probably having overstretched himself as developers tend, and still tend, to do. In 1808 he had mortgaged his Kingsham Farm to the Rev. William Walker for £6,000 and was in debt to Sarah Wyatt Peachey of Bognor[48] to the tune of £4,500. He had bought the advowson[†] of St Pancras in 1801 but sold it on to the Rev. George Bliss for £3,000 in 1816.[49] Selling on the interests in his Newtown sites in the 1816/1817 sale would have helped his financial position greatly, but this was not to be as the sale particulars have been endorsed 'Not Sold' against eight of the lots with a further seven unaccounted for. Around this time William Dearling left the country. The deeds for Friary Close cite the subsequent transactions for a number of these lots and on an indenture dated 21 October 1817[50] Dearling's address is given as late of Oakwood, now residing at Havre le Grace, France. It also shows that he was now running his affairs from there (as an exile?) via a trust managed by his attorney, the Rev. Cornelius Green of Iping. This particular indenture was for the sale of Lots 16, 17 and 38-40 (1808 Lot numbers) by Dearling's trustees to Charles Ewens for £285 and the annexed plan states that Dearling had bought these lots from Crosbie in 1809 in the name of Jno Fookes. Fookes had been a close friend of John Dearling who had left him £50 in his will.[51] All in all Dearling had woven a most tangled plot!

The deeds for Lots 18-21 (1808 lot numbers again) show that they were sold by Dearling's trustees to Susanna Ferris in December 1817 for £150[52] and cite an earlier agreement regarding her father George Ferris who had taken possession of the site and spent a considerable amount of money building upon it, which suggests that at least part of the building,

---

[*] The present Chapel Street was known as Upper West Lane at the time.
[†] The right of presentation to a benefice.

now No 10 St John's Street – Southdown House, which occupied Lots 20, 21 and 38-40, was already there. As such it is surprising that no buildings at all are indicated here on either Fuller's or Bingley's plans but, the fact that both cartographers missed them if they were there, makes a strong case that perhaps they were not. (As the immortal Wilde might have said: to miss them once might be regarded as a misfortune but to miss them twice ....) Southdown House, which was called Ivy Bank prior to 1937,[53] is a rather rambling two-storey flint building, or rather collection of buildings, which has been rendered on its northern flanks. It has been squeezed onto its awkward triangular site across the end of St John's Street and the 1896 OS map (see Fig 46) indicates that it, or possibly its outbuildings, extended up the east side of St John's Street onto lots 20 and 21. These parts of the house were demolished in 1938 to make way for a road connection through to Market Avenue. Its strange form and mixture of details make it difficult to analyse and date precisely and hence to decide whether it should be in this chapter, or early in that covering the post-Georgian period. The building is now occupied by Stride and Sons, auctioneers and estate agents.

Around 1830 on the west side of St John's Street, Lot 26 together with half each of flanking Lots 25 and 27 was developed to provide a fine terrace of three three-storey town houses with full-width basement areas, now Nos 11 to 13 St John's Street. In vertical proportion these houses match the earlier No 14 and were built contiguous with it. Again of yellow brick but this time the narrower (20-foot) frontages are of only two-bay construction and their detailing is different from, and far superior to, that of No 14, with elegant cast-iron balconies to the first floors and railings around the basement areas. As with No 14 the front doors are recessed with steps up to their fine front doors. Basement areas were uncommon in Chichester where below-stairs accommodation was traditionally lit by shallow windows set in the wall at pavement level. At some time after 1822 the streets were renamed yet again, when the names George Street and Cross Street were transferred to Somerstown and the current names substituted.

To add further to the naming confusion Cross Street was renamed New Town, the name which had hitherto been used for the whole development rather than just one of its streets. Accordingly, when the area, rather than the street, was being referred to locals now spelt it as one word – Newtown.

As all this renaming will have thoroughly confused the reader, all the combinations are given in the following table:

Street	1809 Proposed Name	Name 1813 to after 1822	Current Name
main street	Friar Street	St John Street	St John's Street
western street	Paternoster Row	George Street	Friary Lane (but only from 1918- was part of New Town before then)
northern linking street	Convent Street	Cross Street	New Town
southern linking street	Cross Street	Street not built until 1970	Unnamed

We have evidence that some small measure of the exclusivity that Crosbie desired for the New Town was achieved from an agreement[54] drawn up by some of the residents on 4 October 1825. At this time the beast market was held in East Street and the wandering cattle and their unpleasant by-products made for uncomfortable navigation of the streets. Newtown residents wanted none of this and took measures to prevent cattle straying into St John's Street as the agreement records:

> We the undersigned Proprietors of St John's Street and other parts of the extra-parochial lands within the walls of the City of Chichester called New Town at a meeting at held this day at the house of Mr James Rogers* do order that posts and chains be erected at the West and North ends of the street in the same New Town to prevent the cattle on market days from entering and filling up the same – and Mr Wingham and Mr Atkey having consented to direct the necessary operations they are to appoint two persons to attend the said chains so that passengers requiring to enter the streets may not be interrupted and that the expense of the above shall be paid by a rate.
>
> Stephen Barbut
> [??] Nooks
> John Wolfe
> Wm Wingham
> James Carter
> Jas Atkey

Interestingly, the problems with cattle wandering into Newtown had been troubling the Corporation three years earlier, for on 13 December 1822[55] they had resolved that:

> Posts and chains be fixed on both sides of St John's Street in the New Town to prevent beasts getting on the pavement, and that a committee consisting of the Mayor, John Newland, John Murray, Richard Murray, Wm Humphry and James Powell, or any three of them should give directions for the same to be done in a way satisfactory to the proprietors of property in the New Town.

We do not know whether the Corporation's resolution was put in hand (the Common Council Minute book makes no record of completion) but the fact that the residents came up with their own solution suggests that it was not. However, it should be noted that the two proposals were somewhat different in intent; the Corporation just wanted to keep the cattle off the pavements, the residents wanted to keep the cattle out completely.

The James Atkey named in the residents' Agreement was a blacksmith and brewer who moved to Chichester in 1792[56] and founded the Eastgate Brewery. His precise involvement with the Newtown at this time is uncertain

---

* A James Rogers of St John's Street is listed as a painter, plumber and glazer in *Pigot's Directory op. cit.*

11 *Nos 11 to 14 St John's Street. The far house of the four (No 14) was built by 1812; the other three were added later, c.1830, to complete the terrace.*

as he lived in a house on the north side of East Street but his son, also James, came to own four houses in St John's Street* which he left in his will of 1851.[57] It is quite likely that James Atkey Senior was an investor in the Newtown project and bequeathed at least some of those four St John's Street houses to James Junior. The Newtown element of the Atkey Will will be dealt with more fully in Chapter 10 but, without giving all the game away, a likely candidate for the property which James Atkey Senior owned in 1825 is Nos 1 & 2, which were closest to the site of the northern chains for which James Atkey was jointly responsible for the appointment of a chains attendant; the other holder of this responsibility, Mr Wingham, may have been Atkey's tenant.

The year 1830 saw the death of George IV and it was also the year that William Dearling, Newtown's co-founder, died. As we have seen, he left (fled?) the country in 1817 for France and was still living there in 1821, as is recorded on a declaration of trust pertaining to him, but what happened to him between then and his death is, at present at least, a mystery. The Eastgate Baptist Chapel closed permanently in 1954 and was bought by the City Council for use as a meeting hall. In 1999, during repair works to the floor, a number of coffins was found in a vault† including members of the Dearling family.[58] Whilst those of James and John and their wives might have been expected, the finding of that of William comes as something of a surprise. As we have seen, he had not been recorded as a member of the Eastgate congregation and the fact that he had bought the advowson of St Pancras and invested heavily in St John's Chapel might suggest that he had become an Anglican.‡ However, his burial in a Baptist vault would seem to put paid to that hypothesis and point to his investment in the Church of England as having been purely another money-making idea. How had he come back to England – did he come back in the flesh, in which case where had he lived, or was his body returned to the land of his birth? This was a

---

* Fred Atkey (James' great-great-great-grandson) who is researching the family history has discovered no records relating to Atkey involvement in Newtown, so these four houses cannot be identified positively.
† Until 1852 the Baptist Chapel had no burial ground so the vault had obviously provided a useful alternative.
‡ He was baptised as an Anglican in St Andrew's Oxmarket in 1767.

mysterious end to a most colourful life. All the coffins were exhumed from the Eastgate Chapel vault and re-interred in Chichester Cemetery.

Having marked the death of William Dearling it is appropriate to look at that of John Gustavus Crosbie, the true founder of Newtown. When he died in August 1843, by which time he had added a knighthood to his glittering array of titles, he was buried at Donnington alongside Frances who had pre-deceased him in 1835. His son Charles then inherited the estates and his mantle. Although there is no evidence that the Crosbies ever lived at Donnington, or took an active part in the life of the village, the north-west corner of the Trinity Chapel in Donnington Church is given over to several memorials to the family. There is a wall-mounted tablet to John Gustavus himself in which he is described as

> ... having honourably served his king and country in the earlier part of his mortal career, he retired into private life where he fulfilled the duties of an affectionate husband and father, dying loved and respected by all who knew him, but more especially by his nine children who survive to deplore his loss.

Below it is another tablet which records the demises of those later Crosbies down to 1912. A tablet to Frances Crosbie on the adjacent wall describes her as ever warm hearted and affectionate as a wife and parent. Most interesting is a pair of early 19th-century white-marble portrait busts, unsigned and bearing no inscriptions, of a man and woman who, from their positioning, we must also take to be Crosbies. The woman is sited below the tablet to Frances and her hair is in ringlets, whilst the man is sited below the tablet to John Gustavus and he sports a luxuriant set of side-whiskers. Both these hirsute fashions suggest the 1830s so is it not reasonable to presume that the busts are of Frances and John Gustavus? On the chance that they are, a photograph of that of John Gustavus is given as an end-piece to this volume. Interestingly, in the 1970s he was to be commemorated again in the naming of Crosbie Close, a new residential road in Donnington.

And that was it! By 1830, as a Georgian development, the New Town had not really taken off (unlike Somerstown where no space remained unused), although more development did take place in post-Georgian times,* as we shall see in Chapter Ten when we resume the Newtown story. The potential offered by the 61 lots for building a fine New Town of grand town houses was never fully realised.

---

* One house which may well have been built between 1822 and 1830 is No 8 St John's Street which was certainly in existence in 1832. However, as it was subsequently extended, the whole story of this house is covered in Chapter Ten.

Two

John Marsh – A Founding Father

One of the Chapel's founding fathers is so important a character, not only in the life of Georgian Chichester but in Georgian Britain, that he deserves a short introductory chapter to himself. That founding father is John Marsh, barrister, composer, organist, player of the viola and cello, philanthropist, mathematician, astronomer, writer and prolific diarist.

Born on 31 May 1752 in Dorking, the son of a naval captain, he spent most of his boyhood in Greenwich. There he fell under the spell of organ music and also of church bells but his father forbade him receiving music lessons until he was 14 'for fear it interfering too much with my other studies'.[1] Those first music lessons were on the violin, but his subsequent knowledge of composition and the organ was gained by self-education from books and treatises – an inauspicious start to a life that was largely to be devoted to the composition and performance of music. However, Marsh had a brain the size of the proverbial Manchester so this lack of formal musical training was not to be a problem to him and he went on to produce some 350 compositions including 40 symphonies and much organ and church music. He entered the Law as a profession in 1768, articled to a Romsey solicitor, and was called to the Bar in February 1786 after only 18 years but this again should come as no surprise since having brains the size of Manchester is *sine qua non* for barristers.

In 1765 he began to keep a very detailed diary which in later years he wrote up as a journal entitled *History of my Private Life*. This he maintained right up to his death in 1828 and it gives a fascinating first-hand account of life in three Georgian cathedral cities. The manuscripts, regrettably, are in America held by The Huntington Library in San Marino, California but fortunately they can be viewed on micro-film at the West Sussex Record Office. In 1998 Brian Robbins published a volume of the edited *Journals* from 1765 to 1802.* But these, of course, stop short of the St John's period.

From Romsey, where he married, Marsh moved to Salisbury in 1776, becoming involved in the musical and intellectual life of the city until 1783 when he moved the family to Nethersole House, the family seat, which he had just inherited along with other estates, in Kent. Nethersole was

---

* *The John Marsh Journals – The life and times of a Gentleman Composer*, Pendragon Press, New York, 1998.

only six miles from Canterbury so he found the extra-mural challenges
he so needed in that city, becoming director of the subscription concerts
there. However, Marsh soon sold Nethersole and was looking for another
place to move to. His need for intellectual stimulus meant that it had to
be another cathedral city and his friendship with the poet William Hayley
steered him towards Chichester where he bought Hayley's town house in
North Pallant (No 8) for the sum of £1,150. He moved in in 1787 and
was to remain in Chichester for the rest of his life. Chichester then had
a population of only 5,000 souls and would have seemed very provincial
after Canterbury but it provided the sort of challenge to which he could
rise. Once installed he soon became heavily involved with civic, musical
and intellectual activities, becoming director of the subscription concerts
in the new Assembly Rooms in North Street which he ran until 1813. He
also played for Cathedral services but a long-running dispute with William
Walond, the organist, meant that he would only do so when Walond was not
around. The income from his Kent estates was around £1,100 per annum
which was more than enough to ensure a comfortable life in a provincial
city. The diaries for this period carry no mention of his undertaking any
legal duties, which may be because it was of little interest to him and hence
not part of his *Private Life* or quite possibly because his income was such
that he no longer had need to practise law. In any case with all his extra-
mural activities he would have had little time to do so. After the death of
his wife he began to travel widely around the country visiting cathedrals and
advising on improvements to their organs, and was absent from Chichester for
long periods. He got as far as Edinburgh and was a frequent visitor to Derby.

As well as his musical activities, John Marsh was a great philanthropist
and became associated with many good causes in the city. In 1791 he paid
the entire cost of installing an organ in the Assembly Rooms and also
donated five guineas towards the costs of installing chandeliers. He was a
subscriber to the new theatre which was being built in South Street in 1792;
four years later he founded a book club and, as if that were not enough, he
was also a Poor Law Guardian. In view of all this it is not surprising that
he became involved with St John's as soon as the project was announced,
starting with a donation of £25. He later bought two £100 shares which
ensured that he became a Trustee. He was elected a chapel warden at the
opening and retained this post until he died in 1828. His diaries contain
much about the chapel both during construction and its first 15 years of
operation and so his name and words will keep cropping up in the text of
this story.

Unfortunately we have no portrait of John Marsh, although we know
from his diaries that at least two were made. Whilst in London in 1816 he sat
to John Miers* for 'a profile' (i.e. a silhouette) with which he was so pleased
that he ordered a copy as a present for his son Edward. Their whereabouts
is not known. In 1819 he sat to William Owen RA (1769-1825), who

---

* John Miers (1756-1821) was the foremost painter of silhouettes on plaster. At the time of Marsh's visit
his studio was at 111 The Strand.

described himself in 1813 as 'Principal Painter to the Prince Regent'[2] and hence would not have been a cheap artist to commission, but unfortunately the portrait, which featured his house organ in the background, has been lost without trace. Georgian portraits, however, have a happy knack of surviving so it is quite possible that someone, somewhere, has a portrait of an 'unknown musician' by William Owen hanging on his wall which he bought in a sale blissfully unaware of its significance, or perhaps a silhouette by Miers either of which might just be of Marsh. With similar misfortune his house at No 8 North Pallant has also disappeared having been demolished in the 1930s to make way for council offices. However, Marsh did buy No 4 East Pallant for his son John (from the roof of which he observed Saturn with his new telescope) which does survive, providing one link with his domestic life. When Marsh died his interests in the Chapel were kept going by his son John who was already a Trustee. In 1866 the list of pew-holders[3] includes a Capt Edward Marsh whose address is given as Nethersole, Bath. It is unlikely that this was Marsh's own son Edward, who having been born in 1779 would thus now have been 87 – an uncommon age to achieve at that time – and in any case he had entered the Church rather than the services. As such he was probably a grandson who not only maintained the family interest in St John's (albeit as an absentee pew-holder) but also continued the name of the family seat on his house in far-away Bath.

Although for long listed in both *Grove's Dictionary of Music and Musicians* and the *Dictionary of National Biography*, the rediscovery of Marsh's importance as a composer has been a comparatively recent phenomenon but one which has been pursued with some vigour by his followers. On 3 July 1989 Ian Graham-Jones and his Consort of Twelve gave a concert in St Paul's Church, Chichester featuring two of Marsh's symphonies which he had recently edited. Brian Robbins, editor of *The Journal*, gave a lecture on Marsh in the man's old stamping ground, St John's Chapel, on 20 July 2000 as part of the Chichester Festivities. To mark the 250th anniversary of Marsh's birth a ten-day festival was organised between 21 and 30 June 2002 to celebrate the man and his works. It included an exhibition at the West Sussex Record Office, three lectures, five concerts and a walk around Marsh's Chichester. In addition, Marsh's music was performed at four Cathedral services during the period and the pieces remain in the choir's repertoire. Finally, at a reception held on 7 April 2004 to mark the completion of the Chapel's restoration works by the Churches Conservation Trust, the composer's organ music was again heard in St John's played by Ian Graham-Jones and Richard Barnes.

Marsh's music can now be enjoyed on record; in 1989 Ian Graham-Jones recorded five of the symphonies and since then works have been included on CDs by The Hanover Band and the Salomon Quartet. He is now deservedly back on the map.

Three

THE ARCHITECT – JAMES ELMES, AND HIS CHICHESTER CONNECTIONS

Another person whose contribution to St John's merits a short chapter of his own is James Elmes, the architect appointed by the Trustees to design and supervise the construction of the Chapel.

James Elmes was born in London on 15 October 1782 the son of Samuel Elmes who was a builder. After education at Merchant Taylors' School he was articled to the architect George Gibson and entered the Royal Academy School where he showed exceptional promise, winning their silver medal for architecture in 1804 at the age of 22. He exhibited his work at the RA regularly from 1801 to 1842[1] and carried out his work principally from London. Elmes was also very active in trying to establish a professional body to represent architects and in 1806 became a founder member and Vice President of the London Architectural Society.[2] In 1810 he held a meeting at his London house with a view to establishing a Royal Academy of Architecture[3] but, whilst his proposal received widespread support from the leading architects of the day, it fizzled out. Undeterred, in 1819 Elmes was appointed secretary of another fledgling body, this time the Institution for the Cultivation and Encouragement of Architecture. Resolutions were passed at its first meeting which Elmes published in the journal *Annals of Fine Arts*, of which he was the editor, but once again it came to nought.[4] However, the agitations of James Elmes and his peers had established the need for a professional body and it was finally established in 1836 in the form of the Institute of British Architects which achieved its royal charter the following year.

At first it may seem strange that the St John's Trustees appointed a London architect and one whose name, unlike say the Wyatts or John Soane, would have been unfamiliar in the provinces. However, between 1811 (or maybe earlier) and 1814 Elmes undertook a body of work in and around Chichester of sufficient value to warrant his taking a house in Shopwhyke some two miles east of the city. We may not know what brought him to Chichester initially but three of his projects have a common association with William Dearling, who, as we have seen in Chapter One, was a major speculator in the Newtown project. In 1811 Dearling became involved with the Bishop's proposal to establish 'The Sussex Society for the Education of the Infant Poor in the Principles of

12 *James Elmes 1820, by James Lonsdale.*

the Established Church'* and in April 1812[5] offered a parcel of his land in what is now New Park Road to build the boys' school. The architect appointed for this scheme was James Elmes. Both William Dearling and James Elmes were Freemasons and masonic records show that Dearling joined the Chichester Lodge of Friendship on 15 March 1811 and Elmes on the following 3 November when Elmes' address is given as London. Major-General Crosbie is also shown as having joined the same lodge in 1812.[6]

The boys' school was completed in September 1812 but soon proved too small and it was demolished to make way for a much larger building in 1888.[†] It has to be said that Elmes' first architectural contribution to the City of Chichester was not exactly stunning. Standing at right angles to the road, the austere two-storey building was of seven-bay construction with a loggia to the ground floor while the upper floor was lit by five lunette windows set very high up so that the boys inside could not see what was going on outside. With so much blank wall it has all the appearances of one of Blake's dark satanic mills and only the legend Sussex Central School emblazoned across the base of the pediment confirms its purpose to be otherwise. A photograph of the Elmes building exists, taken in 1868 when surrounded by floodwater from the River Lavant. New Park Road always suffered when the Lavant burst its banks and there was serious flooding there in 1960, when your author was a pupil at the Central Junior Boys' School, during which the only way into the school was by being lifted over the (spiked) iron-railings from the adjacent park.

Amongst the various lease assignments pertaining to Newtown is one dated 4 November 1813[7] which gives Dearling's address as Oakwood – previously the address had been Donnington for, as we have seen, he had leased Donnington Manor from Crosbie. Oakwood[‡] is a large five-bay Regency house two miles west of Chichester on the Funtington road which

---

* This was the founding of what was to become the Central Junior Boys' Church of England School.
† A commemorative stone on the front of the building records the founding of the school in 1812 and that it was rebuilt to celebrate the Queen's Jubilee of 1887. It ceased to be a school in 1964 but is now used as the New Park Community Centre.
‡ Now occupied by Oakwood School.

13 *Elmes' Sussex Central Boys' School in 1868.*

Pevsner[8] describes as a 'plain stuccoed box 1809-1812 perhaps by James Elmes who exhibited a design for it in 1811'. From this uncertainty[*] we infer that the drawings are lost and hence cannot be compared with the house, but with the established Elmes/Dearling masonic connection we can be practically certain that it is by Elmes and was carried out for Dearling, no doubt paid for out of the latter's wealth amassed from his property deals including those in Newtown. The house is approached by a drive which is the best part of a mile in length which is a sure reflection of Dearling's wealth. Whether the boys' school or Oakwood came first we cannot be absolutely certain but whichever way round it was, one obviously sprang from the other.

Just across the road from Oakwood is another large stuccoed house called Sennicotts. This was built around the same time as Oakwood for Charles

---

[*] Howard Colvin does not share this uncertainty stating that it is by Elmes and to the drawings Elmes had exhibited.

14   *Oakwood in 2003. Note the un-pedimented Doric portico.*

Baker who retired from the East India Company in 1809. This house is not discussed by Pevsner[9] or Colvin[10] and again the drawings have not survived but it is thought, locally, also to be by Elmes. There is no known Dearling connection but certain internal details support an Elmes attribution and the strongest suggestion that it is by him lies in the pediment on the east front. Of shallow pitch and deeply modillioned, it is what one might term a flying pediment – it gets no visual support from pilasters but rests on the cornice; it 'grows' out of the slope of the roof behind and is itself roofed in slate. The west face of St John's carries a very similar pediment so this could, perhaps, be an Elmes motif. Sennicotts has an un-pedimented Doric portico to its front door, a detail which is also seen at Oakwood.

So now to Elmes' appointment at St John's. One of the shareholders and original Trustees of the Chapel was, perhaps not unsurprisingly, William Dearling* and as St John's in its earlier years had strong masonic connections it was perhaps inevitable that Elmes would be commissioned for this project. Francis Steer, in his Chichester Paper 35 quoting from Howard Colvin,[11] states that the supervision of the works was actually carried out by Elmes' pupil John Haviland since Elmes himself was ill at the time. A collection of Elmes' correspondence with the Trustees[12] has survived and whilst one letter does indeed refer to Haviland as having 'full power and knowledge to attend ...' (i.e to deputise for Elmes) all the letters and the certification of the contractors' accounts are in Elmes' own hand, suggesting that he did in fact play a much more active role in the supervision than has hitherto been assumed. As well as providing details of the contractual problems that Elmes encountered during construction† (which the Trustees' Minutes fail

---

* He bought two £100 shares (see page 35).
† See pages 45-8 where quotations from some of these letters are given.

15   *East front of Sennicotts in 1992. Compare the pediment with that of St John's.*

to do) they give a fascinating insight into the man's character – eloquent, tough with his contractors, deeply wounded when his professionalism was called into question and able to lay the charm upon his clients with a trowel. His portrait at the age of 38, painted by his close friend James Lonsdale, tends to bear this out; confident and expensively dressed, he could easily have flowed from the pen of Jane Austen! Unfortunately, his relationship with the Trustees was to sour when construction of the Chapel ran into difficulties as we shall see in Chapter Four and no amount of his charm seemed to be able to redeem him in their eyes.

Although we might presume that Elmes carried out his Chichester work from his Shopwhyke home, the letters carry a range of addresses which suggest that he rented rooms in the city for use as an office in order to have his drawings and papers near at hand.

>September 1812 – *East Street*
>April 1813 – *Pallant*
>December 1813 – *16 College Hill, London & North Pallant*
>January 1814 – *North Pallant*

Between 1812 and 1814 Elmes was architect to Chichester Cathedral which further increased his Chichester portfolio and detained him from his London office. The most important job he did during this commission was the rebuilding of the top part of the spire which was suffering from the erosion effects of salt-laden gales. He carried out a survey (which must have been a perilous task in those pre Health-and-Safety-at Work-Act days) and produced a specification for taking down the stonework of the top 11 feet below the capstone and rebuilding in Portland stone as well as repairing

16 *Chichester Cathedral from the north in 1811 before Elmes rebuilt the top of the spire.*

and re-gilding the weathercock.[13] This work involved dismantling and reinstating the ingenious pendulum which Christopher Wren had installed in 1721. The pendulum consisted of a heavy weight suspended from the capstone which pre-loaded the stone skin of the spire and thus increased its resistance to overturning under conditions of high winds. Handling this pendulum must have been a great delight for Elmes since Wren was something of a hero-figure to him, and in 1823 he became Wren's first biographer. Elmes' book, loftily entitled *Memoirs of the Life and Works of Sir Christopher Wren, with a brief view of the progress of Architecture in England, from the reign of Charles I to the End of the Seventeenth Century,* included an account of his work to the Chichester pendulum. Indeed, it as a writer on architecture and the arts, rather than as architect of his own buildings, that James Elmes is best known today.

His letter of 17 December 1813 to the Archdeacon,[14] enclosing his bill for the survey and specification for the repair works, is very typical of his epistolary style and characteristically extols the virtues of his economical rates:

> ... hoping it will meet your approbation having made it out at the lowest rate for such cases – usual briefs, charging nothing extra for the height and danger of the service and including (as it does) every charge of mine up to the day of commencing the works. My charge for the future employ will be regulated by the same mode and hope that as the works have begun under me they may be continued so that I bring them to a favourable conclusion.

Naturally John Marsh was a keen observer of the works to the spire and recorded in the diary that they commenced in April 1814 and were completed the following September, when he stated that the spire 'now looked more beautiful than ever I saw it, as the top which was a little warped was now quite straight ...'. Sadly, like the Central Sussex Boys' School, Elmes' work to the spire has also disappeared, destroyed in the collapse of the spire in 1861 following a Victorian act of vandalism in the removal of the stone screen below it. Regrettably, Elmes was not beyond committing acts of vandalism on the Victorian scale himself since in the Lady Chapel he covered Lambert Barnard's delicately painted foliage with yellow wash which, fortunately, later generations were able to remove.

In 1813 Elmes' son, Harvey Lonsdale, was born in Chichester. Taking his middle name from his father's artist-friend James Lonsdale (who was appointed as Harvey's godfather) he also trained as an architect and was more prolific than his father. He is best known for winning competitions to design St Georges' Hall, and the Assize Courts in Liverpool but he died from consumption at the tragically early age of 34.

In 1814 the new Masonic Hall was opened next door to St John's Chapel and it is quite possible that Elmes was consulted over its design. However, there is no record of this and nothing about the building (which has been much altered since the Masons left it in 1824[*]) suggests any association with him. During his time in Chichester Elmes had also undertaken a few small commissions for the Corporation and so had very much made his reputation in the place during his short stay.

After 1814 Elmes was succeeded at the Cathedral by James Baker[15] and, as the St John's Trustees had also dispensed with his services, he seems to have returned to London to practise. However, his career was to establish – or rather nearly to establish – another link with Chichester in a very different capacity some 10 years later. Elmes also practised as a civil engineer and in 1828 was appointed Surveyor to the Port of London. He was elected an Associate Member of the Institution of Civil Engineers in 1829 and contributed to a weighty tome *The Public Works of Great Britain* on the subject of London's Docks and of Thomas Telford's work in particular.[16] This dual architect/engineer role was not uncommon in Georgian times;

[*]See page 17.

indeed, the great Thomas Telford, the first President of the Institution of Civil Engineers, was first trained as an architect and has many fine buildings to his credit.

Chichester was connected to the canal network in 1822 when a branch was constructed from the Portsmouth and Arundel Canal at Hunston to a basin just south of the city. It allowed ocean-going vessels to sail from the harbour into the city centre thus avoiding the need to transfer cargoes to wagons at Dell Quay. The canal route from London to Chichester, though, was pretty hopeless as the Wey and Arun and Portsmouth and Arundel Canals together offered a very slow and circuitous route and it was this last fact which sparked, between 1823 and 1828, three amazing proposals for a 'Grand Ship Canal' to link London with Portsmouth. The first of these schemes was put forward by James Elmes in 1824 for a tidal canal, with very few locks, able to take ocean-going vessels 'of the largest dimensions when fully loaded' and the route took it via Chichester. Later that same year a rival scheme was put forward by N.W. Cundy[17] but in his prospectus Cundy spends almost as much time rubbishing Elmes' scheme as he does extolling the virtues of his own:

> The line pointed out by Mr Elmes, up the vale of the Ravensburn, from Greenwich by Croydon, Merstram [*sic*] Quarries, Mason's Bridge, the County Oak, St Leonard's Forest, Horsham and Slinfold, is about one hundred miles in distance to Spithead with a very long summit of four hundred and fifty feet above the tide level at the ridge near Merstram Quarries; and from the elevation and circuitous route of the three described lines it would require considerable deep cuttings through an under-strata of chalk, lime, and other stone for a considerable distance, and, conveniently, a want of water to supply the summit level, may occur in dry seasons.

This public attack upon his professionalism would have wounded Elmes deeply. A third scheme was proposed by George and John (the younger) Rennie in 1825 but in the event none of them got built and the projects were abandoned in 1828.[18] This is hardly surprising as the Stockton and Darlington Railway had opened in 1825 and the Liverpool and Manchester Railway was under construction, sounding the death knell for canal building. Indeed, the Portsmouth and Arundel Canal succumbed to the London Brighton and South Coast Railway very quickly by 1853. As such Elmes did not contribute an engineering work to Chichester, and St John's alone remains as his memorial within the City.

Elmes continued to work from London until 1848 when failing eyesight forced him to retire at the age of 66. He died 14 years later at Greenwich having outlived his architect son Harvey by 15 years.

Four

RAISING THE MONEY –
RAISING THE CHAPEL

An appeal to raise funds for building the Chapel had been made by August 1811 for Marsh records in his diary for that month that he had put down a donation of £25 and later records that, at the 23 September shareholders' meeting, it was agreed that donors of £100 should become trustees – a requirement which was included in Section I of the Act.

The set of presentation drawings[1] which Elmes gave to the Trustees[*] lists the original 18 holders of £100 shares and their holdings as follows:

Charles Baker	£200	
Rev. George Bliss	£100	
Bishop of Chichester	£100	(John Buckner)
Dean of Chichester	£300	(Combe Miller)
Archdeacon of Chichester	£200	(Charles Webber)
William Dearling	£200	(quoted as being High Sheriff of the County)
Rev. Dr Jackson	£100	
W. Johnson Esq	£100	
John Marsh Esq	£200	
Rev. B Middleton	£200	
Rev. J Moore	£200	
Admiral G. Murray	£200	
R. Murray Esq	£200	
R.B. Pope Esq	£100	
J. Peachey Esq	£200	
T. Rhoades Esq	£200	
William Ridge	£100	
Edmund Woods	£400	

This netted the sum of £3,200 which, when added to the £1,869 17s. 0d. received from donations,[2] gave a total fund of £5,069 17s. 0d., sufficient to get the project started.

Another meeting of shareholders was held on 5 October 1811[3] when it was resolved to purchase the ground to build the Chapel. The negotiations for the purchase were completed by the middle of 1812 and the land was

[*] See page 46.

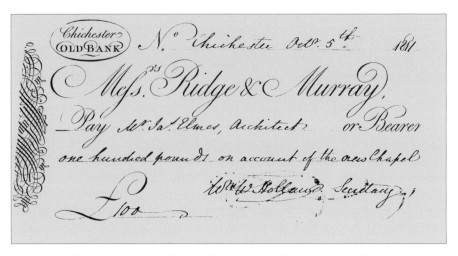

17   *Cheque dated 5 October 1811 from the Trustees to James Elmes.*

later conveyed from William Ridge and his cohorts to the Trustees for £500 by means of a Deed dated 4 January 1813. As we have seen in Chapter One, three 24-foot lots were purchased, giving a site 72 feet wide. The nature of the negotiations is not recorded but it must have involved, or been affected by, the business with Dearling's plot of land. At the same meeting it was resolved that 'Mr Elmes the architect shall be allowed to receive a sum not exceeding 100£ in part of his bill'. This suggests that he had already been appointed and had started work, no doubt in connection with the draft Parliamentary Bill. Indeed the cheque had already been made out on 5 October! James Elmes' design for the chapel will be dealt with fully in Chapter 5.

As an aside from matters St John's, Marsh's diary for November 1811 contains a fascinating entry so typical of his observations:[*]

> on Saturday 30th a slight shock of an earthquake was felt at Chichester, Portsmouth and Bognor at between 2 & 3 in the morning. Being however asleep myself, I did not feel it.

This was manifestation of the Chichester Fault which still makes its presence felt from time to time.

The Bill was enacted on 5 May 1812[4] and Section IV required the Trustees to meet at the *Swan Inn* in Chichester (where else?) on the second Monday after the passing of the Act between the hours of twelve and two in the afternoon 'for carrying this Act into execution'. Section VIII required the Trustees to enter all their proceedings into 'a proper book or books'.

With these requirements they duly complied. The first Minute Book[5] (which lasted until 1902) was a ledger bound in tooled leather with the following fine inscription on the flyleaf:

[*] One of the problems with cranking through the microfilms of Marsh's Journal is that wherever you stop there is something of interest even if it is not what you are actually looking for!

Acts, Orders and Proceedings
of the Trustees of the
Chapel of St John
the
Evangelist
in the
City of Chichester

The first meeting recorded was held on 18 May 1812, in the *Swan* as decreed
by the Act, when nine Trustees were sworn in, after which the meeting
was adjourned. The next meeting was held on 25 May at which six more
Trustees, including John Marsh, were sworn in and James Freeland* was
appointed Clerk. James Elmes was authorised and empowered to treat with
Charles Cooper, the builder, to construct a flint wall along the northern
boundary of the site. What the minute book does not record, but Marsh
does in his diary, is that following the meeting there was a procession from
Council Chamber to the New Town consisting of the Mayor, Corporation
and Trustees to lay the foundation stone (or 'the first stone' as Marsh puts
it) '... which was done by Mr Dearling who made a short speech on the
occasion'. This Mr Dearling was of course William Dearling and his 'short
speech' was reported in the local newspaper, which bore the impressive
title *Sussex Weekly Advertiser* or *Lewes and Brighthelmstone Journal*, for Monday
1 June 1812.[6] In it Dearling expressed his 'gratitude for so flattering a
compliment bestowed upon me' and went on to express the hope that
'the religion of Christ [may] flourish within these walls and may its salutary
effects be abundantly expressed by thousands yet unborn. Under such an
impression I cannot but hail this as the dawn of an auspicious day.'

The following week's issue[7] carried a detailed account of the ceremony
of laying the foundation stone which is worth quoting in full, not only for
its splendidly flowery style of reporting (and over-abundance of commas)
but for the information it contains which is woefully omitted from the
minute books:

> The following ceremony was observed in laying the foundation stone
> of the new Chapel, at Chichester, by W. Dearling Esq. whose address
> on the occasion we gave in our last. The venerable Archdeacon, the
> Reverend and other Gentlemen of the Committee, the Worshipful,
> the Mayor and Corporation in their gowns, attended by all the City
> Officers, the Mace &c. formed the procession, which left the Council
> Chamber a little after twelve o'clock, in the following order:

Gentlemen of the Committee, two by two
Architect
The Mayor and Corporation

---

* James Freeland was a partner in Johnson, Price and Freeland, the solicitors who dealt with the
Parliamentary process.

On arriving at the ground, where the stone, attended by the Master Builder, was suspended by proper tackle, silence was proclaimed, when the Architect, Mr Elmes, acquainted the company with the cause of their assembling, and read the following inscription, which was deeply cut on a plate of fine, milled lead –

The Foundation stone
Of this Edifice
Was laid, on the 25th of May 1812
By
WILLIAM DEARLING Esq
Late Sheriff of this County
Attended by
The Archdeacon, Clergy and Gentry
Trustees of this Building
And the Mayor and Corporation of the City of
CHICHESTER
The Rev. JOHN BUCKNER, L.L.D. Bishop
The Venerable Charles Webber, Archdeacon
WILLIAM NEWLAND Esq. Mayor
James Elmes, Architect.

The worthy Ex-Sheriff then ascended the wall on which the stone was to be placed and delivered the address, verbatim, as given in our paper last Monday.

A new trowel being handed to him by the Architect, he spread the mortar and put the inscription plate, rolled up, into a large glass bottle, with a variety of coins of the present day: Bank and Chichester Tokens, and a Coronation Medal of the King and Queen, and the same being carefully sealed it was deposited in a cavity to be covered by the stone, which was then lowered down, into its proper place and Mr Dearling gave it three distinct knocks, as a master-mason, which was immediately cheered by the workmen and spectators. The Archdeacon and the Mayor assisted in the like manner and their operations were equally honoured, and the return of the procession to the Council Chamber concluded the ceremony.

In the evening the workmen were regaled with a plentiful supper, at the *Golden Fleece Inn.*

The 'new trowel', which had been provided by James Elmes, was an ordinary steel tool rather than a ceremonial silver one, but he had had it inscribed and, after all the knocking had ceased, he presented it to the Lodge of Friendship and it is still owned and cared for by the Chichester

18   *The trowel used to lay the foundation stone.*

Freemasons who kindly provided the photograph in Fig 18. The inscription reads:

This trowel
Which
W Bro Dearling
High Sheriff of Sussex the
courtesy of senior and past
Masters in the Lodge of
Friendship Chichester No 624
laid the first stone of the
new Chapel of St John the
Evangelist in the said City
On the 25th of May 1812
was presented to the afore-
Said Lodge by brother
James Elmes the
Architect of that
Ediface AL5812
AD 1812
D.O.M.*

No sign of the foundation stone is visible today. The newspaper report refers to Mr Dearling and the other worthies 'ascending the wall' suggesting that it was above ground level and hence, unless it was on the south side and covered by the rendering, it must have been installed on an inside face. A Contractor's Bill of Extras† includes an item for the foundation stone[8] viz: 'providing and fixing a bevilled [*sic*] corner foundation stone for the ceremony of laying the same'. This points to its having been cut for one of the canted corners but there is nothing in the Bill of Extras for inscribing it, the reason being, as the newspaper reported, that the inscription was made instead on a sheet of lead which had been rolled up, put in a bottle (what would be termed a 'time capsule' in today's parlance) and hidden in a cavity

* DOM Dominus Omnium Magister – God is Master of All.
† This was of William Brooks who carried out, *inter alia*, the stonework.

in the wall. The foundation stone was thus just a plain stone and in view of this it was not deemed necessary to keep it visible, so it was either plastered over or ended up below the level of the raked floor.

At the Trustees' meeting on 24 July 1812, at which Marsh was not present, it was agreed to accept Elmes' plans and to authorise Elmes to enter into articles of agreement with contractors. The timing of these decisions is a little strange as siteworks were by then well underway, allowing the foundation stone to be laid 'in a wall' some six weeks earlier, so contracts must have already been let to Elmes' drawings and specifications! The tendering process is described in Elmes' report to the Trustees[9] submitted at completion. Elmes had placed notices in the County Press seeking tenders but when the lowest came in at £5,770, which was considerably in excess of his own estimate of £4,823 15s. 0d., it was rejected. Instead Elmes sent the drawings to his London office to seek tenders there as he 'was certain of the correctness of my estimate'. Obviously the Trustees were not impressed with fancy London ways and ordered Elmes to break the works down into packages and seek local tenders from tradesmen who 'might object to making proposals for the whole works'. Accordingly Elmes called in the London tenders and invited local ones from 28 Chichester tradesmen. Two packages were awarded, the first of which was to Charles Cooper of North Pallant who was responsible for the brickwork, plasterwork and slating. This was the same Charles Cooper we met in Chapter One who owned the plot to the north of the Chapel and had developed Cooper Street. The second was with William Brooks of St Martin's for the carpentry, joinery, stonework, plumbing, glazing, painting, smithing,* ironwork and upholstery. The contracts were for £1,363 0s. 0d. and £3,266 15s. 6d. respectively[10] and the Trustees acted as Employer with supervision by Elmes. The contractors prepared their regular accounts and submitted them to Elmes for certification who in turn passed them to the Trustees for payment – or not – as the case might be. The minutes record several authorisations for payment both to the contractors and also to Elmes himself. Having two main contractors on site both under Elmes' direction rather than one being a sub-contractor to the other would be classed as construction management today so perhaps Elmes and the Trustees were way ahead of their time in their contractual thinking. Notwithstanding this, though, the contracts ran into acrimonious difficulties which just goes to show that disputes in the construction industry have a long and dishonourable history.

By September 1812 the timberwork contract was already in trouble and Elmes had to write to the Trustees on the 12th to tell them that he had been 'obliged to employ Mr Francis Daltman to remove and reinstate some of the timbers in consequence of Mr Brooks' breach of contract'. He also certified that £65 7s. 11d. should be paid by the Trustees to Mr Daltman and that the same sum be deducted from Brooks' account.[11] This dispute was to rumble on after the chapel was finished and was not resolved until

_____
* i.e. brass and tin work.

March 1814. The shell of the building rose at an amazing rate for also on 12 September 1812 Elmes certified that Cooper's brickwork had reached roof level and on 4 December he certified payment for Brooks' completion of slating the roof.[12] That roof was to prove a constant source of trouble right up to the present day, as we shall see later.

Section XVIII of the Act left purchase of an organ and a clock to the discretion of the Trustees 'if they shall deem it expedient' and naturally Marsh was very keen for the chapel to be provided with a fine instrument. In his diary he records with obvious sadness that at a special meeting on 5 December with the Trustees (which is not recorded in the minute book) it had been 'agreed not at this time to set on foot another subscription but to defer it until next year after the opening of the chapel'. However, his despondency did not last long for at the meeting on 6 January 1813 the Trustees agreed to purchase an organ from 'Mr England of London'* for the sum of 260 guineas. Whether the fact that Marsh was chairing the meeting brought about this amazing volte-face we can only surmise but England had built the organ which Marsh had commissioned for the Assembly Rooms in 1791 and the specification for St John's was based upon it. However, Marsh's diary shows that another special meeting had taken place (again not recorded) at which the first decision had been reversed and that money for an organ would now be borrowed rather than raised by subscription. In order to house the organ a gallery had to be built at the east end, which entailed creating an opening in the wall and building a canted brick bay, carried on timber beams, above the vestry. This last was a detail that was to be its downfall, almost literally, some 170 years later. Normally in a Georgian church the organ would be sited in the west end gallery but by this stage Elmes' design (which had not allowed for the instrument) had provided a large west window to light the gallery and this would have been eclipsed had the organ been placed there. To pay for this major alteration to the fabric, for which Elmes produced a drawing, the Trustees increased the organ budget to £300 on 16 January and the building work was carried out in February. Marsh himself placed the order for the organ with England and agreed the specification, whilst a design for the organ case was drawn up by Elmes. Marsh twice visited England's works in April and May[13] during his travels to inspect the organ building and to dispense his advice. The specifications of the organ, both as built and as subsequently extended, are given in Appendix C, which includes a photograph taken in 1910 showing how Elmes' case had been extended when the instrument was enlarged.

During the construction work Marsh was a frequent visitor to the site, no doubt making a thorough nuisance of himself, and even when an ulcer in his leg recurred he still insisted on being carried there to see what was going on. His findings are all meticulously recorded in his diaries including, for

---

* This was George Pyke England of the most eminent organ-building family in London at the time.

St. JOHN's CHAPEL,

CHICHESTER.

——

Many enquiries having been made, relating to Pews and Sittings in the above Chapel, (which is now nearly compleated,) the Public are informed that one or more of the Trustees will attend at the Chapel every day during the next week, between the hours of Twelve and One, to receive the applications of all those who are desirous of purchasing, or having Pews or Sittings, and to give such information as may be required respecting the same,

March 30, 1813.

——

MASON, Printer, Chichester.

19 *Notice advising of the forthcoming sale and rental of pews.*

week commencing 4 January 1813, 'At the end of the week the first coat of the ceiling of the chapel was quite laid and the flooring of the galleries began'. In May he also went to Mear's bell foundry in Whitechapel to give directions for casting a bell of 300lbs weight for the chapel, a job he no doubt relished, bearing in mind his boyhood passion for the sound of bells.

This rapid construction meant a rapid spend of the original sums raised by shares and subscriptions so it soon became necessary to raise more funds by the third method at their disposal: the sale of pews. This was empowered by Section XXVIII of the Act but only at such a time that the chapel 'shall be in a sufficient State of Forwardness'. At the Trustees' meeting on 13 March, with Marsh in the chair, it was decided that the State of Forwardness had been reached and that a handbill should be produced informing the public that they should attend the Chapel in person and make application to the Trustees for sale or rent of pews. The notice was printed by Masons of Chichester and issued on 30 March[14] and the sales brought in an additional £1,549 up to 28 May 1814, bringing the total raised to £6,618 17s. 0d.[15] Section XXVI of the Act required the Trustees to maintain plans of the pews and enter the details into a book, whilst Section XXX required memoranda of the sales also to be entered in the book. There is a layout drawing in Marsh's hand[16] which gives his proposed method for classing and letting the rented pews as follows:

> the *front* pews in the galleries, being undoubtedly the best situated both for seeing and hearing and likewise handsomely fitted up they are proposed to form the first class at 30/- per sitting.*

The middle and back rows were, on account of their location, to be cheaper at 24s. and 20s. respectively. Marsh's calculations estimated an annual income of between £434 16s. 0d. and £445 5s. 0d. from pew rents to off-set an estimated expenditure of £330 per annum ... if only his predictions had proved right!

---

* sitting meant per person – when pews were sold they were sold in their entirety.

A bound book[17] for recording the pew transactions was duly produced and entries were laboriously made in full and signed by the parties and trustees. Those who had subscribed £100 or more were to be given first choice of the sittings or pews followed in order by those who donated lesser sums, with those who had donated nothing to the cause getting what was left. This requirement was included in Section XXIX of the Act to ensure that supporters got just reward for their generosity.

Elmes' agreement with the Trustees provided for completion of the chapel in March 1813 but by the end of that month the work was falling behind programme; no doubt the change of site, the dispute with Brooks and the extra work constructing the organ gallery were contributory factors. Elmes had advised the Trustees that completion would now be in June so at a meeting on 12 April 1813 the Trustees resolved that the Chapel should be consecrated as soon as possible after completion. Marsh was requested by the meeting[18] to

> wait upon said Bishop of Chichester with the respectful Salutations of the Trustees that his Lordship should be pleased to appoint such period for the ceremony of Consecration in the month of June as may suit his Lordship's convenience.

Unfortunately this was not to be since more problems began to appear, this time with the brickwork – that on the north side was found to be bulging by two inches. In view of the speed with which it had been raised this should not have come as a great surprise for at that time mortars were based on lime rather than cement which took much longer to hydrate, thus limiting the number of courses which could be raised in a day. Too many and you risked at best distortion and at worst collapse. The bulge caused obvious alarm and no doubt much heated discussion between architect and contractor ensued, but curiously it is not mentioned in the minute book. Elmes sought a second opinion of another architect, Lewis Wyatt,* who, as Marsh records, was working for Lord Selsey (of West Dean House) at the time. This of course further delayed completion and the hoped-for June consecration had to be deferred.

Lewis Wyatt submitted his report to Elmes in a letter dated 9 August 1813.[19] In it he confirms that:

> The north wall is decidedly bulged out at the level of the Gallery floor, probably one or two inches, but whether from the carelessness of the Bricklayers in carrying up uneven or the presence of the timbers is not now easily to be ascertained, it certainly is not workmanlike and the deviation from your original design in the construction of the Gallery floor has rather tended to increase the defect, but not in my opinion sufficient to excite the smallest appearance of danger.

---

* Lewis Wyatt was a nephew of James Wyatt and set up his own architectural practice in 1805. West Dean House had been remodelled by his Uncle James for Lord Selsey in 1805-08.

Wyatt recommended fitting wrought-iron straps between the ends of the floor joists and the wall plates and front beams of the gallery as a strengthening measure and provided a sketch for it. Wyatt was quite satisfied with the capacity of the columns but noted that it was impossible to inspect the roof space as it had been enclosed but opined that, provided the roof had been constructed in accordance with the drawings and from normal timber, he would have 'no doubt of its security'. He closes the report with the delightful assertion

> finding no other external causation of failure, I am generally of the opinion with the additional iron ties I have taken the liberty to recommend that no danger whatever is to be apprehended.

Quite what the deviation from the original was is not recorded, so whether this was something which Elmes had sanctioned or another of Brooks' breeches of contract we will probably never know. Unfortunately more problems were to emerge within nine years when again the workmanship of Messrs Brooks and Cooper would be called into question, but that will be dealt with in due course. Wyatt's observation about lack of access to the roof-space is interesting and it would seem that this was something that Elmes had overlooked rather than another failing of Brooks, since it was not corrected at the time.

Also in August 1813 the organ arrived. It was delivered on the 2nd but, as it was needed for Marsh's grand Music Meeting on the 12th, there was little time to erect and voice the instrument and it was completed only just in time.[20]

By September the Trustees obviously felt satisfied that, having overcome the delays and fears about structural deficiency, they were ready once again to petition the Bishop to attend the consecration. At the meeting of 13 September they agreed the wording of the petition whose lofty words included the following:

> Having purchased a parcel of land on ground ... being in a certain extra-parochial place near the East Street – commonly known by the name of the Friary ... the Trustees in pursuance and according to said Act of Parliament have caused to be erected ... a chapel and a chancel* or a place proper for administering the Sacrament of the Lord's Supper ... the said chapel may be consecrated and set apart for the Celebration of Divine Service according to the usage of the Church of England.

At the same meeting the treasurer was ordered to pay the invoice of Thomas Cox for carriage of the organ from London to Chichester. The Music Meeting and the consecration will be dealt with in Chapter Six but

---

* The Chapel had no chancel so quite why this wording was included is unclear, the proper place to which they refer involved eclipsing the Communion Table with the three-decker pulpit!

with the Chapel all-but complete it is interesting to look at the final costs of construction,[21] as reckoned in May 1814:

		£	s.	d.	£	s.	d.
Purchase of site and interest on purchase money					506	11	6
Builders' accounts	Charles Cooper	1617	12	9			
	Wm Brooks	3759	10	6			
	James Elmes (fees)	377	0	0			
		5754	3	3	5754	3	3
Legal Fees for Act of Parliament and other (Messrs Johnson, Price and Freeland)					540	4	4
Cost of Organ (paid to John Marsh)					295	0	0
Carriage of organ (Thos Cox)					11	2	0
Sundries					51	9	6
Total					7158	10	7

The total funds raised to 28 May 1814 were £6,818 17s. 0d. representing a shortfall of £539 13s. 7d. which was cleared by the sale of more pews, taking pew rents and also from further donations.

Before closing the chapter on construction we need to look at how the dispute with William Brooks was resolved and at another dispute, this time between Elmes and the Trustees over his fee. The financial resolutions of both were included in the final account. Elmes wrote a rather obsequious letter to the Trustees dated 4 September 1813[22] regarding the inability of either himself or Mr Haviland to attend a meeting and he 'begs to apologise for the unexpected absence of us both'. He then goes on to explain that 'the non-performance of the contract which was to have been finished by March led me to make considerable engagements away from my London concerns which will detain me some few days longer'.

He points out that all his work is finished save for certifying the completion of the contracts and valuing the variations thereof and then really pours on the sweeteners,

> but cannot help feeling regret at not being able to attend a committee of Gentlemen from whom I have received so many marks of friendship and I do hope when they take into consideration the money I saved them in the chapel as well as in the Central School* they will readily admit of my apologies.

In the previous three months Elmes had certified the amount to which he considered Brooks to be entitled on account of the quality of his work. This amount, naturally, was less than Brooks had applied for and so the builder had appealed to the Trustees in their capacity as Employer to the contract. The minutes during this period are frustratingly brief and there is no recorded sense of impatience over the delays, but one can infer that The Trustees were not satisfied with Elmes' performance since at this time his final account

* The Central Boys' School (see page 28).

remained unpaid. Had he been toppled from the privileged position that Dearling had bestowed upon him? The Minute Book shows that Dearling had not attended a Trustees' meeting since 5 May 1812, maybe having lost interest in the project after having laid the foundation stone; perhaps the cause of the changed siting of the Chapel had something to do with it.

On 10 December 1813 Elmes submitted his report on the completion of the Chapel to the Trustees, in which he describes the 'various difficulties in altering bad work and removing defective materials' and also the extras. Principal amongst Cooper's claims was the moving of the site of the Chapel from Dearling's land which we encountered in Chapter One of which Elmes, writing in the third person, says:

> The major part of Mr Cooper's extras are occasioned by the removal of the building from Mr Dearling's spot of ground to the present. Because the plans were drawn, the specifications and contracts made expressly for that location which was already excavated of its mould and the soil ascertained by the Architect, neither need the foundations have been so deep – Mr Elmes never was officially informed of the change nor consulted whether the situation was more or less eligible, but the contractor was ordered* to build there and the soil consequently was not examined by the Architect till the trenches above were excavated for the foundations.

Elmes then states that he had set out the building in the trenches 'without knowing till the day of measurement after the building was completed that all foundations were deeper'. This shows, perhaps, a little naivety on Elmes' behalf; surely he should have spotted all was not well when he saw the trenches. He then covers Brooks' claim but ends the report with classic Elmes sycophancy about a presentation set of drawings which is worth quoting in full :

> ... and the Architect requests their acceptance of a finished set of plans, elevations and sections with a description of the building over and above the other perfect sets already drawn for the contractors and the signed documentary set as a mark of his sense of their favours.
>
> Trusting his exertions have been exclusively and unremittingly employed to their interests, have been fortunate enough to meet their approbation, he begs leave to subscribe himself (collectively and individually) with grateful esteem.
>
>
>
> Their very obliged
> And obedient Hble. Servt.
> James Elmes, Architect
> 19 College Hill, London
> &
> North Pallant Chichester
>

---

* Elmes does not say by whom but we must assume it was the Trustees.

Despite their displeasure with Elmes the Trustees were obviously impressed with the presentation set of drawings for they spent £1 6s. 0d. in getting them bound!

On the 17th of that month, when Elmes wrote to the Archdeacon[23] in connection with his work surveying the cathedral spire, he added:

> PS the committee of the new chapel meet on Monday next to consider my deduction from Mr Brooks' bill of extras, which was finally reported by me last Monday.

This had nothing to do with the spire project but was a paving of the way for a Trustees' meeting, for the Archdeacon was a Trustee. Elmes was obviously offended by Brooks going behind his back and wrote a long letter[24] to the Clerk of the Trustees dated 1 January 1814. He starts, once again, apologising for his inability to attend at the Trustees' meeting that day this time on account of having to go to Singleton to conduct business with the Duke of Richmond (he obviously thought that a person of rank had a higher priority) and also that he is also 'much confined at home/ Shopwhyke about an extensive design in London'. He refers to the business with Brooks:

> I can say no more than that I did not make any award and report until after long deliberation – and find no motive for altering it nor can I give him any farther explanation – I have awarded him an ample sum and I have done justice between the Trustees and him therefore I must decline any further investigation. If the Trustees feel disposed to reward him with any gratuity over and above his estimate and extras I can have no objection.

He then passes on to the more delicate matter of his own fee:

> About my own account I cannot but express surprise that the Trustees who pay the contractors their extras, refuse me mine. On the score of the agreement it was for the contract only and for that to be finished by the first of last March and I have charged nothing extra upon the additional length of time, but merely my percentage upon the expenditure which is so just and equitable a demand that I cannot recede from it – Was the agreement set aside and all additional things as drawings,* extra office, extra length of time, attendance, writings &c, &c charged that I have done I am certain that my bill would have been much, very much more, but I made out my bill on plain simple principles & which I can prove to be moderate and does not amount to a fourth part of what I have been (to my own satisfaction) – the means of saving to the Trustees. I hope on reconsideration they will order it to be paid to me. ... I cannot conclude without saying that I

---

* These would have included the design of the organ loft which was an extra.

did hope that it would have been paid without remark, but also that some acknowledgement would have been made of my additional trouble & zeal which I declare without fear of contradiction. I never spared where the interests of the Trustees were at stake.

However, even claims were dealt with in a gentlemanly manner in those less-hurried times, and Elmes ends his letter:

Mrs Elmes joins me in best compliments and usual good wishes to Mrs Freeland and Yourself which nothing but her indisposition and my absence from Chichester would have prevented us from paying in person, & which we will, with your permission, take the earliest opportunity of doing.

   With the usual compliments of the season, believe me, Dear Sir,
With sincerity & esteem
And very best wishes
James Elmes

His heartfelt grievance so eloquently expressed and his seasonal greetings caused the Trustees at their meeting that same day to order the payment of £28 'being the balance remaining due to the sum of £360 agreed to be paid for drawing designs and superintending the building of the chapel' but nothing in respect of his claim for extras. Only five Trustees had attended and they were obviously not in a generous mood despite the festive season still being upon them. It was not until three meetings later, on 4 March 1814, that the Trustees resolved both claims; Brooks was ordered to be paid £598 5s. 3d. as his last instalment but 'as reduced by Mr Elmes'. As for Elmes himself it was agreed that he would be paid a further £17 'for his additional trouble in superintending and surveying the extra work done at this chapel'. Elmes' friend Dearling was not at these meetings to support him which may have been because he was planning to leave, or had already left, the country as we saw in Chapter One.

    Unfortunately the settlement of Elmes' account was not to be the end of the construction disputes, for in 1822 defects found in the roof and flooring caused the Trustees, who had obviously no intention of forgiving Elmes, to suspect him of having colluded with his contractors to use inferior materials – but we are getting ahead of ourselves. That will be covered in Chapter Six.

    With the building complete, it is now time to have a look at the Chapel Elmes had designed.

Five

THE ARCHITECTURE OF THE CHAPEL

Note: This chapter, as well as being part of the narrative, is designed
to be used as a stand-alone guide to the chapel and hence needs to
describe what is seen today as well as what was originally built. Thus,
whilst the changes which have occurred since 1813 are described
here, the reasons behind them will be dealt with more fully in the
appropriate chronological chapters, to which references are given.

THE EXTERIOR

Elmes' Chapel is octagonal in plan which straightway gives it a distinctive
air. An octagonal plan had been used in 1767 by the architect Thomas
Lightoler, albeit within a rectangular edifice, in his eponymous Octagon
Chapel in Bath. During his Salisbury years of 1781 to 1783 Marsh visited
this chapel (a proprietary like St John's) many times and occasionally played
the organ there for services.[*] He could not have failed to be impressed by
the layout and Lightoler's superb plasterwork and it could be that Marsh
influenced Elmes in choosing this shape. However, whereas Lightoler used
a regular octagon, Elmes elongated it, the plan area being 50 feet by 80
feet.

It is built of white brick which was an unusual choice for Chichester
at that time but, although the builders' accounts are fairly detailed, the
supplier is not named; however, the schedule included in the articles of
agreement with Cooper specifies 'best white Southampton, Bewly or
Lymington Bricks'.[1] White bricks were being made at both Littlehampton
and Worthing at this time so one wonders why they were not sourced more
locally. The slate roof is of the characteristic shallow pitch for a Regency
building, hipped to all sides and resting on wide, modillioned eaves. Both
levels of the chapel are lit by large round-headed windows, the present ones
being of steel put in in 1949 to replace the wrought-iron originals which
were damaged during the war.[†] As can be seen from Fig 20 they are a fairly

---

[*] The first organist at the Octagon was William Herschel, the celebrated astronomer with whom Marsh
was friendly. Their common interests in music and astronomy would have made for some stimulating
after-dinner conversations in Bath.
[†] See page 104.

20   *The west front of the Chapel in 1910. The railings and gates have been reduced in height and trees have grown up in the forecourt.*

good copy but the individual panes are larger. The south side of the Chapel is rendered which was done not long after the opening in an attempt to overcome penetrating damp. At the east end of the Chapel the vestry and coal store was contained in a somewhat inelegant lean-to structure above which was a canted bay forming the organ loft. Fortunately, because of the lie of the site, the lean-to could not be seen from any road and so did not distract from the general effect. The organ loft was demolished in 1980 when it became unsafe but the scars of its outline can be quite clearly seen.*

* See page 150.

21 *The east end of the Chapel in 1971 showing Elmes' rather inelegant treatment of the vestry. Above it can be seen the organ loft, added as an after-thought, which has been stabilised with tie-bars whose S-shaped patress plates can be seen. The organ loft was demolished in 1980.*

Most of the architectural inventiveness was invested, naturally, in the west front facing the street which was given a Greek-Revival treatment. There are three separate entrances, the reasons for which we will come to later. The main entrance is in the west wall and has double doors approached by two steps. Brooks' account[2] lists the front door as having been grained 'to resemble wainscot'.* The doorframe is set in a reveal within a moulded surround comprising two Doric pilasters supporting an entablature in low relief with cylindrical guttae to the frieze. This is all detailed in the Brooks' account, where it is described as being made of 'Roman Cement'.† On top of the entablature seven Portland stone balusters sitting in a recess support

---

* i.e. oak.
† A hydraulic mortar made by mixing lime with crushed tiles or volcanic ash invented, as its name suggests, by the Romans and possessing great strength and water resistance.

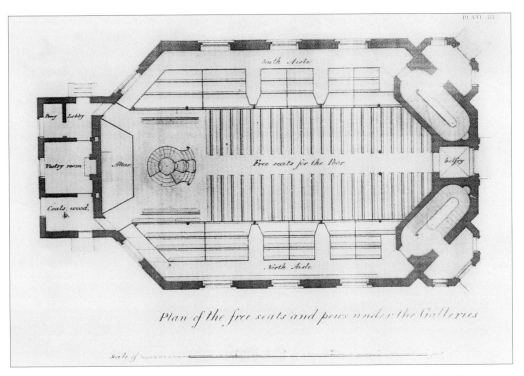

PLATE III

South Aisle

Porr Lobby

Vestry room   Altar

Free seats for the Poor

belfry

Coals, wood, &c.

North Aisle

Plan of the free seats and pews under the Galleries

Scale of

22 *Elmes' ground-floor plan of the Chapel showing the two classes of seating. The pulpit is shown on the more usual east-west axis as constructed but was later altered, for reasons unknown, to the current arrangement.*

the cill of the west window. Over the west window is the 'flying pediment' which, as we have seen in Chapter Three, closely matches that at Sennicotts. It occupies the entire width of the west wall and is roofed in slate which is blended into the roof slope behind. The crowning glory, literally, is the Portland stone campanile which sits over the pediment. Its design is based on the choragic monument of Lysicrates which the Greek-Revival architect James ('Athenian') Stuart had published in his *The Antiquities of Athens, Measured and Delineated by James Stuart, FRS and FSA* in 1762. It consists of six Corinthian columns surrounding the cylindrical bell chamber under a domed roof, the whole lot set off by a handsome weather vane. The single bell carries the legend 'T. Mears of London fecit 1813'.

Back at ground level the other two entrances to the Chapel were via projecting canted porches on the north-west and south-west walls, each having a single door and approached by a single stone step. The porches, lit by sash windows, were rendered in Roman Cement from the start and the specification[3] requires that in applying the stucco the builder should 'joint and stain as near the colour and fashion of Portland Stone as possible'. Against the north porch can be seen the sole remaining wrought-iron boot scraper, a very necessary adjunct, for St John's Street was not made up until well into the 19th century.

The forecourt was paved in York stone and separated from the road by a handsome set of iron railings which can be seen in the photograph at Figure 49. There were three sets of double gates with ramped tops carried by brick piers, rendered with Roman Cement and topped with Portland Stone caps. Curiously the railings are not shown on Elmes' drawings but they are listed in Brook's account as costing £155 0s. 10d. and were supplied by a Mr Smith.[4] For some unrecorded reason in 1894 the height of the railings, gates and piers was reduced to the level of the lowest part of the ramp on the gates, as can be seen in Fig 20. Later still in the 1940s the whole lot was removed as part of the war effort, an act of wanton vandalism since history has revealed that little, if any, of the thousands of tons of iron work so removed was ever used. The burnt-off remains of the railings can be seen in the kicker and the bottom bearings of some of the gates are still in the ground. After the war a hedge was planted to replace the railings and in the 1950s a 'wayside pulpit', a glass case containing an open Bible, stood next to the pavement.

For the new Chapel Elmes had produced an elegant and dignified design which was easily, and still is, the best thing in Newtown.

The Interior

Although the Act of Parliament set out the self-supporting commercial basis on which the Chapel was to be run, it contained a sting in the tail for the Trustees, since Section XXV required them to provide at least 250 free seats for the 'Use and Accommodation of the Poor'. As such the accommodation was to be in two classes: private subscribers had spacious box pews in and under the gallery, whilst the poor were given closely-spaced bench pews in the centre of the ground floor.

Entering the Chapel by the main entrance today we see a rather different view from what Elmes had intended because the entire ground-floor accommodation was replaced by the present Victorian pine pews in 1879.[*] Fortunately a superb photograph[†] taken of the old order has survived (Fig 23) which shows what it should look like. The private box pews face inwards and are raked up towards the rear to ensure that everybody got a good view. The Trustees met their philanthropic obligations to the poor by providing rather Spartan open-backed benches facing the front on either side of a centre aisle. Exactly 250 free seats were provided but this represented a large percentage of the total capacity of 622½[‡] and hence a considerable loss of potential income. Ironically, the free seats could only be reached by the more impressive centre entrance and there was no way of getting from the free into the private areas except by going back outside and re-entering by one of the porches. The classes were kept strictly segregated and

* The benefactor who funded this act of Victorian vandalism, Douglas Henty, is commemorated by a tablet set over the west door.
† The date is not given but the Chapel has a rather abandoned look about it which suggests it was taken during the 1871-4 closure (see Chapter Seven).
‡ Quite where the half seat was, or how Elmes calculated it, is uncertain.

23   *The interior of St John's c.1871 showing the raked box pews under the gallery and the open-backed benches which constituted the 'free seats for the poor'. All this was lost in the 1879 re-pewing. On the front of the gallery can be seen the first gas-lighting fittings installed in 1836.*

you will notice that the box pews, as well as being raked, are set at a higher level than the seats for the poor, presumably to avoid the rich having to inhale the vapours arising from their less-fortunate brethren. The front pews downstairs were the cheapest in the house! When the Victorian pews were put in the floors under the galleries were lowered and the new pews mostly faced the front. A match-boarded dado was installed against the wall.

The atmosphere within the Chapel is one of light and space, it being well lit by the large windows which have only plain glass. Many Georgian churches of this type were fitted with stained glass in Victorian times but, for reasons we shall appreciate later, this did not happen here. The gallery runs right round the perimeter of the Chapel and is supported on slender, reeded columns which are of cast iron save for the two under the organ which are timber. All the columns are topped with plaster palm leaves, which would not have looked out of place in the Royal Pavilion along

the coast in Brighton, whilst the front of the gallery is of American Black
Birch. The well created by the gallery is rectangular which rather negates
the sensation of being in an octagon but in his design Elmes had thought
of this; the east gallery was originally set some six feet further back than it
is now and the corners were splayed parallel with the walls. It was altered
early in 1818 to accommodate additional gallery seating and in so doing the
splays were lost. The present 'stone'* colour of the walls dates from the 2003
restoration and is based upon evidence provided by paint scrapes[5] which
have revealed the decorative history of the building. The builders' accounts
do not mention the original colour which is because the walls were left to
dry out before being painted. The Trustees' Minute Book[6] records that on
27 July 1814 it was agreed that the Chapel would be coloured 'on 8 August
next, the colour shall be determined by the Trustees'. Marsh's diary entry for
29 August refers to his playing for the first time since the Chapel reopened
after a three-week closure which had been 'to allow the walls to be coloured
for which they were not dry enough the preceding year'.

Dominating the interior is the magnificent three-decker pulpit. No
Georgian church was complete without one but, whereas most were
ripped out by Victorian 'improvers', this one, fortunately, has survived. It
is made of American Black Birch, as specified by Elmes, but who made it
is not recorded. Elmes' ground-floor plan of the Chapel (Fig 22) shows the
three desks on the conventional east-west axis but at some time they were
altered to the present north-south arrangement and a close examination
of the lowest (clerk's) desk reveals where the original side door has been
filled in. It had previously been assumed that the pulpit was rearranged at
the same time as the Victorian re-pewing but the 1870s photograph clearly
shows that it had already happened. Once again the Trustees' Minutes fail
to record why or when such important alterations to the fabric occurred,
especially as it would have been quite expensive. The top deck is cylindrical
and supported on a barley-twist column which splays out at the top into
five acanthus brackets. It is approached from behind by a long winding
staircase, the soffit of which is plastered and cleverly painted with 'trompe-
l'oeil' panelling. From the top deck the minister could see, and be seen by,
those in the Gallery and he could also see the clock, set into the front of the
west gallery. This clock, of which only the face now remains,[†] was supplied
by the Chichester maker Thomas Wilmshurst who had his premises in East
Street. Mr Weller, the upholsterer, provided an estimate[7] which shows that
the pulpit was lavishly appointed with a crimson-covered stool and deep
quilted hair cushions to the minister's and clerk's seats.

Sited as it was in the middle of the east end and being widely spread
the pulpit completely eclipses the Communion Table which is set on a dais
against the east wall. The balustered communion rail is mahogany with gates
at the centre. However, even though it was hidden away, Mr Weller supplied

* Stone was used as the wall colour until the end of the 19th century when dark pink was adopted. The
pink was last used in the 1928 redecoration after which the walls became white.
† The movement and bezel have been stolen.

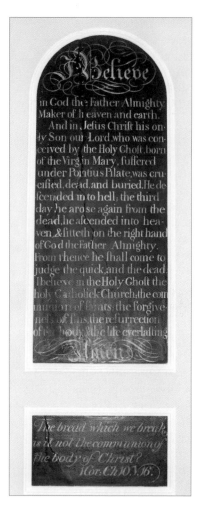

*24 One of the painted panels above the
Communion Table.*

some plush furnishings for the Communion Table including a Brussels carpet, fringed cushions (two of goose-feather), two Ottomans, six hassocks, a deep silk fringe and eight silk tassels. All this was supplied in crimson[8] and must have looked quite sumptuous. On the wall above the table are eight plaster panels with gold lettering on a black background, the large round-topped ones contain the Lord's Prayer, Ten Commandments and the Apostles' Creed, whilst below them are small rectangular panels containing texts, one of which, from Proverbs Chapter 22 verse 2, is particularly apposite: 'The rich and poor meet together: the Lord is the maker of them all'. What it does not point out, of course, is that here at St John's they had to meet together separately! These panels, although shown on Elmes' drawings (see Fig 25), were not completed until 1815, as Marsh records in his diary for 9 September:

> I went into St John's Chapel to see the Commandments which with the Lord's Prayer & Creed had during my absence been handsomely painted over the Communion table with gilt letters upon a black ground.

Apart from some minor repairs to cracks these handsome panels have survived intact.

It will be noticed that there is no font in the Chapel and this has always been the case, for Section XXI of the Act forbade the carrying out of Baptisms along with marriages and the churching of women. It would be standard practice for such duties to fall to the parish priest rather than a minister of a proprietary chapel but in the case of Newtown, from which many of St John's congregation came, this provided a conundrum, since being extra-parochial its inhabitants had no dutiful parish priest upon whom they could call.

It is the combination of three-decker pulpit, no apparent altar and no font which leads many visitors to assume that St John's must be non-conformist rather than C of E. This should not be surprising for very few similar places have retained their original ethos, albeit at St John's many of the fixtures have been altered.

To view the gallery we will go outside and re-enter, as would a wealthy Georgian, through one of the porches. The floor of the porch is stone flagged and well lit and ahead a door gives onto the stairwell which

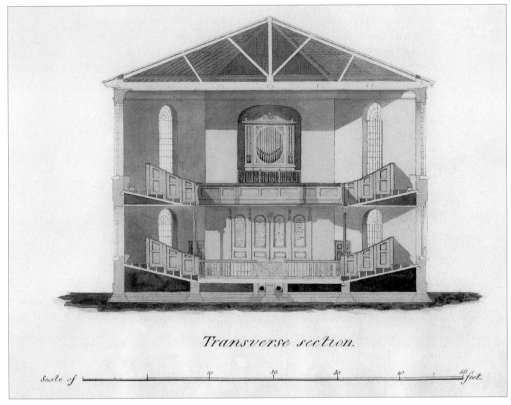

25 *Elmes' colour-washed transverse-section drawing of the Chapel. The two heating ducts can be seen under the central aisle. Note the organ case which Elmes had designed for England's instrument.*

has semi-circular ends. To one side is a door which led into the private accommodation downstairs, the door, as with all others, being described[9] as of 'yellow deal, six panelled square framed – and hung on pivots to open both ways and covered with Green Baize'. Under the stairs were sited the coal stoves which fired Elmes' under-floor heating system. The stoves vented downwards into earthenware ducts which ran through the sleeper walls under the centre aisle and provided warm air into the ground floor through 'brass valves' whilst the galleries were warmed by the hot air rising from the stoves themselves. At least that was the theory; in practice it does not seem to have been very effective for on 7 January 1814 Marsh records that the oil froze in the chapel lamps. The under-floor ducts vented into chimneys built into the walls at the east end of the Chapel so the draughting of the system may not have been terribly efficient. It was replaced with gas radiators, the presence of a large cast-iron specimen of the latter being the reason for the shorter pews half-way along the main aisle.

The geometrical, open-string staircase is particularly elegant. It is built of softwood but with a mahogany handrail, supported on stick balusters,

26   *The gallery as it is today.*

ending in a scroll above the 'snail' of the bottom step. Half way up there is a niche set in the wall which, contrary to the beliefs of many visitors, did *not* contain a devotional statue (a statue? at St John's? Perish the thought of such a thing!) but an oil lamp. The head of the stairs is roofed over with a false ceiling springing from the timber screen which has a baize-covered sliding door guarding the entrance to the gallery. Before going through the door it is worth looking back at the wall behind to see where the curved profile of the stair well ends abruptly and awkwardly, being overtaken by the octagon of the main building, before the ceiling level was reached. Quite whose fault this setting-out error was we do not know!

Passing through the sliding door we enter into the gallery and can now get an impression of what the ground floor would have been like when the Chapel was built. Up here the box pews have survived and they are ranged on three sides of the gallery in rows of three, raking up from the front and accessed from aisles against the walls. They are much lower than box pews were in the 18th century and, whereas 18th-century deal pews would have been painted, these have been stained. Brooks' account[10] includes for 'Colouring deal partitions of pews and oiling with boiled coloured oil, making and cleaning and fixing the same to all of the church make the deal imitate the Birch* – all to be varnished'. For this he required £16 5s. 6d. It does not require too close an inspection to see that the joinery in

---

* i.e. the American Black Birch of the pulpit and gallery front.

27 *One of the gallery sliding doors in its undressed state, photographed during the 2003 restoration works.*

the pews is not of the highest quality; indeed, the whole ensemble looks rather flimsy but they are spacious and comfortable. Elmes had specified that the deal should be one inch and a quarter thick. Another example of the quality of workmanship was evidenced by the sliding door. Under the baize covering the timber panelling was left in its rough-sawn state, the man who made it relying on the fact that his work would never be seen.

Originally the pews had lockable doors which, to accord with Section XXVI of the Act, carried the number of the pew. At some stage they were taken off; possibly the flimsy construction meant that they were destined for a short life anyway, and the numbers were painted on the pew ends. Unusually the locks were on the door jamb rather than on the door itself and close examination will reveal the keyholes and imprints of the hinges. The specification[11] called for six master keys to be provided for the use of the 'pew openers'. The eagle-eyed may also spot that some of the pew ends have been moved around as evidenced by the altered numbers and the fact that some of the keyholes are not adjacent to the doorways. When new, the box pews were quite lavishly appointed, the front ones having crimson-upholstered book boards with a valance hanging down whilst the owners were free to add their own effects such as extra book-shelves and hat pegs – one at the west end even has a drawer under the seat. Owners too would have provided tasteful cushions to improve their comfort. In 1817 brass rails (now replaced in painted steel) were added to the front of the galleries.[12] To add to the overall comfort Mr Weller[13] supplied roller blinds to be fitted to the south-facing windows to cool the interior on hot days.

Along the walls of the aisles can be seen the continuous bench which was provided for the use of the families' servants. Once again we see a social divide: servants were a cut above the 'humble poor' seated in the centre down below and hence were able to enter through the much-vaunted side doors but were not sufficiently elevated to be permitted to sit in the box pews. Resting their backs against the wall (as they had to) obviously brought problems from the mess caused by the paint rubbing off onto their Sunday-best clothes, so in 1820 the Trustees agreed that 'rush matting of a suitable width should be fixed above the servants' seats against the walls of the chapel'.[14] One can imagine that the servants were most grateful for this act of munificence. Below the benches the wall plaster was stained and grained and a portion of this can still be seen in the south aisle at the east end, including the damaged remains of a signature and the date, May 1812, scratched into the wet paint.

As built, the gallery at the east end was narrow and only accommodated the organist and the ten singing boys, the organ being entirely housed within its recess. Mr Weller supplied crimson cotton drapery to hang in front of the organ.[15] However, in order to increase the capacity of the Chapel, the gallery was extended forward by six feet early in 1818 which allowed six more box pews[16] to be installed and two pews in front of the organ for the singing boys (see page 71). The organ itself was moved forward to allow an opening to be made in the floor with a ladder down into the vestry below. In the late 19th century the east-end box pews were replaced with Victorian bench pews of a similar style to those downstairs but of them nothing now remains. It is likely that the displaced box pews were broken up to provide the spare parts which enabled the aforementioned alterations to some pew-ends to be carried out.

Siting the organ in the east is an unusual feature for an Anglican church for organs were normally put with the choir at the west end so as to lead the congregation, like the Duke of Plaza-Toro, from behind. This was, as we have seen, because the organ was an after-thought and the design of the Chapel could only be adapted at this end. The organ was dismantled when the organ loft, whose outline can be seen on the east wall, was demolished in 1980 (see page 150) but the case, which was by Elmes, had been discarded in the 1940s as it was riddled with worm. It is hoped that one day the organ will be rebuilt and reduced back to its original specification without a pedal board and using only England's pipework.

The vast ceiling was originally plastered and decorated with three large plaster rosettes along the long axis described in the Specification[17] as being 'three handsome flowers, two of three feet and one of five feet, the two smaller ones to have large circular holes in them to serve as conductors to the ventilators'. A view taken in the Chapel in 1923 (see Fig 38) shows the eastern rosette. In 1927 the plaster ceiling was replaced by varnished pine match-boarding (see page 102); the central rosette was retained and given a wooden surround but the other two were removed. Decoration was provided in the form of timber ribs with rosettes at their intersections but the varnished pine, together with the Victorian pine pews below, provided a surfeit of the stuff which did absolutely nothing to enhance the interior, it being a material more appropriate for a sauna bath. In the 1990s the

28 *Surviving pneumatic gas switch. The gas industry's last attempt to compete with the convenience offered by electricity.*

Churches Conservation Trust, for some strange reason, removed the ribs and rosettes from the ceiling and painted the match-boarding white (as it is at the present), a treatment which has no historic precedence, neither restoring the original plaster nor preserving the 1927 scheme. Still, historic or not, it has to be admitted that the match-boarding does look much better painted than varnished and, viewed through half-closed eyes, it can give a hint of how it might have originally looked.

The Chapel was lit by oil from the start, apart from candle brackets attached to the organ and pulpits, and Elmes specified[18]

> ... a branch of three Patent Lamps, glasses, chains and brackets complete to each column. A large brass chandelier, iron chains and apparatus complete with 20 Patent Brass Lamps----- two dozen of single patent brass lamps to be fixed against the wall where directed.

The bills for oil were considerable. Chichester was one of the first towns to be lit by gas and the Trustees installed gas lighting in 1836 which can be seen in the 1870s view at Fig 23. At this time the incandescent mantle had not been invented and early forms of Argand burners, which produced a naked flame protected by a glass, were suspended from the front of the galleries. Gas pressure was unreliable in 1836 and fluctuations could cause some alarming leaps in the height of the flame which must have added considerably to the excitement of those sitting in the front gallery pews. Never satisfactory, the gas lighting was replaced three times before being ousted by electricity. Relics of the gas era remain in the form of standards in the gallery and downstairs of two pneumatic gas switches attached to the columns in the rear pews. These would have activated a remote valve and pilot light in the gasolier above and still give a satisfying *ppffff* when activated.

Six

GEORGIAN ST JOHN'S 1813-1830

The inauguration of any new Georgian venture would be seen as just cause for an elaborate bun-fight and the opening of St John's was to be no exception, for John Marsh organised a two-day 'Music Meeting' as he called it – actually two days of concerts – for which tickets would be sold. Planning for this began in May 1813, no doubt in anticipation of an early completion of the Chapel, but curiously the Minute Book makes not one mention of it so Marsh's diaries provide the only source of information. In May he records:[1]

> Having at the late meeting of the Chapel Trustees made the proposal of having a music meeting at the opening of the chapel by way of raising something towards the organ making for it, which being agreed to* I immediately wrote to Messrs [illegible], Goss, Vaughan, Boyce and Ashley advising of it and to Mr Sibly† as leader ...

In June he records that a committee had been formed to manage the Music Meeting and that advertisements would be put into Portsmouth and Lewes papers and handbills printed for distribution. Although no minutes exist of this committee either, part of one document has survived in a recycled form, the back of it having been used for one of Marsh's pew-rental schemes.[2] It carries a list of subscribers to the concerts (incomplete as it is torn off) which includes: Admiral Murray, Rev. Mr Walker, The Lord Bishop, The Dean, The Archdeacon, Mr Toghill and Mrs Marsh. All paid £1 5s. 0d. except Mrs Marsh, against whose name there is no entry! Toghill was a bass lay-vicar in the cathedral choir so it can be seen that The Close provided the initial support. The committee met on 22 July and agreed the ticket prices which were to be 7s. in the galleries and 5s. downstairs.

The dates finally set for the Music Meeting were 12 and 13 August 1813, but as we saw in Chapter Four the organ had arrived only just in time and in order to house the orchestra it was necessary to build a temporary stage in front of the pulpit, the work being instructed as an extra on Brooks'

---

* As it is not recorded in the Minute Book, the rest of the Trustees obviously did not rate this as importantly as Marsh!
† Stephen Sibly was organist at St Thomas' Portsmouth and also an accomplished instrumentalist. He often performed at Marsh's subscription concerts.

The INDUSTRIOUS 'PRENTICE performing the Duty of a Christian.

Pſalm cxix Ver: 97.
O How I love thy Law it is my
meditation all the day

29   The Industrious 'Prentice performing the Duty of a Christian, *engraving by William Hogarth.*

contract and costing £52 11s. 4d.[3] On 2 August Marsh visited the chapel (in his chaise owing to continuing problems with his leg) to 'give directions' in respect of the platform. Despite this close supervision the carpenter who constructed the platform, Mr Cobden, managed to cause some damage to the fabric; Cooper's final account[4] includes an extra for 'making good to mouldings and pillars ... broke by carpenter at Music Meeting'.

Although no printed programmes survive we can learn much about the meeting from reports published in the *Hampshire Telegraph*.[5] On the 12th *Messiah* was performed complete followed in the evening by 'miscellaneous concerts' in the Assembly Rooms and ending up with a ball. The next day the morning concert was a selection of sacred music by Handel and Pergolesi plus excerpts from Haydn's *Creation*. The evening events took place in the Assembly Rooms again in the same form as the previous day. The *Hampshire Telegraph* did not send their Arts Critic (or the Georgian equivalent thereof) but did print a second-hand review:

> We hear that the Musical Performances at Chichester, under the conduct of Mr Sibly, went all in a brilliant style.

The soloists are listed who included:

> Singers
> Thomas Vaughn (Tenor)
> Mrs Vaughn (Soprano) – [Thomas Vaughn's wife]
> John Jeremiah Goss (Counter-Tenor)
> W Elliot (voice not specified) [from London]
> Master Hobbs (Treble) [from London]
> Master John Goss (Treble) [from Chapel Royal, London]
> Chichester Cathedral Choir (boys and lay-vicars)
>
> Instrumentalists
> Edward Sibly (2nd Violin)
> C. Ashley (cello)
> William Boyce (double-bass)
> Richard Cudmore (viola)
> Mr Hyde (trumpet) [from London]

The organist throughout is listed as Thomas Bennett and since Stephen Sibly conducted it looks as though John Marsh took no leading role on the day. Books of words of *Messiah* and the selections were printed and sold at 6d but none of these has survived either. Amongst the soloists the presence of two John Gosses* must have been confusing; of the two the treble (b.1800), went on to become Sir John Goss and organist of St Paul's Cathedral and composer of the popular hymn-tunes to *Praise my soul the King of Heaven* and *See amid the winter's snow*. This occasion seems to be the first recorded complete performance of *Messiah* in Chichester so the opening festival was something of a ground-breaking event for the city.

Unfortunately, despite the careful marketing and the glittering line-up, the concerts were not a financial success being under-subscribed, as Marsh's diary entry for the first night records:

> We were however seriously disappointed in the numbers – which did not much exceed 200 in the galleries and at most 40 below at 5/-, tho the former wo'd have contained 300, the latter nearly 400. This was probably owing to a variety of circumstances, the chief of which was ...

He then undergoes some soul-searching to identify the probable causes which included 'rumours having circulated about the bulging walls';[†] there were rumours that the plasterwork had not dried out;[‡] it was the Prince of Wales' birthday 'which was being celebrated in Brighton and Portsmouth with balls and parades' and that took away the military; the County Assizes

---

* Sir John Goss's great-grandson assures me that the two were not related.
† This, as we have seen, was no rumour but Marsh does refer to Lewis Wyatt's report giving the all-clear – the results of which had obviously not spread far enough abroad.
‡ Again, no rumour – the walls were not coloured until the following year as a result.

were to be held in Lewes on 13th which took away the lawyers; the Prince of Wales had come to Brighton ten days previously which had given rise to rival concerts elsewhere. Unfortunately, the second night fared no better and the whole venture cost nearly £390 against the receipts of £264 10s. 0d. The deficit of £125 had to be made up by the committee of whom 11 paid £10 each whilst Marsh, magnanimously, stumped up £15 resulting in his being some £20 out of pocket overall.

The Trustees' petition to the Bishop for the consecration of the chapel was approved by the said Bishop and the consecration and dedication took place took place on Friday 24 September 1813 between the hours of 11 and 12 noon. The Bishop, attended by the Cathedral Chapter and various other clergy of the Diocese, made his way to the Chapel and the ceremony is duly recorded in the Act of Consecration:[6]

> the Bishop with his said clergy in their proper habits entered the said Chapel and proceeded up to the middle thereof repeating the 24th Psalm alternately, the Bishop one verse and the clergy another, to the Communion Table ...

Once he arrived at the Communion Table the Bishop seated himself within the rails and received the conveyance of land after which the Registrar read the sentence of Consecration which the Bishop signed. The service continued with the psalms for the day followed by Holy Communion at which the Bishop presided. Following the 100th Psalm the Archdeacon preached the sermon after which the Bishop gave his blessing. Marsh records that he played for the service as no organist had yet been appointed and that the cathedral choir sang the psalms. He also felt that the Archdeacon's sermon was 'excellent' and he comments on how full the Chapel was. The Chapel was first used for public worship the following Sunday, 26 September, but without an incumbent minister as none had been appointed, largely because the post had not yet been advertised by the Trustees.

A Notice seeking applicants for the post of minister was posted in the *Lewes Telegraph, Portsmouth Telegraph, The Courier* and the Oxford and Cambridge papers advising them to appear for interview on 18 October. In the interregnum the services were administered by the Rev. G.F. Heming who was obviously impressed with the place for in November he donated a clock.[7] At the 25 October meeting John Marsh was elected a chapel warden, a post to which he was to be re-elected every year until his death in 1828.[8]

The minister was appointed on 18 October in the person of the Rev. Stephen Barbut on a stipend of £80 per annum and he began his ministry on the following Sunday. Barbut, who had been born in London in 1783, was an Oxford graduate[9] and very active in the work of the Society for Promoting Christian Knowledge, the Church Missionary Society and the British and Foreign Bible Society.* Since there was no clergy house he had

---

* He was elected local secretary of the BFBS in 1816 with John Marsh as treasurer.

to make his own provisions for a dwelling but fortunately he was a man of means, for he was able to buy Hobbs' large house in Friary Lane in 1820 which he then named St John's House.* Barbut was a very popular man both in his ministry and his local good works in schools and the new Infirmary.†
It is reported that in his time pews were bespoken for years in advance of a vacancy occurring and that those with no pew would stand outside to hear the service;[10] surely a fitting testament to the esteem in which he was held.

So, what were those early services like? So much has been made of the zealous evangelicalism and hour-long sermons which were a legendary feature of the Chapel that many assume not only that St John's had always been like it but that it had been built the way it was because of it. In fact, neither assumption is true. The Chapel was built to suit what passed for the normal style of Anglican worship of the period and some of the features of its services, as revealed by the Minute Books and Marsh's diary, would actually have been regarded as fairly high for the times. The zealous evangelicalism was in fact established in Victorian times, as we shall see in Chapter Seven, but, whilst this caused the layout of the Chapel to be retained, it was not the origin of it.

To understand the layout of St John's we need examine this 'normal' style of Georgian worship and put the two into context. The Protestantism expounded by the Georgian Church of England flowed from the 1662 *Book of Common Prayer* which permitted a fairly broad-church approach to services. On the one hand choral services were held in cathedrals and college chapels, albeit to standards that were not what we would expect today (Marsh made some very scathing remarks about the choir and organist of Chichester Cathedral when he first arrived in 1787), whilst on the other the evangelical wing could pursue their services with as little ceremonial as they wished. The Prayer Book also specified those Feasts and Holy Days which were to be observed during the year. Most churches occupied the middle ground but all services would be regarded as decidedly low by today's standards. *The Book of Common Prayer* had as its principal services Morning and Evening Prayer which were prescribed to be used 'daily throughout the year' and accordingly the Psalter was divided up on a monthly cycle to ensure that all 150 psalms were used. The Order for Holy Communion, or 'The Lord's Supper' as it was more popularly known, featured later on in the book and the rubric only required each parishioner to communicate at least three times a year. As such the facilities for administering Holy Communion were far less important than those for reading Morning or Evening Prayer and preaching, so the layout of a church reflected this. The reconstructed St Pancras Church of 1750 serves as an illustration of how old-style Anglican churches were being used at the time. Although of fairly recent construction, its design was decidedly old-fashioned, following as it did the medieval nave-plus-chancel plan, but its interior layout was

---

* Now Friary Close – see page 15.
† The Infirmary, later the Royal West Sussex Hospital, was founded in 1784 moving into the present building (now converted into fashionable flats) in 1826.

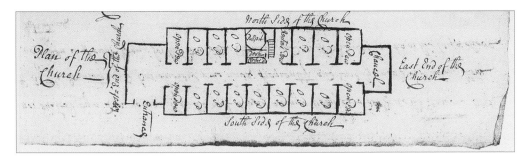

30   *Floor plan of St Pancras, c.1780.*

contemporary, copying that which had been applied to genuine medieval churches by this time.[11]

The interior of a nave/chancel church was treated as two separate rooms. Morning and Evening Prayer were conducted in the nave so the box pews were arranged to face the three-decker pulpit rather than the east end of the church. As can be seen from the floor plan (Fig 30) the pulpit at St Pancras was situated in the middle of the north wall, a fairly common arrangement. When Holy Communion was celebrated the congregation moved into the chancel, facing the Communion Table (the term 'altar' was not yet in use in protestant circles) at which the priest presided.

The reconstructed St Pancras was an anachronism because the favoured design for a new Georgian church was classical with a wide nave and only a vestigial chancel, if any. In such a church the focal point for the congregation was still the three-decker pulpit but it was generally placed centrally at the east end where it would eclipse the Communion Table which lay behind it. The box pews would be arranged facing either inwards or forwards, as appropriate, so as to give the best view of the pulpit. The original layout of St John's was thus the height of fashion, providing exactly what was required for Georgian Church of England worship.

In the conducting of services a minister would be assisted by a parish clerk. The parish clerk occupied the lower desk from which he led the congregation in the responses and saying or singing of the psalms; for the latter the verses usually alternated between clerk and congregation. The minister would occupy the middle desk from which he would read the Order for Morning or Evening Prayer following which he would ascend into the top desk, the pulpit proper, to preach his sermon. In Hogarth's *Industrious 'Prentice performing the Duty of a Christian* (Fig 29) we see a three-decker in use in a rather stylised church, but Hogarth has made an error in having all three desks occupied at once where in fact only two would have so been. What Hogarth's engraving also captures is the fact that services were generally pursued with a certain lack of dignity; indeed, this same lack of reverence often led to the Communion Table, when not in use for its intended purpose, being employed as a convenient receptacle for coats, hats and sticks whilst the Communion rail and steps provided useful additional seating during the sermon!

Whilst the Toleration Act of 1688 had granted freedom of worship to most Dissenters,* the practising of Roman Catholicism remained illegal until 1791 but even after that there was much fear, especially amongst evangelicals, of Roman superstitions and Popish practices. Included amongst the latter category was the wearing of surplices which were condemned as being 'Popish Rags'.[12] Surplices were common in cathedrals for both clergy and choir but in most parish churches the minister would wear a black Geneva gown with preaching bands as can be seen in Hogarth's *Sleeping Congregation* (Fig 31). Choirs in parish churches were normally of the 'Cock and Hen' variety, highly mixed in respect of sex and age and invariably of low ability.[13] What they lacked in musicality, however, they made up for in enthusiasm, and being housed out of sight in a west gallery they would have no need of robes of any kind, least of all surplices. As we shall see, St John's was not to follow the norm in respect of its choir.

Returning now to St John's, the Trustees, at their October meetings,[14] agreed that the times of the services should be fixed at 'half-past ten o'clock' for Morning Prayer and 'half-past six o'clock' for Evening Prayer except on 'Sacrament Sundays' when the morning service would commence at ten. Sacrament Sundays, when Holy Communion was administered, were held on the third Sunday of the month as well as on the Feast Day of Easter and quite possibly on other Feast Days as well. On 31 October the Trustees agreed that Rev. Barbut should be permitted to use the Chapel once a week during the winter for delivery of evening lectures and these duly took place, and continued to do so, throughout his ministry at St John's. Marsh's recorded observations on the services are, as to be expected, predominantly connected with the music over which he obviously had a strong influence and there is little about Barbut's sermonising. Marsh, however, was a very keen 'ecumaniac' and enjoyed visiting Dissenting chapels both in Chichester and elsewhere to hear sermons; on a visit to Bath in 1815 he complains of hearing a sermon at the Countess of Huntingdon's Chapel which lasted for an hour and six minutes.[15] We can be certain that if Barbut had made a practice of such marathon preaching in Marsh's time we would know about it!

Just as there was no incumbent minister when the Chapel opened there was no organist either, so Marsh held the fort. Marsh records in his diary that on 25 October a letter was read out from the former cathedral organist William Walond who had offered himself as a candidate for the post of organist 'gratis for the first year on account of the infant state of the chapel funds'. Once again this is not recorded in the brief minutes of that meeting nor is another meeting on 6 November when Marsh met with the Trustees to choose the successful applicant. There were only two candidates, Walond and Thomas Bennett, the latter being the current cathedral organist. Marsh records that Bennett was elected 15 to one, no doubt with some relish since

---

* Chichester was well endowed with Dissenting chapels. At the time St John's opened, there were established meeting places for Quakers, Baptists, Presbyterians, the Countess of Huntingdon's Connexion, and Calvinists.

31   The Sleeping Congregation, *engraving by William Hogarth. The minister wears a black Geneva gown. The clerk seems to be more interested in the personable young lady beside him than the sermon.*

Walond and he were old adversaries having never really patched up an old quarrel dating back to 1788. Bennett did not resign his cathedral position even though holding both posts was going to be something of a challenge, so Marsh deputised for Bennett at whichever place Bennett wasn't. The question of Bennett's availability must have been raised by the Trustees at the interview and we can only surmise that Marsh was quick to propose this 'Cox and Box' arrangement, since he records:[16]

> As Mr Bennett was always engaged at the Cathedral on Sunday mornings, he could not have undertaken the office of organist at St John's if I had not agreed always to be there of a morning whilst at Chichester and in health, his deputy Brown also being confined to the Cathedral at that time as a singing man.

This arrangement not only headed off the appointment of the dreaded Walond but also suited Marsh personally – he was now free to play at both the Cathedral and St John's but without the tie of being incumbent organist at either place. Marsh's diaries show that they regularly alternated turns at both places and not only in the mornings. Bennett's salary was £20 per annum and he had the free use of a pew in the south gallery adjacent to the organ. The salary rose to £25 in 1817 after Bennett agreed to keep the organ in tune and provide additional instruction to the singing boys.[17]

With both Marsh and Bennett at the helm it was inevitable that a sound musical tradition would be established and, rather than a run-of-the-mill 'Cock and Hen' choir, Bennett recruited and trained a choir of ten 'singing boys',* whom he instructed twice a week. The singing boys sat in the organ gallery and on great occasions they would be augmented by the cathedral choir. In March 1818 the Trustees voted to furnish the singing boys with white surplices 'to be worn on Sundays and on Festival and Feast Days' – this was a very advanced thing but there are no records of revolts against the use of such 'Popish Rags!'. What this Minute also reflects is that the Feast Days of the Book of Common Prayer were being observed and that festivals were held. One such festival took place on 27 June 1815 when the two Societies of Chichester Freemasons descended upon St John's in procession. The Freemasons' minute book[18] describes in florid terms how the procession from the Guildhall was led by the Band of the Sussex Local Militia in full uniform and how the 'Rt Worshipfull & Revd Br S.J. Tufnell' gave a discourse 'which displayed so great a fund of Masonic knowledge'. Marsh attended the service, taking part in the playing, but his account[19] is somewhat different (he was not a mason) concentrating as it does on the music which included his own setting of Psalm 133 and the Hallelujah Chorus from *Messiah* in which the cathedral choir took part with both him and Bennett presiding at the organ console. He records that the Chapel was more crowded than he had ever seen it.

The William Gruggens, father and son (see page 17) were able to spare enough time from their surgery and banking to play a major part in the running of the Chapel. William Senior was elected a Trustee in December 1817 and the following Easter was elected as chapel warden for the minister, a post which he held alongside John Marsh until he (Gruggen) died in 1827. William Gruggen Junior was sworn in as Trustee on 20 April 1824, the same day as John Marsh Junior, so both 'juniors' served alongside their illustrious fathers until the 'seniors' were duly called to rest. When William

---

* The use of robed boys' choirs in parish churches and proprietary chapels was very unusual at this time; they are generally associated with the Victorian Oxford Movement – see page 79.

Gruggen Senior's time was up his son took his place as chapel warden at Easter 1828, and remained in office until 1860 when he retired.

The first major alteration to the interior was proposed at the Trustees' meeting on 2 December, namely bringing the east gallery forward between five and six feet and a subscription was set up to raise the necessary funds. What the Minutes (as usual!) do not record is the reason for it, to provide much-needed extra seating capacity; a drawing[20] shows that six extra box pews were provided together with two bench pews for the singing boys who were now placed in front of the organ. A sub-committee, which included John Marsh, was set up to superintend the operation and in his diary Marsh records that the work commenced on 26 January 1818. If evidence were needed of the demand for accommodation in St John's it can be found in the Pew Rental Book which shows that four of the new pews were already spoken for in November 1817, before construction had begun. A previous proposal of February 1814 to erect two galleries 'for the accommodation of the girls educated in the city' was not executed but may well have been destined for this site. The east gallery was further altered in June that year[21] when the organ was moved forward by six inches to allow access from the vestry below the organ loft, thus giving the organist a faster route to his post after having discussed the order of service with the minister. Unfortunately the price paid for this was that one of the singing boys' pews had to be abolished and accordingly their number was reduced from ten to six, which can hardly have been good for the leading of the singing.

Problems with the fabric began to be encountered from an early stage. Ventilation of the Chapel was discussed by the Trustees in April 1818[22] when it was proposed that the east and west rosettes be replaced with ventilators and a cupola provided in the centre of the roof. In addition, to counteract penetrating damp, it was proposed to render the south side of the Chapel in 'composition grey lime'. The cupola idea was abandoned but the rendering went ahead. In 1819 Elmes' failure to provide access to the roof-space was rectified when two trap doors were provided adjacent to the bell turret and the windows were altered to open from the bottom, 'it being found inconvenient that the windows should continue to be opened at the centre'. In July the first of several roof repairs had to be carried out on the south face. 1822[23] was to prove a crisis year for fabric problems and one which was to force the Trustees to consider taking legal proceedings against Elmes and the contractors. In April steps had to be taken to cure a damp problem in the wall over and behind the organ* whilst the following month the Trustees ordered that the slates on the south face of the roof should be removed and replaced with 'a superior type of slate called "Duchesses".† The last straw came in August when dry rot was discovered in the floor and George Draper,‡ who was now architect to the Trustees, was instructed to ascertain the state of the floor joists and to report to the next meeting.[24]

---

* Marsh records damp affecting the organ in January 1814 but this was during a very cold spell.
† Duchess was in fact a slate size rather than type – sizes being named after female ranks of aristocracy, a Queen, naturally, being the largest.
‡ George Draper produced the designs for the rebuilding of St Bartholomew's Church, Westgate, begun in 1824 but not consecrated until 1832, the Corn Exchange and the Infirmary.

Draper duly took up part of the floor and found that the rotting joists, rather than being of oak as specified, were of the much cheaper chestnut, and unseasoned chestnut at that. Similarly it emerged that the slates used on the south face of the roof were not the 'best Tavistock Rag or other slates of equal goodness to be approved by the architect'. This was enough to cause the Trustees to suspect that Elmes had been in collusion with the two contractors in supplying inferior materials and, no doubt, to their mutual benefit. The previous souring of relationships between the Trustees and Elmes doubtless hastened this suspicion, so they agreed to seek Counsel's opinion to recover the costs of the remedial works under Section XX of the Act. The barrister appointed was Samuel Marryatt of The Temple. Marsh, having a conflict of interest, would have been ineligible to act for the Trustees in a legal capacity even if he had wanted to.

The lengthy preamble to the case drafted by the clerk to the Trustees[25] points out that Elmes, as the architect appointed to superintend the erection of the Chapel, had specified the materials to be used and that he had been empowered to alter the specification and determine any dispute which may arise over the payment for such changes and that both parties to the contracts would abide by Elmes' decision. It then tells how the slates and floor materials had been found not to accord with the specification causing remedial works to be necessary. It also states that the Trustees had approached both Brooks and Cooper, the contractors for the timberwork and roof respectively, to find out why the changes had taken place, the findings being recorded as:

> The answer given by both of them is that the whole of the Works were carried out under the inspection of the Architect who was at liberty to cause, and in some instances did cause, such as he felt to be improper to be removed. And with regard to the substitution of Chestnut for Oak Mr Brooks alleges that the change took place not only with the direct and positive approval but at the request of the Architect.

As Elmes had certified in his comprehensive completion report that '... the whole was complete according to the terms of the Contract ...', the Trustees felt that they were on firm grounds with their proposed action, alleging:

> ... Having an idea (although it cannot be proved) that there must have been some agreement or misunderstanding between the builders and the Architect which induced the latter to sacrifice the interests of his Employers.

Strong stuff indeed but curiously, although they had sought explanations from the contractors, they did not approach Elmes for his side of the story, a fact which was not to be lost on Counsel when he delivered his verdict. Mr Marryatt, in his obfuscatory opinion,[26] felt that any case for breach of

Contract would have had to have been made within six years calculated from 1812 or 1813 (i.e. by 1819 at the latest) and felt it to be 'very singular' that the use of improper slates should have passed unobserved for about ten years. Indeed, he felt that the slates having been passed by Elmes

> will afford a strong presumption that they were of equal goodness ... unless it should turn out that the Architect was being paid by the Contractor as well as the Trustees [!].

His views on the timberwork were similar. He ends by saying:

> This case does not suggest that any Enquiry has been made from Mr Elmes, either to his having in fact approved of the substituted joists or slates or as to his reasons and motives ...

What he was tactfully pointing out to his clients was that their case was inconclusive and would not stand up in court. The opinion was read out by the clerk at the Trustees' meeting on 4 December, but the reactions are not recorded, only that the verdict was accepted and the chapel wardens were ordered to take steps to repair the rotten floor joists at a cost not exceeding £15. That is the last time that Elmes is mentioned in the Minute Books and no doubt he remained unforgiven by the Trustees as the problems were to continue, as we shall see later.

In 1823, the Trustees agreed that two new galleries should be erected over the staircases at the west end '... under the inspection of Mr Draper, the Architect, the expense not to exceed £50'. This was not carried out but the plan showing the new east gallery pews[27] also indicates, albeit roughly, the position of these proposed west galleries. They were to occupy the whole space between the bell-ringing area and the window on both sides of the Chapel. Stairs are indicated on the plan but they would need to have been very steep as the galleries would have had to start above the level of the stair-heads. Perhaps the impracticality of the proposal or Draper's estimate put paid to it.

Marsh spent much time and energy on St John's as is evidenced by his diary entries and the Minute Book, and was obviously a dutiful Trustee and chapel warden as well as deputy organist. He regularly attended Trustees' meetings, frequently taking the chair, and continued to be in charge of the pew sales and rentals. His own first pew was No 6 downstairs in the middle row, south side, next to the pulpit, which he rented for £5 15s. 0d. in 1813.[28] Then when his son Edward flew the nest he bought a smaller pew, No 30 in the middle row on the north side,[29] for £92. In his diaries he records several other changes to suit his personal arrangements including moving back to the south side, No 9, in 1818. Marsh continued to be a philanthropist and his proposal to carry out improvements to the organ at his own expense received the Trustees' 'entire approbation of such attention' at the meeting of 6 April 1825, but there is no record of the work having been carried out.

When his beloved wife Elizabeth died in January 1819, Marsh filled the vacuum by travelling even more widely and hence started to absent himself from meetings and also, no doubt, from his organ playing at both St John's and the Cathedral. Unfortunately his health began to deteriorate in 1827 and in that winter, owing to the poor weather, he was largely confined to 8 North Pallant. The winter then turned into a very hot spring which sapped his strength, but he was taken in a chair to St John's on Whit Sunday to receive the Sacrament. Feeling a little better by Trinity Sunday he decided to play for a service, as he records:[30]

> Thinking that now I could attend the morning service at St John's, I on June 1st went there in a chair & arriving just as the bell had struck out, could take my own time in mounting the stairs & traversing the South Gallery, through which I went to the organ loft. For fear however that I might not feel myself when there, so well as I expected, I desired Mr T. Bennett would also attend, who accordingly sat in his own pew adjoining the organ loft, but though I felt it pretty warm part of the time, 'till I got the organ blower to go and open the outer door at the bottom of the ladder, I yet went through the whole duty as well as I usually did & without any particular inconvenience.

He seems to have revived after this and resumed his travels but by September he began to go downhill and he died on 31 October 1828 at the age of 76, a remarkable innings for a Georgian. He was buried in the family tomb in the churchyard of All Saints in East Pallant, since the Act forbade burials in the grounds of his beloved Chapel. His tomb is described by Lindsay Fleming in his Chichester Paper on Chichester's little churches* as follows:

> Stone sarcophagus with hipped top and panelled sides and ends on six balls, resting on a stone two-tiered base. [Inscribed] Elizabeth Catherine Marsh; John Marsh 31 October 1828, aged 77: Sophia, daughter of J.H. Packenshaw Esq and wife of John Marsh, 12 January 1824 aged 41: Charlotte, Sophia and Anna, infants.

Despite his major contributions to the founding and running of St John's, his passing is neither marked nor lamented by the Trustees, or if it was it is not recorded in the Minutes. The only mention is on 12 May 1829 when one John Price was elected as a Trustee 'in place of Mr J. Marsh (deceased)'. What an ungrateful bunch! However, the *Hampshire Telegraph* carried a fitting obituary:[31]

> Died at his residence, in the North Pallant, Chichester, yesterday at midnight J Marsh Esq. His loss will be felt by every class of the community as he was a most liberal contributor to, as well as an active agent in, every benevolent or useful undertaking.

* CP5 *The Little Churches of Chichester* 1957.

Before closing this chapter on the Georgian era it is worth a brief look[*] at the finances for running the Chapel throughout the period, which reveals the challenges faced by the Trustees. In July 1813 the treasurer produced accounts which revealed a surplus of £473 10s. 10d. but by April 1814 this had dropped to £8 10s. 9d.[32] Despite the full congregations and the waiting list for pews, income was insufficient to maintain the services, suggesting that Marsh had got his sums badly wrong, so in September 1814 the Trustees agreed to increase all pew rents by 1s. per sitting at the expiry of the current leases. This put the cost of the dearest sitting up to 27s. per annum. The construction of the new east gallery pews meant a boost in income and a surplus of £58 13s. 4d. by 10 June 1818 but the cost of continuing changes to the fabric led to a fall in the surplus to £8 8s. 0d. by April 1821. The first deficit is recorded on 17 April 1827 with £7 17s. 5d. being due to the treasurer, unfortunately the first of many, as we shall learn in later chapters. At this same meeting Charles Ridge[†] was appointed treasurer, with the deficit making an inauspicious start to his reign. However, a year later he had managed to turn the Trustees' fortunes around and amassed a surplus of £25 18s. 7d. whilst a year later this had risen to £54 3s. 8d. Typical outgoings for the treasurer in connection with the upkeep of services included £26 1s. 0d. for oil in 1815, £3 0s. 9d. on candles in 1816 and £1 13s. 0d. for the six singing boys in 1822.[33]

The death of George IV in 1830 brought the official end to the Georgian era and marks a convenient place to end this stage of the story, with John Marsh and William Dearling both dead and James Elmes out of favour and back in London. The Georgian era had seen the founding of the Chapel and a successful start to its ministry but the Victorian era is now almost upon us, bringing with it a considerable change in both fortunes and outlook.

---

[*] Lengthy looks at financial matters are too tedious for a book of this nature.
[†] A member of the Ridge family who owned the Chichester Old Bank in which William Ridge, one of the investors in the New Town, was a partner.

Seven

VICTORIAN ST JOHN'S 1831-1900

As every schoolboy (including this ageing one) knows, the Victorian era did not commence until 1837 but the William IV years of 1831 to 1836 are neither sufficiently distinctive nor numerous to form an era in their own right which can separate the Georgian from the Victorian. For my money they are much more aligned stylistically to the latter than the former (taste was rapidly going downhill by 1830), so I have included them in this Victorian chapter.

The 1830s were beset with financial problems (or 'challenges' in today's management-speak) for the Trustees which were to set the scene for the rest of the period. A balance of £54 3s. 8d. in April 1830 had fallen to £1 10s. 3d. a year later and in April 1832 it was decided by the Trustees to levy a rate upon pew owners* of one shilling in the pound in order to fund both repairs to the Chapel and interest payments on loans.[1] It had also been proving difficult to pay the dividends due to the shareholders so the Trustees were badly in debt. At a special meeting on 30 April 1835 the agenda was '... to consider the propriety of raising by sale of pews a sum sufficient to pay off the amount due to several shareholders'. At the meeting William Gruggen generously made application to have all his shares paid off by the Trustees and the Trustees resolved to make out securities for delivery to nine other shareholders. This obviously worked, for by April 1836 the balance was back up to £48 12s. 10d.[2]

The oil lighting of the Chapel which had remained since the opening was ousted in 1836 when the Trustees agreed to accept Mr Cazaly's £60 estimate to install gas, the money being raised by private contributions. The subscriptions only netted £50 so the Trustees had to agree to make up the balance, but unfortunately on completion of the work Cazaly's account came to even more than the estimate (the reason for the excess is not recorded) but as a sweetener Cazaly did offer to put up an additional lamp in the gallery 'free of charge'.[3] The lighting installation, which was described in Chapter Five, can be seen in the 1871 view of the interior (see Fig 23) and consisted of Argand burners hung from the parapet of the gallery.

---

* Section XLVI of the Act allowed such a rate to be levied in times of insufficient income – normal practice in a proprietary chapel.

John Marsh Junior, who was a Trustee, died in 1839 bringing to an end the link with its most distinguished founding father. Further financial gloom was reflected in a deficit of £50 5s. 10d. which was announced at the same Easter Tuesday meeting. Once again a rate had to be levied, this time of 6d in the pound, which restored the business to a more even keel for three years until another serious dip in April 1842 when a deficit of £59 17s. 0d. accrued. At the Easter Tuesday meeting the treasurer, Charles Ridge, resigned. We do not know whether this was on account of the size of the deficit or a reflection of the fact that the Ridge and Newland Bank, of which he had been a partner, had failed the previous year and therefore he might not be considered a fit person to have at the financial helm! Either way, his resignation was accepted but matters still did not improve and in 1844 interest on £3,200 remained unpaid, so once again a one shilling rate, which brought in £104 5s. 0d., was levied. By 1851 more heavy repairs were required to the Chapel and the lowest estimate of £84 10s. 0d. could not be matched by funds so the money had to be raised by a further one-shilling rate. The poor shareholders were being brutally shown how precarious their investment was and surely many pew-holders, faced with these constant levies in addition to the initial purchase price, must have been eyeing the new church of St Peter the Great which was rising out of the ground in West Street and heeding the rumours that the sittings there were to be absolutely free. Rates were levied again in 1855, 1857 and 1858, in which year a bigger crisis loomed: the Reverend Stephen Barbut, who had been minister since the opening in 1813, tendered his resignation. He resigned over a disagreement and a point of principle about the chapel's finances and had written an open letter to the congregation explaining his reasons. This last action had antagonised the Trustees who, after debating the issue at a special meeting on 4 November, produced a printed resolution to be sent to Barbut. A copy of this was pasted into the Minute Book and it gives their perspective on the dispute:

> ... the Trustees desire to express their deep regret at the cause of such a vacancy; – viz, the resignation of Rev. S. Barbut: and at this, the earliest opportunity which has occurred since the fact of such resignation was made public, they further desire to express to Mr Barbut the high respect they entertain for him and their grateful appreciation of his long and faithful services.
>
> Nor is it with less regret that they have learnt, from a letter addressed by him to the congregation, one of the grounds (and, as Mr Barbut states, not a weak one) which has induced him to take this step: viz 'that he is, as it were, standing between the Trustees and the possibility of an improvement in their financial position of which improvement there could be no reasonable prospect as long as he continued in the office which he had just resigned': and that 'such an opinion had been intimated in no very ambiguous terms at a vestry meeting' 'a shaft', Mr Barbut remarks, 'which was not likely to miss its mark'.

> The Trustees are deeply pained that Mr Barbut should give credence
> to the statement that such an opinion was ever promulgated and
> accepted at a Vestry Meeting ... to their knowledge and recollection,
> not a word that could be construed into ought disrespectful to, or
> mistrustful of him, was ever uttered at any of their Vestry Meetings.

Minister and Trustees seemed to have locked themselves into a war of printed
words, trying to upstage each other as being the most hurt by the other's
sayings. Despite whatever really instigated the dispute, it is interesting to
reflect on why Barbut might have felt himself to be so in the way of 'financial
improvement'. This surely can only have been by way of his drawing his
rightful salary – had he been approached unofficially at that vestry meeting
to take a salary cut, one wonders? We know he was a wealthy man from
his purchasing of Hobbs' large house in Friary lane in 1820* so perhaps
the Trustees felt he could have afforded it. Anyway, Barbut's resignation
was accepted by the Bishop and his long and successful ministry, which
had lasted for 45 years from the opening, sadly ended on a sour note. He
then seems to have retired but remained as Prebendary of Ferring in the
Cathedral until his death in 1869.[4] He was persuaded by the Trustees to
cover the interregnum for which he was paid the princely sum of £20. A
slightly different slant on his departure was given some ten years later on his
death in September 1869 in a tribute[5] carried in the *Chichester Advertiser*.

> When he had passed by some years the allotted boundary of three-
> score years and ten, his failing bodily powers warned him that it was
> time for rest, and in 1859 he determined to resign his post at St John's
> Chapel where he had done a great and good work, the fruits of which
> will never be lost. And now after ten years of comparative retirement
> the time has come and he has been summoned away ...

This view might well have been tempered by hindsight but one thing was
certain, although the Chapel had always been unstable financially, pastorally
Barbut had been a much-needed rock for his flock. His departure ushered
in a period of great instability.

Stephen Barbut's place was taken by the Rev. Edward Whitehead,
another Oxford graduate who had been born in 1813 and previously held
the post of minister to the proprietary Laura Chapel in Bath.† It appears
to be he who introduced the zealous evangelicalism to St John's which
was to last until the Chapel closed, fending off the effects of the high-
church Oxford Movement and causing the Chapel's layout to be preserved.
In view of this it is appropriate here to take a brief look at the Oxford
Movement, which was having such an enormous impact in the Church of
England during this period, so as to understand why it failed to have any
effect upon St John's.

---

* See page 15.
† This chapel, taking its name from Laura Pulteney, daughter of the developer of Pulteney Bridge and
Great Pulteney Street, opened in 1796 and closed in 1890. It was demolished in 1907.

32 *The Rev. Stephen Barbut. In this view it can be seen that he had by now fully adopted Victorian fashions and tastes.*

As we saw in Chapter Six services in Georgian times were all very 'low' by today's standards, concentrating on the preaching of the word and often exhibiting a lack of reverence during services. The Oxford Movement was started by John Keble who made his famous *Assize Sermon* on national apostasy in 1833 with the assertion that the Church of England was a true branch of the Catholic Apostolic Church.[6] It proposed a return of reverence and dignity to services and the placing of a greater emphasis upon the Sacrament of Holy Communion, this last requiring the congregation to focus upon the altar rather than the pulpit. Another feature of the movement was the establishment in parish churches of robed choirs of men and boys sitting facing each other in choir stalls across the chancel and performing the sort of music hitherto only heard in cathedrals or Oxbridge college chapels. These ideas inflamed the evangelical wing who saw it as the introduction of ritualism and popery and hence something to be resisted, even though the Tractarians argued (not always convincingly) that their ideas did not contravene the rubric of the Book of Common Prayer. The degree of acceptance of the ideas, however, varied. Along the coast in Brighton the ritualism was taken to incense-laden, theatrical extremes in the new anglo-catholic churches being built there, with Holy Communion being termed 'Mass' and the priests being addressed as 'Father', all of which became known, in a parody of the local railway company, as the 'London Brighton and South Coast Religion'. In most cases the effects were far less extreme; Morning and Evening Prayer remained the principal services but there were few churches from which the box pews and three-decker pulpits were not ripped out to be replaced by bench pews facing the altar, along with choir-stalls inserted into the chancel and candlesticks and a cross placed on the altar. Georgian churches which had no chancel were reordered so as to provide a sanctuary of some sort – but not this one!

The evangelical tradition had been firmly established at St John's by the time the Oxford Movement reached Chichester and its advances were staunchly repelled by the successive ministers where the evangelical *Hymnal Companion to the Book of Common Prayer* continued to be used rather than the increasingly-popular *Hymns Ancient and Modern* of 1861 which was associated with the Tractarians.[*] Although a robed boys' choir and observation of all Feast Days had been established in Georgian times, both were quietly dispensed with, doubtless being considered too 'high church', but the Chapel's three-decker was left untouched, continuing to eclipse the altar upon which no candlestick was ever to set foot – or rather base. As such its by-now unusual layout was to remain until the Chapel's closure.

In 1860 Whitehead requested the Trustees to enlarge the vestry to accommodate a Sunday school which was agreed to but, for financial reasons, could not be taken forward. Financial problems continued to dog the business of the Chapel and more rates had to be levied, six times between 1863 and 1866.[†] After two successive deficits poor William Gruggen resigned as treasurer and Charles Halsted[7] was appointed in his place. The continuing financial problems also affected the organists. Thomas Bennett had died in 1848[8] and had been succeeded by his son Henry at the same £26 salary. As part of the belt-tightening exercise he agreed in 1859 to take a reduced salary of £18 but this was short-lived as he resigned in October 1860, possibly having regretted his decision. Richard Wills was appointed in his place at £18 per annum in March 1861 but only lasted three years as he too resigned. John Knapp was the next organist who took up office in March 1864 but his salary was only £12 for the first year! As with Wills he stuck it out for three years before resigning – there is no record in the Minute Book of his first-year salary having been reviewed so he too obviously decided that he could not afford to go on. There is no

---

[*] Ironically, *Hymns A & M* became the 'middle-of-the-road' hymnal after the introduction, in 1906, of *The English Hymnal* which was quickly adopted by Anglo-Catholics.
[†] The owner of pew no 9 is given in the calculation sheets (WSRO Par 39/53) as Capt Edward Marsh (John Marsh's younger son) whose address is shown as Nethersole House, Bath. Nethersole was the name of the Marsh family seat in Kent.

record of a successor having been appointed or of any discussion about it. We can only assume that doing without an organist was seen as a necessary economy. Whilst on the subject of music it is interesting to note that the Minute Books contain very few references to the choir. We know not when the choir of boys established by Thomas Bennett disappeared; however, there is an entry for April 1868 recording thanks to a Miss Lunn 'for her services in the choir' which suggests that the boys had long since been dismissed. They were replaced by an adult mixed and non-robed choir who sang from the east gallery, arrayed either side of the organ.

By 1867 there had been several defaulters against paying the rates (including Steven Barbut who does not seem to have surrendered his pew on his resignation) and at the Easter Tuesday meeting the Clerk was instructed to instigate proceedings under the Act to force them to pay up. This particular meeting was fraught with difficulties for not only was it was recorded that the Rev. Whitehead had '... placed his resignation at the disposal of the Trustees', Knapp the organist had also done likewise. The problems with the minister seem to have been financial and we can only assume that, once again, the Trustees had been unable to pay his salary. A resolution was passed that Whitehead be requested to continue his ministry to which he agreed but it was a shaky arrangement. By March 1868 poor Whitehead had been reduced to threatening proceedings against the Trustees for his arrears and expenses.[9] Things were rapidly coming to a head and in the following May Counsel's opinion was sought as to how to deal with the defaulters and whether the affairs of the Chapel could be dealt with under the Winding Up Acts – i.e. could the 'business' be closed down?

The opinion of Mr Frederick Merrifield QC was duly sought and submitted.[10] In respect of the defaulters he opined that there was a case for applying for a Distress Warrant to recover the arrears but warned on the other hand that the Trustees were liable to be sued by the minister in the name of the treasurer in respect of their own defaulting. As far as closing the Chapel he felt that this could not be achieved 'without legislature'; in other words the Act would have to be repealed or amended. In June, as a result of this opinion, two pew-holders, Messrs Duke and Johnson,[*] were duly visited with the majesty of the law whilst the problem with Whitehead was settled out of court when the Trustees wrote to him[11] advising that his stipend due on 24 of the month 'would be paid in a fortnight'.

The Rev. Whitehead tendered his resignation again in April 1870 but this time he obviously meant it as he asked that the letter be forwarded to the Bishop. The Bishop eventually accepted the resignation and the incumbency was declared vacant on 23 January 1871. However, no advertisement for a successor was placed. Although a rate of 2s. had been imposed the previous April, the Trustees were obviously not in a position to commit themselves

---

* William Duke was a solicitor whilst William Johnson was the builder who occupied the former timber yard next door to the Chapel. Johnson did much work for the Trustees so this recalcitrant attitude must have carried a severe business risk for him!

to funding another minister's salary and hence persuaded Whitehead to cover his own interregnum for free, which he did until 19 February 1871 when he finally withdrew his services. A Mr Garrett of Winchester covered the service for 26 February 1871[12] after which the chapel closed for public worship. Nothing is recorded in the Minute Book about how the pew-owning congregation were told what was to happen to them but with the relatively new churches of St Paul and St Peter the Great now available in addition to the little churches there would have been plenty of alternative – and free – places for them to attend Divine Worship.

Although the Chapel was no longer in use and its ministry had ceased, the Trust had not been wound up and the Trustees continued to meet even though they had effectively ceased trading. They continued to pay dividends to the shareholders and caused two more long-standing debtors to appear before the JP of the city in 1872. Indeed, from reading the Minute Book it would be difficult to detect that anything was amiss; only the lack of appointments of wardens on Easter Tuesday gives a clue that things were not quite normal.

In 1874 a mood of resurgence began to stir within the Trustees and in January it was decided to make an offer to the shareholders to buy out their holdings at £20 each. The solicitors Greene and Malim drew up a document,[13] which was sent to each shareholder and pew-owner, containing a proposition with an attached agreement which could be signed and returned.

The wording of the proposition explains the scheme so succinctly it is worth quoting in full:

Sir____

ST JOHN'S CHAPEL, CHICHESTER

We are authorised by a few Gentlemen who are deeply anxious to see this chapel once more open for the celebration of Divine Service therein, to submit the following proposition to the Shareholders and Pewholders with a view to that desirable end:

1. AS TO THE SHARES. Our Clients are willing, in the event of their being able to obtain all the Shares, to purchase the same at Twenty Pounds per Share.

2. AS TO THE PEWS. With a view of extinguishing private ownership and vesting all the Pews in the Trustees, they are prepared to accept Surrenders of the Pews and their accompanying liabilities.

This offer is conditional upon the terms being accepted by all parties interested, as well Shareholders as Pewholders; unless, therefore, all assent, the proposal will be abandoned.

Although this offer is entirely independent of pecuniary considerations, we may mention, with regard to the Shares, that one of the largest shareholders was a short time since offered Ten Pounds per Share for eleven Shares; and we need not inform Pewholders that the Pews are not only valueless but are encumbered with heavy liabilities.

We shall be obliged by your filling in, signing and returning to us, on or before the 2nd of February next, the enclosed form, stating whether you assent to the proposal or not.

The proposal was indeed an interesting one. Eliminating privately-owned pews would not remove the Chapel's proprietary status but as all pews would all now be rented a higher income would ensue; the *quid pro quo* for the erstwhile owners being the loss of those 'heavy liabilities' to which the offer refers, namely being forced to pay rates over which they had no control. At their meeting of 10 June 1874 it was reported that the 'majority' had accepted and eight days later a sub-committee was set up to 'take into consideration the present general position of the Chapel and what can be done for the future ...'.

The sub-committee reported back on 4 July that the majority of the pewholders were willing to surrender their interests and suggested that the Trustees use this as the first step towards reopening the Chapel. However, nothing is recorded in the Minutes about how the shareholder matter was dealt with. Whilst it is not clear whether the required unanimous support was obtained, the shareholders did bind themselves by deed not to take any interest until the minister had received £200 of his stipend. On reflection, however, it was realised that after paying all the necessary running costs of the Chapel there would still be no balance of funds to pay the shareholders. So five 'Gentlemen' bought out the entire share stock for £750 which was then settled upon three of their number who agreed to abide by the requirement under a private trust deed.[14] These two results were sufficient to start the preparations for the reopening.

That entry in the minute book for 4 July 1874 is the first which acknowledges the fact that the Chapel had actually been closed! The suggested reopening was accepted by the meeting and steps were taken to find another minister who was chosen on 27 November 1874 in the form of George Blisset MA. who was vicar of St Thomas the Apostle, Wells in Somerset. Blisset was appointed on 14 February 1875 and the chapel prepared to reopen for business. The Easter Tuesday Trustees' meeting on 30 April 1875 recorded the slender balance of nine shillings and fivepence but nonetheless the Trustees went ahead in appointing Mr Bradley as organist at £30 per annum and Mr Daniel Lee as 'Chapel Keeper' at £20 per annum as well as instructing the treasurer to advance to Rev. Blisset £30 as one quarter's salary. Nothing is recorded about the reopening so one assumes that, unlike the opening in 1813, this was a very low-key affair with no concerts or banner-waving. The offertory book[15] carries an entry 'St John's reopened on Feb 14th' and records that on the following Sunday the 35 Communicants gave £1 9s. 9d. The paucity of information in the

Trustees' Minute Book at this period is partly compensated for by the existence of a memorandum book[16] spanning the years 1875 to 1892 which contains, *inter alia*, draft minutes which for some reason did not make it to the actual book.

Blisset's seemed to have been a successful appointment and he must have appreciated his time at St John's as he donated a stove for warming the Chapel and bestowed 'numerous other gifts' upon it, for which thanks were duly recorded in the Minute Books. Despite this his ministry was to be short-lived for he resigned in October 1876, leaving the post vacant once again. He was succeeded by Francis Gell whose last incumbency had been as rector of Llyswen in Breconshire[17] but this too was to be brief since he resigned in April 1878 to take up a new living in Kent, all of which must have been rather unsettling. The reasons for the short-lived appointments cannot be inferred from the minute or memorandum books but one strongly suspects that difficulties with salaries again lay at the heart of it. Despite these financial troubles the organ was rebuilt in 1877 as a memorial to Charles Hayllar, a wealthy butcher who had been a chapel warden and lived at 8 St John's Street.* He had apparently long desired the organ to be 'restored' (*sic*) and 'looked forward to making it a really sound and efficient instrument'.[18] Yet another appeal was launched to pay for the work which was carried out by a Mr Hayward and a brass plate was affixed to the organ to dedicate the work to Mr Hayllar.

The next minister, nominated on 25 May 1878, was George Furness-Smith, a young man of 28 taking up his first appointment. His style of ministry was enthusiastically evangelical as is demonstrated by some of his writings in the *St John's Magazine*. In January 1879 construction of the Chichester to Midhurst branch of the London Brighton and South Coast Railway had commenced and the new minister was keen to carry out missionary work amongst the navvies who as a breed were widely regarding as an ungodly lot. In the June 1880[19] magazine he wrote:

> The workmen engaged on the new railway to Midhurst have lately elicited the interest and sympathy of the Chichester public to a large degree. It is recognised that for a class of men from the very necessities of their work so different in their habits and mode of life from other classes, a peculiar and separate agency is required and a Scripture Reader has accordingly been engaged who will work exclusively among them. Mrs Duke of North Pallant will gladly receive donations of money and daily and weekly papers, Bands of Hope and other periodicals will be acceptable.

Despite all this laudable missionary work the navvies still caused havoc in the area with their unruly behaviour and many were the arrests for drunkenness and assault. However the 'interest and sympathy' for the navvies of which

---

* See pages 120-3 where the history of this house is dealt with in detail.

Furness-Smith wrote was real as had been witnessed by a public subscription to fund the provision of a meat tea for them at the *Dolphin Hotel* on 9 April 1880, at which the Dean gave an address and the choir of St Peter the Great sang.[21] It is recorded that a number of ladies had volunteered to preside and no doubt St John's was well represented in their number.

Another ungodly lot were the Goodwood race-goers but they were accorded only condemnation rather than compassionate mission in his magazine editorial[175] for August 1880:

> We shall be congratulating ourselves that race week* is past and gone for this year ... Whatever may be said in defence of the races as they might be, it is a too-patent fact that they bring together a large number of dissipated and disreputable characters of whom it is a relief to be rid ... moreover, however enabling as a spectacle a horse-race may be conceived to be, the race course and the betting ring are so intensely allied that the influences must be pronounced to be of a demoralising character.

Unsurprisingly George Furness-Smith's zeal also extended to condemnation of the demon drink† and in November 1880 he formed at St John's adult and juvenile branches of the Church of England Temperance Society[22] whose objects, he cited, were 'the recovery of the intemperate and the prevention of intemperance'. Meetings were held twice-monthly featuring 'readings and recitations and plenty of singing'.

The year 1879 was quite a momentous one for St John's Chapel, being marked not only by Furness-Smith's ministry but also by two major projects both funded by generous benefactors. The interior of the Chapel was changed dramatically when Douglas Henty offered to re-seat the ground floor at his own expense. The builder, Mr Fielder, had drawn up a proposed scheme in which the box pews and open-backed benches were ousted in favour of typically Victorian pine bench pews virtually all of which faced the front. He retained the geographical location of private pews under the galleries and fee seats in the middle, separated by a low partition, but internal communication between the classes at the back of the Chapel was now possible. The four pews at the centre of the Chapel were built shorter at their inner ends so as to accommodate heating apparatus but Fielder's drawing[23] is incomplete at this point; the inner ends have not been drawn in, suggesting that the new heating arrangements were undecided. There is another drawing[24] entitled 'New proposed position of stove' which shows (in elevation only) a huge coal-burning stove of the type normally supplied to cathedrals which would be sited under the west gallery to vent in two directions to the outer walls by cast-iron pipes suspended from the ceiling.

---

* Until well into the 20th century there was but one race meeting a year at Goodwood – always in the summer.
† This was a little insensitive, if not hypocritical, as the congregation included two generous brewing families, the Atkeys and the Hentys.

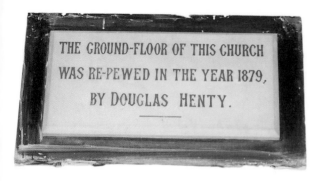

THE GROUND-FLOOR OF THIS CHURCH WAS RE-PEWED IN THE YEAR 1879, BY DOUGLAS HENTY.

33 *The tablet over the main door commemorating Douglas Henty's 1879 gift of the new pews.*

There is no evidence, physical or written, that this scheme was adopted and one can imagine the Trustees' reaction to an installation of such ugliness – besides which, being situated at the back, it would have been rather ineffective. Eventually a large gas radiator was installed in the middle. Fortunately for posterity the pulpit and Communion rails were left untouched by Fielder's re-ordering scheme.

The work, which also included redecoration, cost Mr Henty £326 and seems to have been accomplished with surprisingly little disruption to the daily round and on only one Sunday, 25 May, were services unable to be held, being transferred instead to the Assembly Rooms.[25] The return to normality was enthusiastically heralded by Furness-Smith in his June editorial:[26]

> When we assemble together in one place, with one accord to wait for the promise of the Father, may we be filled with the Holy Ghost! May He humble us at God's footstool revealing to us the exceeding sinfulness of sin!

Reflecting in July after a month of the new arrangements Furness-Smith points out that the new arrangements had overcome his perceived shortcomings of the former box pews:

> It is true, the semi-privacy which our ancient pews afforded has been missed by some* ... the same cause which makes more observable the presence of those who attend, also makes more conspicuous the absence of those who stay away.

The other major scheme was the provision of a schoolroom which resulted from an act of munificence by another member of the congregation, this time Mr George Paull. George Paull had been elected a Trustee in April 1861 and later became the minister's chapel warden. The schoolroom was built on land already owned by the Trustees to the south-east of the Chapel adjoining the southern boundary wall and Mr Paull laid the foundation stone on Whit Monday 1879. It was completed in July at the cost of £239 10s. 7d. and on 18 July[27] the workmen were 'very pleasantly entertained within its walls'; we can be fairly certain that this entertainment did not involve the dispensing of any alcoholic refreshment! The new schoolroom permitted an expansion of the Chapel's work amongst children and young people. Six

---

* Of course it would be – that was part of the charm of box pews.

Sunday-school classes were provided (three each for boys and girls) meeting twice at 11am and again at 2.30pm.* Midweek there was a young men's meeting held on alternate Wednesdays, the secretary being Fred Atkey, great grandson of James Atkey the brewer and Newtown investor we met in Chapter One. Unfortunately the conduct of these meetings was not always as orderly as might have been hoped. Reporting that the 1880 meetings were to be suspended after Easter until the Autumn the magazine[28] hopes '... may God pardon all the faults and failings which have attended their meetings'. We are not told what these faults and failings might have been but we can imagine that it was too delicate a matter for the pen of GF-S. Other midweek meetings took place on Tuesdays at 8pm on a monthly cycle: general prayer meeting, general Bible reading, mission prayer meeting and lastly a community meeting.

Also that year a subscription library was started, run by Mrs Malim and containing some 350 books, of which 80 had been provided by George Blisset's sisters. Subscribers paid the princely sum of 1d. a month to borrow one volume a week which could be kept for 14 days and changed on Tuesdays. Defaulters were levied a fine of a halfpenny and this provided a useful source of additional income – the accounts for the financial year 1887/8 show that a total of 6s. 7½d. was netted from absent-minded readers.[29]

1879 also marked the death of Mrs Barbut, widow of Steven Barbut. Mrs Barbut had continued as a member of the congregation and was living in St John's Street; a valuation of her effects for probate[30] shows that the house† was very well appointed. Paying tribute to her in the magazine Furness-Smith extols her link with the past '... yet so lively was her interest in the present with its doings, so warm her sympathy with the young, that few indeed would suspect that her best years had been lived before locomotives were heard of'. This oblique reference to her prime years being in a long-past era seems rather tactless – perhaps it was the headiness of his youth which caused him to write with so little regard for the sensibilities surrounding females' ages.

An important contributor to the ministry of the Chapel at this time was the distribution of the magazine *Home Words*. This was published nationally by the 'Hand and Heart Publishing Office', in London under the editorship of Rev. Charles Bullock BD and its contents of poems, uplifting stories and improving articles on religious observance was a characteristically Victorian blend of fervour and mawkish sentimentality. A flavour of it is given in this extract from a poem by the Rev. James Page entitled *The Book of Common Prayer*:

---

* The custom of Sunday school meeting twice was still observed in the 1950s when your author attended the same.
† Steven Barbut had, as we saw in Chapter One, bought Hobbs' large house (St John's House) in Friary Lane in 1820. The valuer's notebook, however, lists Mrs Barbut's house as being in St John's Street so St John's House must have been disposed of by then. As St John's Street was not then numbered we cannot identify which house Mrs Barbut lived in.

> I have a casket, stored for me
> With jewels rich and rare
> By sainted, martyred, ancestry
> My Book of Common Prayer
>
> O Book, beyond all price to me,
> Save ONE, beyond compare
> My Church's glorious liturgy
> My Book of Common Prayer

Home Words was intended to be issued with a local parish insert to form a parish magazine and at St John's this was done, the two being sold as *The St John's Magazine* and extracts from some of these have been quoted above. At the end of the year it was possible to send the collected works back to the publisher to have them bound 'at wholesale prices of 15d.' in blue cloth with the Chapel's name on the cover; Mr Paull acted as agent for this at St John's.[31] Two such volumes for the years 1879 and 1880 have survived and are in the collections of the Chichester District Museum.

The new beginnings offered by the reopening and the various acts of munificence improved the financial status of the Chapel for a while and there was much outward giving to missionary work both at home and abroad on account of the almost unbelievable generosity of the congregation. Nonetheless, the heavy cost of providing the services was ever-present and in 1881 a collecting box was installed[32] adjacent to the middle door 'for contributions towards expenses'. The years 1879 to 1881 did seem to be restoring a measure of overall stability, but it was to be short-lived.

The year 1881 was marked by two resignations. The first was of Mr Angel the organist who was 'given notice to resign' (i.e., he was sacked) 'the trustees feeling that the singing of the choir is not equal to the requirements of the congregation'. He was replaced in December by William Dean on a salary of £30. More serious was the resignation of George Furness-Smith in July, marking the third short incumbency in a row. Once again we do not know the reason for the departure. Furness-Smith's time seemed to have been most successful but he was young and probably had higher ambitions. After leaving St John's he held a number of posts within the Church Missionary Society before returning to parish work as rector of Kedleston in Derbyshire in 1916,[33] his last appointment before retirement. Furness-Smith was replaced by Rev. William David Cowley DD who was elected on 20 December 1881, having previously served for 23 years as chaplain on the Bengal Establishment.[34] His was a popular ministry which was fortunately set to last for much longer than the three short terms of his predecessors put together.

The heating problem was tackled again in May 1883 when the Trustees proposed a vote of thanks to their two benefactors, George Paull and Douglas Henty, for their 'kind and liberal donation for defraying the expenses of the gas stove' which we can assume was the vast cast-iron gas radiator which can be seen in the interior view of 1923 at Fig 38. Unfortunately the legacy of James Elmes and his contractors surfaced again in early 1884 when a superficial inspection by Mr Vick[35] the builder revealed that the bell needed to be re-hung to remove the risk of collapse, the vestry chimney required repairs, the roof needed a detailed examination and the problems with ventilation had not gone away. In addition, redecoration was required inside and out and it was decided that (unspecified) alterations were desirable to the second- and third-row pews in the galleries. Whilst an amazing £114 4s. 0d. was raised in donations a further £22 15s. 3d. was needed to meet Vick's bill. As 2 February was the tenth anniversary of the reopening of the Chapel it was decided to launch an appeal in connection with the planned commemorative services and a printed notice, detailing the problems, was issued to the long-suffering congregation. Once again, the faithful members dug deep and the collections at the two services netted £32 16s. 0d.[36]

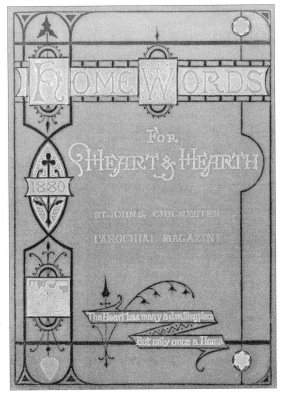

34 *Cover of the* St John's Magazine *1880. Note the incorrect use of the term 'parochial'.*

Without access to magazines for this era we have less evidence of the life of the Chapel but we can be certain that the style of the ministry did not change and we definitely know that the perceived threat posed by the Oxford Movement continued to be kept at bay. The printed accounts which appear in the Minute Book after 1888 give some clues as to the activities. Mission work was well supported, including the Church Missionary Society and the Zenana Mission, whilst regular scriptural knowledge competitions were held, which included a separate class for servants! However, despite all this mission work, in April 1885 the trustees voted against apportioning seats to the militia[37] as 'it would not be within the meaning of the Act'. There were annual 'treats' for the choir and the Sunday school for which funds were raised from the ever-generous congregation. Destinations included Arundel, Hayling Island and Singleton Arboretum. Travel was invariably by train, that to Singleton being by way of the new Midhurst branch whose navvies, when it was under construction, had been so carefully ministered to by St John's. The most adventurous outing was to West Brompton in 1887 to visit the American Exhibition, the aquarium and to partake in a steam-boat trip on the river. The total cost for the 37 participants was a staggering £13 5s. 9d. The following year the trip was to Singleton again for the more modest outlay of £3 6s. 6d.! William Dean resigned as organist in April 1886 and was replaced by Mr J. St Clair at a salary 'of not less than £25'. At the same time it was agreed to affiliate St John's to the Parochial Choirs Association, a Victorian equivalent of the Royal School of Church Music.

The generous George Paull died in April 1886 and the Trustees duly recorded their appreciation which was inscribed on a separate page of the Minute Book – the first time this had happened. It ran:

> The Trustees desire to record the long and valuable services rendered to themselves and the congregation by the late George Paull who was for many years a Warden of the Chapel and a member of the congregation from its commencement, whose long life was faithful in good works and deeds and kindness among them, especially among the young and whose steady and consistent Christian life should be had in remembrance. The Trustees record Mr Paull's strenuous and successful efforts in procuring the reopening of the chapel which remained closed from 1870[*] to 1875: his numerous and substantial benefactions towards the improvement of the fabric and the maintenance of Divine Service; his gift of a schoolroom and a substantial bequest of £50 to be applied to the benefit of the same.

Fifty pounds does not sound a very substantial bequest by today's standards but in 1883 Paull had already set up a trust account in the bank in the sum of £400 to be invested and applied together with all interests arising therefrom 'at his absolute discretion' but primarily for the endowment of the Chapel.[38] The Trustees elected to use the £50 for enlarging the schoolroom for which purpose a sub-committee was set up. The lowest tender received was from William Johnson (next door to the Chapel)[†] in the sum of £75 which, with additional improvements to the existing fabric, came to £93 14s. 1½d., fully £43 14s. 1½d. short of Paull's bequest. Despite this it was decided to award the contract in the hope of raising the necessary funds, no doubt once again from the long-suffering congregation. How the money was actually raised is not recorded but it may have been drawn from the Paull Trust.

That same year, 1886, brought forth another kind benefactor whose generosity was to have the most lasting effect upon the income of the Trustees. Miss Farndell had offered to convey her house, 68 North Street[39] (then numbered 24), to the Trustees 'for the endowment of the chapel and used in such a way as the Trustees might think fit'. Needless to say, the offer was accepted and it was decided to rent the property and use the income to supplement the minister's salary in accordance with Section XL of the Act.

---

[*] This is an error – the closure actually took place in 1871.
[†] Johnson had acquired Cooper's old yard – see page 133.

By April 1887 the deeds of Miss Farndell's house, a substantial Georgian property, were vested in the Trustees.

Yet more substantial repairs became necessary in the summer of 1888 for which Mr Vick's tender was accepted in the sum of £66 10s. 0d. Curiously his tender was not the lowest; that submitted by William Johnson was two pounds less, but the Trustees elected on ballot not to accept it[40] – perhaps the memory of Johnson's defaulting over pew rates still rankled! The final costs were higher than the tender and so another appeal was launched with special services to raise the necessary £71 15s. 0d. As an inducement to attend these services (and to dig deeper into their pockets) the congregation were advised that the anthems to be sung would be 'The Glory of the Lord' by John Goss* in the morning and 'The Lord hath done great things' by Henry Smart in the evening.[41] The melodramatic works of Messrs Goss and Smart were more highly regarded in those days so it was probably worth a try. More improvements to the gas lighting were carried out in 1890 but estimates varying between £110 and £150 to improve the heating were rejected as being too great, so the work was deferred.

Charles John Atkey, another grandson of James Atkey the brewer, resigned his trusteeship in April 1889.[42] He had returned to Chichester in 1885 to manage the Eastgate Brewery and became mayor in 1875. He had been elected a Trustee in 1874 but as he had not attended a meeting since May 1878 his interests must have been diverted elsewhere.

Dr Cowley had kept his ministry going for just over ten years when he decided to resign and at the meeting on 19 April 1892 the saddened Trustees resolved:

> This meeting received with deep regret the announcement made to them this day of the resignation of the Rev. Dr Cowley as the Minister of this chapel and having considered the circumstances connected with it earnestly request that he may be induced to be reappointed to the vacant benefice.

Once again the reasons for the resignation, which had already been accepted by the Bishop, are not given, but at an emergency meeting nine days later with Bishop Tufnell in attendance a letter from Dr Cowley was read out:

The Elms, Chichester
April 23 1892

> Dear Sir
>   As the members of St John's congregation, including several of the Trustees have kindly expressed their desire that I should continue to minister amongst them I most willingly consent to offer myself for re-election.

* This was the John Goss (now Sir John) who, as a treble, had sung at the St John's opening concerts in 1813.

It is a measure of the esteem with which Cowley was regarded that the appeal for him to stay had been made (it had not happened with the three previous resignations) and Cowley was obviously touched by it, hence his assent to stay on. The draft Minute Book carries a printed 'memo for the congregation of St John's' about a scheme for quarterly augmentation collections to provide Dr Cowley with a stipend of £225 per annum. The collections were to be made on the last Sunday in each quarter and it was 'hoped that the quarterly collections will augment the stipend and meet the expenses without the need for any special annual collection'. So once again it seems that problems with paying the stipend were probably the reason for the resignation and yet again an appeal was made to the ever-generous congregation to pay up. Such were the joys of attending a proprietary chapel – it was a very expensive alternative to the parish church.

However shaky the finances, the Trustees had always been careful to have the accounts printed and audited but they received an unexpected challenge from Messrs Drewitt and Wyatt the accountants who carried out an audit in 1893. They were critical of a number of issues including the fact that the 1892 accounts had shown a deficit of £11 18s. 8d. due to the treasurer (i.e the treasurer had been paying out of his own pocket) which had been ignored in the 1893 figures. This, Drewitt and Wyatt opined,[43] 'appears to us unjust and ungenerous on the part of the Trustees'. In a reply the Trustees acknowledged most of the criticisms and declared that the shortfall to the treasurer would be made good.

Meanwhile Dr Cowley's health had deteriorated (could this have been a reason for his resignation?) and in a period of illness lasting over four months services were taken by Rev. Wilberforce from Chelsea and the Rev. Falconer from Stowmarket, the latter, hardly a local man, holding the fort for three months.[44] Regrettably Cowley was not to recover and died in December 1893, the first incumbent to die in office. A testimonial collection raised 60 guineas, which was presented to Cowley's widow, and the search began for his replacement. A proposal was made at the Trustees' meeting on 10 January 1894 to erect a monument to Cowley in the Chapel but it was resolved to be inexpedient as none had been erected for Steven Barbut who had been similarly popular.* The debate continued and a counter-proposal to provide the monument which was carried by four votes to three. The monument which consisted of a brass plate fixed to a marble tablet was installed on the south east wall it reads:

IN MEMORY OF THE REVEREND
WILLIAM DAVID COWLEY, DD
FOR 12½ YEARS THE MINISTER OF THIS CHAPEL
WHO DIED 25Th NOVEMBER 1893, AGED 62

THIS TABLET WAS ERECTED BY THE CONGREGATION

* The reason for this should not have been surprising after all; Barbut had left office following a dispute with the Trustees.

The replacement minister was William Ferris who had previously been at Thorney Abbey in Cambridgeshire and his salary was to be made up of the £120 required by the Act increased to £200 by Queen Anne's Bounty plus the surplus from pew rents. To this would be added the (unspecified) income from the rental of 68 North Street. This arrangement, or at least the last part of it, proved to be a difficulty for Ferris as 68 North Street had been empty for 12 months and was thus not producing any income. He wrote to the Trustees in February 1895 urging them to find a tenant.[45] A Mr Turner had applied for the tenancy but wished to have a shop front installed, the cost of which would have to be met by the landlord. Unfortunately the negotiations fell through and the Trustees were rapidly heading towards another financial crisis. One economy was to withdraw the choir from the Parochial Choirs Association but this might also have been prompted by the Association being seen as too high-church for St John's. From their Easter Tuesday meeting in 1896 the following strange minute arose:

> It was found that the income from the chapel was insufficient to provide the agreed stipend to the Minister and the Clerk was directed to write to Mr St Clair and Mr Lee and ask whether they would consent to any, and what, reductions in their present salaries.

That the making of such an approach could even be considered seems incredible but make it they did and Mr St Clair, the organist, offered to donate £5 of his £25 salary whilst Mr Lee, the custodian and bell ringer, agreed to undertake all his duties, including pew letting, for £15 rather than his rightful £20. What sterling people made up the St John's family! Unfortunately this belt-tightening was insufficient to prevent Ferris resigning after only two years in February 1898 and taking up the post of Perpetual Curate at Christchurch Worthing.[*] However this appointment was conditional upon the existing Worthing incumbent, Charles Hole, coming to St John's in his place but Hole, very inconsiderately, died the following March. This seemed to render the whole arrangement ineffective but the Bishop decided that as he had already appointed Ferris when Hole died the arrangement would stand[46] – Ferris made his escape and St John's was once again vacant.

The man chosen to lead St John's into the new century was Rev. Joseph Monti who was then at St Jude Mildmay Park, Islington, London[47] and he was appointed on 12 April 1898. Monti's ministry was to continue the evangelical tradition and fend off the advances of the Oxford Movement as we shall see in the next chapter. The constant financial crises did not prevent a further rebuilding and enlargement of the organ by Hele and Co. in Monti's first year, but curiously this is not recorded in the Minute Book – we only know of it from the printed order of the special service[48] held on

---

[*] Christchurch Worthing will feature in this story again in Chapter Ten as it was the construction thereof in 1843 which caused the bankruptcy of John Elliott who was the contractor for the construction of the Chichester Corn Exchange in 1832.

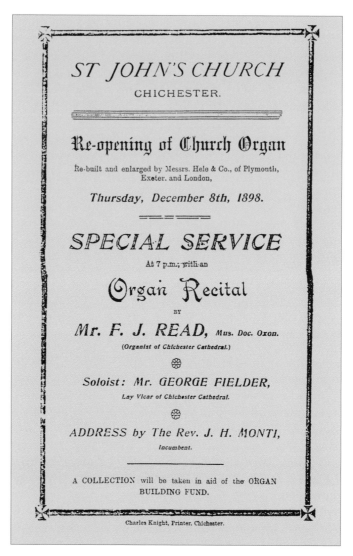

35   *Cover of the order of the special service to commemorate
the rebuilding of the organ in December 1898.*

8 December 1898. The printed accounts had always had a separate entry
for an 'organ building fund' so we can either assume that it had reached the
necessary level or someone had left a legacy for the purpose.

The organ recital was given by Dr Frederick Read who had been
appointed organist at Chichester Cathedral in 1897, a post which he held
until 1902 and then later returned for a second stint between 1921 and
1925.[49] The service consisted of shortened Evening Prayer followed by
the organ recital and rounded off with hymns during which the obligatory
offerings for the Organ Building Fund were taken. The programme for the
recital was:

Symphony from 'Saul'	Handel
Priere and pastorale	Guilmant
Recitatives: 'For behold darkness'	
'The people that walked in darkness'	Handel
Voluntary in D Minor	Stanley
March in B Flat	Silas

The recitatives from *Messiah* were sung by George Fielder who was a bass lay-vicar in the cathedral choir. The order of service also contains the specification for the rebuilt organ which is given in Appendix C.

Penny-pinching was still the order of the day and it was agreed in May 1899 to remove the duty of cleaning the schoolroom from the chapel custodian and make it the responsibility of the Sunday School superintendent – presumably with no hint of remuneration! Staying with finance and before leaving the Victorian era it is interesting to look at the declared figures in the printed accounts for the two principal sources of income from the congregation – pew rents and collections – for some of the years 1888 to 1900:[50]

Pew rents and collections 1888-1900

Year	1888	1889	1891	1894	1895	1897	1900
Pew Rents	286-6-10	210-3-2	195-10-0	179-17-8	163-6-3	157-1-6	144-19-6
Collections	29-9-1	201-4-4	109-10-0	25-10-0	27-8-5	25-1-7	32-18-8
Total	233-0-7	411-7-6	305-0-0	205-10-0	190-14-8	182-3-1	177-18-2

This shows a steady decline in the number of rented pews indicating a reducing congregation and a corresponding erosion of income. In 1851 the Religious Census showed that income from pew rents was £320, nearly double what it was to become in 1900. The curious apparent drop in giving after 1894 probably results from a change in the accounting practices following the highly critical audit the previous year. It is probable that from 1894 the collection figures comprise only the Sunday-by-Sunday offertories and exclude those made in response to particular appeals.

The new century seemed set to provide more challenges for the Trustees – and it certainly did.

Eight

NEW CENTURY AT ST JOHN'S 1901-1945

There are two schools of thought over when a new century begins – namely the '00' or the '01' year. I am firmly of the latter opinion which is why I believe we celebrated the Millennium at the wrong time and why this 'New Century' chapter begins in 1901.

At the first Trustee's meeting of the new century, on 16 April 1901, the opinion was recorded that 'the repairing and enlarging of the church organ and new seating in the east gallery is very satisfactory and that the organ is greatly improved in power and tone'.[1] Whether this is a belated reference to the 1898 rebuilding which, as we saw in Chapter Seven, had taken place apparently unnoticed by the Trustees, or whether there had been yet another (unlikely) rebuilding is uncertain. On another musical note it was resolved to introduce psalm singing at Morning as well as Evening Prayer. The Rev Monti was obviously concerned that this might be seen as a weakening of his impeccable evangelical credentials, so he wrote in the May Magazine[2] that:

> the introduction of psalm singing is not done because we are less Protestant and faithful to Christ, but because as both Church and Bible allow it, we feel that, if all will enter into it with heart and soul, it may be made to embody a great and mighty shout of praise to God.

The threat posed by the Oxford Movement was still seen by Monti to be ever-present. He had preached on 'ritualism' in March 1899 and in the July 1901 magazine[3] he felt moved to write to his flock warning that:

> Every day reveals the need for us to abstain from the great advance of ritualism which is hurrying the age to its final fearful struggle and calling loudly for God's wrath.

This fulmination may have been occasioned by the construction of St George's Church in Whyke* which was to be firmly in the 'London Brighton and South Coast Religion' tradition, or even aimed at the Dean of Chichester Cathedral. Dean Randall had begun, in 1894, to increase the

---

* Designed by J.E.K. and J.P. Cutts, the new church was consecrated in 1902 to augment the old parish church of St Mary's Rumboldswhyke which was now too small for the growing parish.

number of celebrations of Holy Communion and also introduced a measure of ritual to the cathedral services. This last was not popular in all circles and on 6 October 1900 the evangelical rector of St Pancras interrupted a cathedral service in protest for which he was disciplined by Bishop Wilberforce.[4] Unfortunately, shortly after writing this letter, poor Monti was struck down with a painful throat complaint necessitating treatment by an eminent London specialist. In letters written to his flock he describes the problem variously

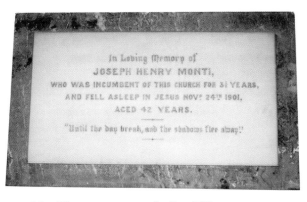

36   *The monument to the Rev. J.H. Monti on the north-east wall of the Chapel.*

as an ulcer and a growth and we can be fairly certain that the poor man had contracted throat cancer. Whilst this seemed to have been successfully operated on he then went on to contract jaundice which lingered much longer than he expected. In another letter, in November 1901[5] he wrote:

> Today I have seen a special doctor, and in a few days he hopes to say whether the stoppage is that of ordinary jaundice, which should have been cleared up long ago and is now giving rise to other complications, such as bringing up of blood or whether it is caused by swollen glands in the stomach, which are painfully in evidence all over my body ... God bless you, and let us not live one moment away from Christ until we see him face to face ...

That was the last letter he was to write for he died on 24 November at the age of only 42 and was buried at Woodford in Essex. The Trustees resolved to erect a memorial tablet to Monti and this was duly executed in marble and mounted on the north-east wall opposite that to Dr Cowley.

The replacement for Monti was Charles Edward Steinitz who was appointed in February 1902. He was to be as legendary a minister as Barbut and was to remain in harness for a similar length of time. Born in Camberwell, London on 12 October 1862 his previous placement had been as curate at St Margaret's proprietary chapel in Brighton* where he had been for four years.[6] 1902 not only marked the beginning of a new chapter in St John's history it also marked the close of another – literally – as the Trustees' Minute Book which had been in use since 1812 was full, the last entry being for 16 December.

The new Minute Book was a plain-paper ledger bound in calf with a tooled leather cover and was to last until 1985 when new technology

---

* St Margaret's Chapel near Regency Square was opened speculatively in 1824 to the design of Bernard Gregory. It was demolished in 1959.

37   *The Trustees' Minute Book 1903 to 1985.*

– typing – overtook hand-written minutes, something which drafters of the Act (which required the minutes to be entered into a book) had not foreseen!

The new book and new minister did not, unfortunately, herald a new period of financial stability. The balance at Easter 1903 was only £6 5s. 6d. but with some pew rents still owing. In addition, with 68 North Street still empty and not yielding any income to augment the minister's stipend, the Trustees felt that they should donate £5 of their slender balance to Mr Steinitz as compensation. The Trustees had received a tender from Vick the builder for installing a new shopfront in No 68 but at £110 this was seen as too large an outlay – not altogether surprising when their bank balance was now down to £1 5s. 6d. A year later the Trustees were in debt to the treasurer and ideas were sought for fund-raising activities, including organ recitals, to relieve this embarrassing position. Unfortunately a year later there was still £10 19s. 8d. owing to the treasurer; indeed there was not to be a balance-in-hand until 1909 when the dizzy sum of £2 1s. 5d. had accrued.[7] The Dean, as a Trustee, suggested at the 1910 Easter Tuesday meeting that the 'present foundation of the chapel be entirely revised' with a view to substituting collections for pew rents, i.e. removing one of the essential tenets of the Act. The Dean pointed out that an Order in Council would be required to sanction such a change but his suggestion found no proposer; probably it was seen as too radical an idea. However, another useful legacy came the Trustees' way in 1911 when Mrs Eliza Powell, a former member of the congregation, left £500-worth of shares in the Chichester Gas Company. This was a fair-sized investment for 1911 and the not-inconsiderable income from it was to be used to augment the minister's stipend.[8]

1912 marked the centenary of the founding of St John's and despite the precarious financial position a suitable project to mark the occasion was sought: it came in the form of an extension to the schoolroom. The schoolroom had been built at the south-east corner of the Chapel but there was still space on the Trustees' land to extend it eastwards. The design[9] was produced by W.A. Osborn and Sons of 45 North Street and provided for the building to be extended back to the former city wall (with a folding partition to divide the enlarged hall) and also an outside WC. The work was estimated at £173 and went ahead funded principally from public subscriptions. The centenary of the opening the following year was marked on 24 and 25 September but only with 'special services' and no repeats of the opening bun-fights which had caused John Marsh so much angst. The service on the first day featured two sermons;[*] the second preacher, Herbert Brooke, had been minister of St Margaret's Brighton[10] when Steinitz was serving there as a curate.

Daniel Lee the chapel keeper retired in 1913 and in his place a Mr Furnell was appointed as 'Chapel Clerk' at a salary of £20 plus £1 for bell-ringing and the cost of his laundry (!). With a new broom (so to speak) the Trustees decided to set out Mr Furnell's duties in writing[11] so as to ensure they got the most from their outlay. These were:

1. Collect pew rents, every quarter. Give receipts and fill in counterfoils. Pay over (same day) to the Treasurer, Mr Bowler. Refer applicants for seats to the Churchwardens [sic] and report to them as soon as possible.

2. Attend all services in church [sic] Welcome visitors and supply hymn and prayer books as needed.

3. Fetch Communion plate from Incumbent's or Churchwarden's house and return same properly cleaned. Place all Communion requisites on the Holy Table. Unused wine to be replaced in bottle.

4. See that surplices[†] and Communion linen are washed when required

5. Sweep floors and dust seats every week. Wash all over once a year in the month of May

6. Keep porches and outside clean and tidy. Not responsible to trim bushes.

7. See that gas and radiators are lighted in proper time according to seasonal temperatures.

8. Open doors half an hour and ring the bell for 15 minutes before each service. Wardens appoint an assistant for bell ringing.

9. Let Mr Fleetwood (Chapelwarden) know of broken windows and other needed repairs; also when last bottle of Communion wine is opened.

Mr Furnell was going to be kept very busy earning his £20 per annum! Note that in this job description the Trustees have used the term 'church' rather than 'chapel'.

[*] As the tradition at this time was for hour-long sermons this could have been a somewhat lengthy service.
[†] The reference to surplices is interesting. Despite the popish associations of this garment it had been the custom from 1894 for the minister to wear cassock and surplice during the office and then to don a black Geneva gown for delivery of the sermon.

The long-serving organist, John St Clair, died in 1920 and it was resolved that Miss Hoare would be appointed in his stead at the same £20 salary that St Clair had been paid for the last 34[*] years. However, under her the music of the Chapel underwent a resurgence and in the 1920s there are several bills for the purchase of new anthems.[12] Some measure of the quality of the singing in the 1920s can be gleaned from this article which appeared about St John's in the *Bognor Post* of 27 October 1928:[13]

> The church is also noted for its choir, which is voted by all vistors who have any pretensions to musical ability as one of the best in the City. Congregation and choir alike sing every hymn in four-part harmony and it is an impressive rarity to find such really fine singing in such a comparatively small church.

That same article describes beautifully the nature of the services themselves during Steinitz's incumbency:

> There is no altar and the services are conducted with the utmost simplicity.

> The prayers possess an intensity of feeling, what they lack is rhetorical flourishes, all verbal ornamentation is rigidly eschewed.

> The Rev. Steinitz has been at St John's for nearly nine years and the work he gets through would surprise those who do not know his inexhaustible energy.

The last comment is particularly apposite; Steinitz was now 66 but his unflagging energy was legendary. Although he had no parish to look after, his ministry to his extra-parochial flock and his involvement with missionary works was to keep him fully occupied until his death. A study of the Service Registers[14] during Steinitz's incumbency shows that he seldom used visting preachers and equally seldom repeated his sermons. In March and April 1928 he presented a series of sermons linking the Thirty Nine Articles of Religion of the Book of Common Prayer to the Scriptures. However, the fear of Catholicism had not gone away for in December 1928, using Revelation xvii verses 6-18 as a text, he preached on the subject of 'Antichrist – the Popery'.

More insight into the 1920s services, but this time through the eyes of a young boy, is provided in a short memoir[15] written by Victor Hoare:

> The service for a boy of 10 to 13 was rather dull, we always sang all the psalms set for the day and nearly always the Litany all through. The incumbent, the Rev. Charles Steinitz, read the services from the middle pulpit, read the lessons from the bottom one and before the sermon he would go into the vestry and take off his surplice and preach from the top pulpit. Everything was very quiet, nobody ever spoke except in a very low whisper.

[*] In 1937 – 17 years later – Miss Hoare's salary was still only £20!

38 *St John's decorated for harvest festival, 1923. The Chapel seems to have been taken over by triffids. Note the gas radiator in the centre of the floor. Beyond the gasolier can be seen one of the three plaster roses that were lost when the ceiling was replaced in 1927.*

This same memoir also reflects on the Sunday School.

> My Great Uncle Henry Holder was superintendent and very strict.
> We would start by singing choruses such as 'Jesus bids us shine' and
> 'I will make you fishers of men'. The small children went into what
> is now the kitchen* and had their story time, while the older ones
> assembled in small groups for their lessons.
>
> When Sunday School had finished we were expected to go into
> church for the first part of the service. My uncle would stand with
> his hand on the opposite side of the door so we had to duck under
> his arm. He always seemed to pick on me and say 'why are you not
> going to church this morning?' I would say 'Mum wants me to do
> something'. But I did go to church sometimes and sit upstairs with
> my auntie Doris.

Inevitably the new century brought a new crop of problems with the fabric
and in September 1924 an appeal was set up to raise funds to cover the
£244 tender for extensive repairs to the roof and campanile. The appeal
raised an amazing £285 13s. 3d. which more than offset the final cost of
£272 6s. 3d., so the surplus was paid into the Paull Trust Fund.[16] The
ceiling was the next headache for in January 1927 it was reported by the
chapel wardens as being in a dangerous condition. The vast ceiling had
been plastered by Charles Cooper† when the Chapel was built so whether
the imminent collapse was due to the quality of his workmanship or to
some other cause we shall never know; it was decided to take it all down
and replace it with match-boarding for an estimated £180. Once again
a subscription was raised to cover the cost and once again a surplus[17]
(£12 19s. 6d.) was able to be paid into the Paull Trust after settling the
final account. The oppressive effect of this varnished pine match-boarded
ceiling has been discussed in Chapter Five, but why this strange finish was
chosen is a mystery. The following year the Chapel was redecorated and the
walls were again painted pink and the surrounds to the panel mouldings
over the altar were picked out in blue.[18]

No 68 North Street was also costing much in repairs and in 1926 the
Trustees authorised the wardens to open negotiations with the tenant over
the possibility of his purchasing the property and sought the clerk's opinion
about the effects of such a sale upon its charitable status. The results of
neither are recorded but fortunately this important source of income for
augmenting the minister's stipend was retained in the Trustees' portfolio.
The stipend was increased by £25 in April 1927 and in 1931 Steinitz
was given an additional £25 gratuity by the Trustees, paid for out of the
favourable (for once) balance of accounts. This generous act was to be
repeated in 1935[19] but only to the tune of £10.

---

* i.e., the east end of the hall, beyond the folding partition.
† Cooper's workmanship had been called into question during construction when one of the walls
bulged – see page 43.

39 *The interior looking east in 1943 showing the pine match-boarded ceiling. Note the gas lighting and the high polish to the pulpit.*

S.T. Clemens was the contractor selected for the next package of works carried out in 1939. This involved painting the exterior and it is interesting to note that the estimate[20] included for graining and varnishing the two main entrance doors – the same decorative scheme as had first been applied when the Chapel was built. The works also involved alterations to the front 'free' pews, the first three of which on each side were turned through 90 degrees so as to face each other[21] for the use of the choir who were to move down from the east gallery. The cost of this work was £59 10s. 0d. for the redecoration plus a further £1 12s. 6d. for creating the new choir stalls, all paid for out of the income from the Paull Trust Fund. After this little in the way investment was carried out for the duration of the War.

40 *The Communion Table and rails in 1943. The table is set out for northwards celebration with the Prayer Book set on a crimson cushion. There are no candlesticks nor Cross.*

Considering its proximity to both Tangmere and Thorney Island aerodromes it was surprising that Chichester suffered only three major air raids. None of these had affected Newtown. However, St John's and adjacent houses were to suffer some war damage but as the result of allied, rather than enemy, action. On 11 May 1944 an American Liberator bomber, fuelled and carrying a cargo of bombs, got into difficulties over Chichester so the crew pointed the aircraft out to sea and bailed out. Unfortunately it circled round and returned to the city crashing onto the site of the Roman amphitheatre behind the cattle market where it exploded.[22] Mary Gough, who lived at No 8 St John's Street where her father had his doctor's surgery, was on her way home from school and witnessed the whole event, which is recorded in her diary[23] for the day:

> Saw Liberator crash and crew bale out. Plane landed at 4 o'c on Electric Laundry. Peter [her younger brother] home by ½ hr. 1 Guide hurt at St John's School. I was in school ground. A lot of windows out. Went to cadets at 6 o'c, helped to clear up the Parson's house [i.e. The Rectory, 9 St John's Street].

She arrived home to find the windows of their kitchen blown in. The blast had crossed the open expanse of the cattle market with no intervening buildings to lessen it, and in addition to damaging houses it blew in some of the windows on the south side of the Chapel and brought down part of the ceiling in the schoolroom. The ARP reports[24] disclose that there were four bombs on board when the Liberator crashed, one of which exploded but the others could be defused. The City Electric Laundry and several houses around the Cinder Path were said to be very badly damaged, 18 were detained in hospital and a 15-year-old girl lost her life.* One dreads to think what the toll might have been had the bomber come down in the city centre, especially without warning at that time of the afternoon.

Despite this potentially cataclysmic event, which no doubt caused some inconvenience to the congregation, nothing is recorded in the service register or minute book.† The accounts book[25] has two related entries: £1 0s. 6d. was spent on 21 new gas mantles and one nozzle 'due to war damage' whilst S.T. Clemens were paid £34 15s. 1d. for 'first aid repairs'. These repairs are not specified but are likely to have included temporarily making safe the windows and the schoolroom ceiling which were not properly rectified until 1949‡ and 1947[26] respectively, the delay being caused by the exceedingly slow process for obtaining grants for the repair of war damage.

At the Trustees' meeting on 25 April 1945 the motion was carried to express the Trustees' sympathy with the minister's illness and the 'hope that he may shortly be restored to health'. As Steinitz was now 83 years old and still in harness he might be forgiven some illness but the post-war era would soon see the end of his ministry and the beginning of the most turbulent period of the Chapel's history.

---

* Two more people died subsequently from the effects of the crash.
† The crash was not reported in the press either as such events were deemed to be bad for morale. The ARP reports provide the only public written record of what happened.
‡ See page 111.

Nine

St John's:

Struggle for Survival, 1946-1973

With the war over the Trustees might have hoped for a period of calm but any such was to be short-lived for, in 1947, other storm clouds began to gather on the horizon. In August Mr Fleetwood, a chapel warden since 1908, died and was succeeded by Mr S.C. Bacon who very quickly learned of the difficult times that lay ahead of him when an inquiry was announced, under the Union of Benefices Measures (1923-36), in respect of Chichester parishes.[1] This inquiry was to address, *inter alia*, the amalgamation of the benefice of St John's with that of St Pancras. It was agreed at the Trustees' meeting on 22 September 1947 that Mr Bowler be nominated as a Commissioner for the enquiry and that the chairman of the PCC,* The Rev. Steinitz, be empowered to sign the joint nomination on behalf of the Council.[2]

Naturally the Trustees were alarmed by this threat to the continued existence of St John's so at their meeting of 30 March 1948 they made this resolution:

> That the Trustees of the Chapel of St John the Evangelist at their meeting held on the 30th day of March 1948 entirely disagree with the proposal to amalgamate the Chapel of St John with the living of St Pancras in the event of the death of the present Minister as they consider the Commission set up has no jurisdiction over the said chapel which is governed by the provisions of Act of Parliament 52 Geo III Chap 71 entitled 'An Act for building a chapel in the City of Chichester in the County of Sussex'.

The gloves were proverbially on. Putting their trust in their constitution as a proprietary chapel, they wielded the Act and sat back to see what would happen. At the same meeting they had voted an increase in Rev. Steinitz's stipend to £325 per annum, back-dated to 25 March, but unfortunately poor Steinitz died in October and so saw little benefit from it. His funeral took place on 31 October 1948 and was conducted at St John's by Bishop George Bell, as Mr Bacon reported in his letter[3] to the parishioners dated 25 November:

---

* This is the first mention of a Parochial Church Council. As a proprietary chapel run by a board of trustees and with no parish there was no need for a PCC, so this body must have been set up to give the congregation a wider say in the conduct of the services.

> We all appreciate our Bishop's kind action in taking the funeral service at St John's and for his personal testimony to our late Minister. The service was, we feel sure, exactly what the Rev. Steinitz would have wished and many messages have reached us expressing appreciation. The organ and singing was an inspiration to us all.

The music[4] included the hymn 'The sands of time are sinking' and the anthem 'What are these that glow from afar?' by John Stainer. The Trustees generously agreed to pay Steinitz's widow the full stipend up to the end of the year[5] and the wardens were instructed to arrange clerical cover for the services during the interregnum. Most of the interregnum services were taken by a Rev. H.A. Lea who was paid £3 3s. 0d. per Sunday plus 3s. 9d. for his train fare from Worthing.[6] There is no mention of any proposal to erect a memorial tablet to Steinitz and certainly none was provided. As Monti who had only been in office for three years had warranted one, how much more so did Steinitz with an amazing 47 years? This does seem an incredibly mean inaction.

Later in that same letter Mr Bacon, in a rallying cry to the congregation, acknowledges the 'many and varied problems affecting our church* [which] come crowding upon us' and also the need to find suitable accommodation for the new minister. The Trustees advertised the vacancy as if the threat of abolition did not exist and considered the applications received at their meeting of 2 January. However, they did not make up their minds until 19 April when they elected to appoint the Rev. M.G. Newton on a salary of £400, accommodation (rented) having been found for him at 37 St Paul's Road. Maurice Newton, educated at Pembroke College Oxford, must have been aware of the difficult times that lay ahead and this may of course be the reason for the delay in the appointment, but, if it was, it is not recorded. The evangelical zeal was still in evidence as is witnessed by another of Mr Bacon's letters to the congregation dated 30 April 1949[7] – just as the clocks were going forward – which he ended:

> With the coming of longer and brighter days, many and varied are the seemingly legitimate reasons why the Evil One will keep us from God's house. Let us be on our guard and seek by prayer and Christian service to keep our lamps burning.

All seemed to have gone quiet on the amalgamation front but the threat reared its ugly head again in 1952 when a vacancy arose for the rector of St Pancras. At the Trustees' meeting on 10 December representatives of the Diocesan Pastoral Reorganisation Committee attended to explain the implications of the St Pancras vacancy for the amalgamation which were

> very fully explained by the Archdeacon and after considerable discussion the Archdeacon announced that he would render a full report to his committee and communicate the result to the Trustees.

---

* It is interesting to note that at this time St John's was being referred to by its members as a church rather than a chapel.

This once more put the Trustees into turmoil and an emergency meeting was called on 24 February 1953 which is recorded in (unusually) great detail in the Minute Book. The Rev. Heath, who was a Simeon Trustee* with which body the advowson of St Pancras rested, attended the meeting to hear the Trustees' views on the type of incumbent they would prefer 'in the event of the benefices becoming united'. The recommendations made by the Diocesan Pastoral Reorganisation Committee were also read out namely:

> (a) An immediate union between St Pancras and St John.
> (b) St Pancras to be the Parish Church
> (c) St John's to become a chapel-of-ease
> (d) Sunday services to be held at St Pancras
> (e) Amalgamation to take effect from the next vacancy at St John's
> (f) Adult education work to be carried out at St John's
> (g) The Simeon Trustees should have the first and third appointments
>   and the St John's Trustees the second appointment.

Mr Bowler stressed that the majority of the Trustees were against the union and asked the Chairman of the Pastoral Committee to consider the matter further before making a decision. Rev. Heath stated that the St Pancras PCC had requested 'a married priest aged about 45 and who would take the north side† and continue evening celebration of Holy Communion and be keen on youth work'. Mr Bowler continued the opposition by questioning the doctrinal basis of the Simeon Trust and the Minutes continue:

> The Trustees made the traditions and practices to which they had become accustomed abundantly clear: amongst other things it was pointed out that at St John's the congregation did not turn east for the Creed, they take the north side for communion and did not have anything on the Holy Table.‡

In making this last defence the Trustees did themselves no favours since they had demonstrated that their traditions were very closely aligned with those at St Pancras, a fact which would remove, rather than place, obstacles in the way of the union. The Archdeacon then stated that the Church Commissioners had informed the Bishop that a union would be

---

* The Simeon Trustees are an evangelical body taking their name from Charles Simeon (1759-1836) of Cambridge. They bought out the advowsons of key churches to ensure that only evangelicals were appointed when the incumbencies fell vacant.
† The Book of Common Prayer rubric stipulated that the priest, when celebrating Holy Communion, should stand at the north side of the altar. This was in order that the congregation could see what he was doing with the bread and wine. The Oxford Movement (see page 79) introduced the Roman Catholic practice of the priest standing facing east so that his actions were obscured. Since that time northwards celebration had been a point of principle amongst evangelicals.
‡ The same BCP rubric stipulated that The Table should be covered with a fair white linen cloth and makes no mention of candlesticks, another thing that came in with the Oxford Movement and hence roundly denounced by evangelicals. Interestingly, though, St Pancras had applied for a faculty in 1944 to install candlesticks and an altar cross there.

legally possible since any Act of Parliament could be overthrown by making another Act. The revealing of this feature of the parliamentary process rather flattened the Trustees' first line of defence, showing that they could no longer shelter behind their constitution. One can only imagine that the Trustees went home downhearted but they were not yet ready to admit defeat and wrote an appeal to the Bishop[8] on 5 March. Meanwhile the Church Commissioners had prepared a draft scheme for the union which was discussed at a special Trustees' meeting on 5 October. Once again the Trustees were in fighting mood and the Minutes,[9] again long and highly detailed, record the main points of the campaign:

(a) St John's is not a dead or dying church
(b) St John's is not, and never has been in debt[*]
(c) That nothing in the Scheme is mentioned about what is proposed to be done with the chapel of St John (they refer to the earlier chapel-of-ease proposal and their fears that it would in fact be closed)
(d) That closure of St John's and discontinuation of regular worship there could not be said to be furthering the work of the Church.
(e) That if a union is to take effect it would be best for both churches to be used for Sunday worship (they proposed that the incumbent preside alternately morning and evening with a student taking the services at the other.
(f) That at the public inquiry into the possible arrangements of Chichester City parishes in January 1948 the Archdeacon had promised that St John's would be left alone.
(g) Whether the Church Commissioners could close down St John's in view of its constitution (i.e as a proprietary chapel)

It was then reported that at the Church Council meeting on 29 September a resolution had been made to record strong opposition to the draft scheme of union and the secretary had been instructed to forward a copy of that resolution to the Church Commissioners.

The Trustees then made their own resolution, carried unanimously, as follows:

That this meeting of the Trustees entirely approve of the action taken by the Church Council and that the Clerk be, and he is hereby requested, to prepare and lay a case before Counsel for his opinion on the matter, particularly with regard to the Declaration of Trust executed on the acquisition of the shares on the re-opening of the Chapel[†] and to settle the formal objections to the scheme for the union for forwarding to the Church Commissioners.

So once again the St John's Trustees had sought Counsel's opinion in a dispute, echoing what their predecessors had done in the case against Elmes

[*] This is not strictly true as we have seen – perhaps the Trustees had forgotten about the contents of the previous Minute Book!
[†] See page 83.

some 130 years previously. Having left no stone unturned the meeting was then adjourned *sine die*, pending Counsel's opinion on the issues raised.

They met again on 24 October when the somewhat embarrassed Archdeacon challenged the Minutes and the recording against item (f) that he had promised that St John's would be left alone. Tactfully referring to the Minute as containing 'a slight inaccuracy' he pointed out that he was not able make such a promise and wondered whether the words had actually been taken from a press report! The Minutes also record that Counsel had given his opinion but do not say what it was. A conference then took place with Bishop Bell whose compassion for the Trustees and their cause resulted in an undertaking that he would give a written direction that services should be held at least once on each Sunday in every year and would request the Church Commissioners to amend the Scheme so as to provide for this. In a letter to Clarence Hoare, one of the Trustees, dated 20 November 1953 Bishop Bell wrote:

> Dear Mr Hoare,
>   Arising out of our conversation the other day, I wrote to the Church Commissioners explaining the situation and have now received a reply, a copy of which I enclose. I very much hope that you and your colleagues may regard this as satisfactory and that on this basis you will be prepared to acquiesce in the proposals.
>   George Cicestr.

Things at last seemed to be turning in the Trustees' favour but unfortunately there was one snag which the Bishop had failed to point out, but did so four days later:

> Dear Mr Hoare,
>   I forgot to mention in writing to you that there is a financial aspect with regards to the provision of Sunday services at St John's when the union takes effect. Would St John's be willing to fund the payment necessary for the taking of their services?
>   George Cicestr.

The Trustees agreed to meet the Rev. Jack Marshall, the new rector of St Pancras, to discuss the financial aspects and the clerk was instructed to respond to the Bishop saying that the Trustees were giving 'earnest consideration to the scheme'. Unfortunately more trouble was at hand when the minister, Maurice Newton, gave notice to the Archdeacon that he was seeking another living, the reason given being that he could not carry on at a stipend of £400 with no clergy house and the Trustees unable to offer a higher salary. In April the final blow was struck when the Bishop wrote to the Trustees stating that Rev. Newton had accepted a new living in Chelmsford Diocese and the resulting vacancy at St John's meant that the union with St Pancras would now be going ahead. At their meeting of 17 December the

Church Commissioners' Notice to the Queen regarding the union was read out, as was Counsel's opinion. This last was that an appeal would be unlikely to succeed unless St Pancras would join in with it – which their PCC had already voted not to do. Consequently the Trustees had to admit defeat and decided not to proceed with an appeal. The Order made by the Queen was published in the *London Gazette* on 4 February 1955 and the union went ahead. St John's became, pastorally at least, a chapel-of-ease to St Pancras. However, the trust was not wound up and the Trustees continued to fund the cost of repairs to the Chapel and meet the expenses of holding services just as though it were still a proprietary chapel. By 1953 there was only one pew-holder left (Miss Faith) who contributed £2 in rental. Rent from 68 North Street yielded £60 and the gas stock produced £30 19s. 6d.[10] All the remaining income came from the congregation in the form of collections and donations but during this period the trust funds remained in credit.

At the start, perhaps inevitably, it was not an easy marriage between the two benefices and at the first meeting attended by the rector, Rev. Marshall, the Trustees made it quite plain that they considered it to be the incumbent's responsibility to provide *every* service at St John's *every* Sunday but did agree to provide £400 per annum (the stipend they had paid Rev. Newton) towards the salary of an assistant curate or other ordained minister. Unfortunately the rector's proposal was to appoint a lay reader instead of an ordained man so the Trustees made a complaint straight to the Bishop. The ever-patient Bishop Bell replied that this really was a matter for 'mutual consideration' between the two parties (which it was) and finally the Trustees agreed to the appointment of Captain Walker, of the Church Army, as the assistant. St John's and its faithful congregation then began to settle into their new existence. It had been agreed that one fifth of the PCC membership should be elected from the St John's congregation in order to give them a voice in the decision-making process.

During the time that this battle had been raging the Trustees were still investing in the Chapel. The troublesome gas lighting was ousted by electricity in 1948, the work being carried out by a local firm, T.F. Lummus, and the war damage to the windows* was finally made good. S.T. Clemens, another local builder,† supplied and fitted new steel windows in wooden frames for the sum of £743 10s. 7d. of which the War Damage Commission agreed to pay £400.[11] The reason for the shortfall in funding is not recorded but as all the windows were replaced it is likely that the Commission would only pay for those which had actually been affected by the blast, leaving the Trustees to fund the rest. In 1950 the organ was rebuilt and enlarged for the last time. The work was carried out by Hele and Co but the case had already been discarded (it was infested with woodworm) which left all the pipework exposed and looking rather untidy, as can be seen in the view of the interior in Fig 44.

---

* See page 105.
† Still in business.

41 *The interior of St John's in 1971 viewed from the pulpit. A curtain has been put over the west window to avoid the preacher being dazzled on summer evenings, whilst curtains at ground level protect against draughts emanating from the entrances.*

The rebuilding was carried out as a somewhat belated memorial to the late Rev. Steinitz and the opening recital was given on 3 October 1950 by his son,[12] the distinguished musician Dr Paul Steinitz. Paul Steinitz was to return to Chichester 25 years later when he conducted the London Bach Society and the Steinitz Bach Players in a performance of Bach's *B Minor Mass* as part of the Chichester 900 Festival. In 1951 S.T. Clemens returned to clean and repaint the interior of the Chapel for £85 0s. 0d. which work was completed on 20 February[13] whilst in March the Misses Hoare funded the installation of new carpet. Estimates for replacing the gas heating with electric radiant heaters were obtained in 1956 but the work was deferred, not being undertaken until 1961. These heaters and their somewhat inelegant asbestos backing boards can be seen in Fig 44.

The ghost of James Elmes continued to stalk the roof. In July 1957 C.W.L. Pile were paid £184 3s. 1d. to strip and re-slate part of the southern section of it, and they returned in April 1960 to carry out more repairs to exclude pigeons 'which are now invading the roof'. In April 1962 considerable damage occurred to the organ from a roof leak and a year later a loan of £300 had to be obtained from the Diocesan Board of Finance for yet more roof repairs.[14]

No 68 North Street was the major source of income for the Trustees during this period. In 1958 its rental value was assessed as being £475 per annum on a full-repairing basis and the Trustees elected to retain rather than sell the premises. In 1959 the Diocesan Chancellor opined that under the united benefice the augmentation clause* of the Act (Clause XL) was inoperative and that the income from No 68 could be used for keeping

---

* This clause allowed the Trustees to use gifts or other income to augment the minister's salary and/or to endow the Chapel.

the Chapel in repair but not for the maintenance of an assistant curate, the cost of which should be met by the congregation not the Trustees! In 1959 the ground floor of No 68 was converted into a shop and leased to Rays Hardware[15] whose business remained a feature of North Street until 1970.

The schoolroom, as well as providing accommodation for the Sunday School, also yielded more income from its hire to carefully selected local bodies[16] – The Chichester Art Society's request to use it for their meetings was declined in 1954 (the reason is not recorded) but the 15th Chichester Boy Scouts were permitted to hire it one evening a week for 7s. 6d. per week 'including electricity'. In April 1957 the Judo Club were evicted and the Scouts' rent increased to 10s. per week but the Trustees elected to invest £100 in new chairs* for the building, no doubt hoping to attract a better class of clientele. Unfortunately by 1965 the schoolroom was beginning to show its age for, as reported in the *Chichester Observer* of 17 September, a Mr E.R. Walter of the PCC took charge of an appeal to raise £4,000 to renovate the church hall (as it was now called) the money being needed, he stated, to eliminate dry rot, damp-proof the building and replace the heating system. The report ends with his statement that the parishioners had, in the last three years, 'given £3,000 towards the curate's house and major repairs to the rectory, and so to appeal for another £4,000 now is asking rather a lot'. This seems to have proved a masterpiece of understatement as no work is recorded in the Minute Book as having been ordered. In July 1966 when repairs, estimated at £363, were required to the roof the Trustees, not having sufficient funds, suggested to C.W.L. Pile the builders that they could be awarded the contract provided the payment could be spread over three years! Piles declined to enter into such a contract (one has to admire the Trustees for trying this on) but fortunately the Diocesan Board of Finance came up with a loan which enabled the work to proceed.

The Sunday School continued to thrive during the 1950s and, although not so strict as it was in the 1920s,[†] was still held twice every Sunday. In the morning children left Mattins just before the sermon began and filed into the schoolroom to sing CSSM choruses before being split into various age groups. Clarence Hoare and his wife were the leaders and, in typical Sunday School style, stamps on a Biblical theme could be earned leading to possible awards at the annual prize-giving ceremony. Singing was accompanied by harmonium of which there were two magnificent, but rather wheezy, specimens in the schoolroom whose players automatically beat time via the rhythmic knocking of the pedals.

At this time the annual Sunday School treat was an outing to Littlehampton to which children, parents and much of the congregation were invited and for transport Southdown double-decker buses would be hired.

---

* Your author remembers them well – they were heavy tubular-steel chairs with canvas seats which were uncomfortably scratchy against bare legs.
† See page 102.

42 *St John's Sunday School Christmas party, 1956. The cleric is the Rev. Marshall, the St Pancras rector, and seated on his right is Clarence Hoare. Captain Walker is in the middle with the (unidentified) girl on his knee. Your author is standing on the bench at the right-hand end of the middle row, next to his eldest sister, Daphne. What would today's Fire Officer say about those decorations?*

Having secured a separate, if not independent, existence within the new organisation services at St John's seem to have carried on as normal but relationships with the rector, Rev. Marshall, appear to have been a little strained. In 1957 the rector wrote to the Trustees suggesting a possible re-arrangement of the pulpit and reading desks but at their meeting on 23 April this was rejected by the Trustees. The following year the rector had moved the Communion Table – where to is not recorded but we can surmise that it was in front of the pulpit – and on 8 October 1958 the clerk was instructed to 'write to the Rev. Marshall and inform him that the Holy Table should be replaced in its former position at the east end of the Chapel'. In 1962 the rector requested that two surplus pews, which had been moved into the schoolroom, be transferred to St Pancras to replace two which had perished from the attentions of wood beetles. Once again the Trustees refused to acquiesce; the clerk was instructed to write to the rector[17] informing him that 'The Trustees very much regretted that they were unable to consent to the pews being used to replace those in St Pancras Church'.

In October 1962 the Rev. Marshall was succeeded as rector by Rev. John McKechnie and relationships between Trustees and incumbent seem to have improved. A diary sheet for September 1963 shows that morning and evening services continued to be held in both buildings but whilst Holy Communion was held weekly at St Pancras it was only celebrated once a month at St John's – on the third Sunday at 12.00 noon.

A choir list for 7 October 1962 (see Fig 43) reveals that at Mattins and Evensong the canticles and psalms were still being sung to chants and that choir practice was held half an hour before the service.

At Easter 1963 Good Friday services were only held at St Pancras but on Easter Day both places had a full complement of services, those at St John's being:

11.00am	Morning Prayer
2.30pm	Family Service
6.30pm	Evening Prayer and Holy Communion

1963 was, of course, the 150th anniversary of the founding of St John's Chapel and at the Trustees' meeting on 16 April plans for celebrating this event were discussed. Once again it was not to be a festival to rival that for the opening in 1813 – far from it – the 'celebrations' were to be limited to guest preachers at the services on the Sundays 22 and 29 September! On the morning of the 29th a new curate, Rev. M.A. Richardson, was ordained in the Cathedral whilst for the evening service the two congregations combined in St John's. However the *Chichester Observer* in an article about the anniversary did announce that Francis Steer, the County Archivist, 'was hoping to produce a Chichester Paper* to coincide with the anniversary but the history is incomplete. It seems that information about the church is in short supply'. The same article reports that there were 60 persons on the St John's electoral roll and that the income derived from offertories was about £600 per annum. At the 16 April meeting the Trustees agreed to deposit 'numerous old records' relating to the Chapel at the record office.† The small size of the congregation in the mid-1960s (in 1961 the average number of communicants had fallen to 21[18]) meant that the gallery was abandoned and the top deck of the pulpit no longer used, the clerk's desk being used as a lectern and the minister's as the pulpit.[19] During this period the Chapel was being used by students from Chichester Theological College for preaching practice.

At the Trustees' meeting of 16 February 1967 a discussion took place which marked the beginning of the end of St John's. It was reported that the PCC had discussed the amalgamation of 'the two congregations as a matter of grave concern to both churches'. The discussion is recorded as:

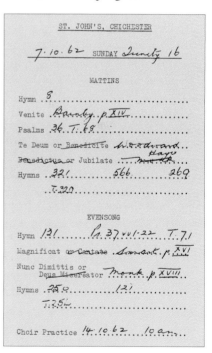

43 *A St John's choir list for October 1962.*

---

* It was published later in 1963 as CP 35.
† How fortunate that they did – it solved Francis Steer's shortage of information and made research for this present volume possible.

Should we continue to meet for worship separately within a short distance of each other having the same ministry and churchmanship, using two buildings with the duplication of manpower, expenses etc- [which] presented a bad image to people outside the Church.

The rector had put forward three alternatives:

1. Unite in St Pancras Church
2. St John's be made the Parish Church with all worshipping there
3. Both buildings be disposed of and the money raised be used towards a new church

The PCC, it was reported, had decided to investigate option 3.

Although relationships between the two congregations now appeared to be more cordial, both having acknowledged their similarities rather than differences, the Trustees once again felt that their building was under threat and passed the following resolution:[20]

We are in general sympathy with the idea of the two congregations uniting for worship. In view of the impossibility under existing law of demolishing St John's and the extreme improbability of permission to demolish being granted under any future law, the Chapel Trustees would be very willing for St John's Chapel to be used in any way which met the wishes of the combined congregations. The Trustees would welcome the opportunity of a joint discussion with the Bishop.

In other words only Option 2 would be acceptable to the Trustees; the gloves were about to be put on again.

A meeting was duly held with the Bishop[21] on 28 March 1967 at which he had ruled that the Order in Counsel made in 1955 to hold two services at St John's could not be set aside but that he could, pending his decision about which building should be the parish church, give the rector dispensation from holding Morning Prayer 'at St Pancras' so that the combined morning service could be at St John's! At the same meeting the resignation of Rev. McKechnie was announced, his having accepted a new living in Reading, so the Trustees had to cope with a change of incumbent (and possibly ideas) at a very critical time. The new incumbent was to be the Rev. Alan Lindsay MA, who was appointed on November 1967.

The Bishop attended the meeting on 6 February 1968 when it was agreed to ask Mr Tyler, the architect, to produce a report on the repair work that would be necessary to make St John's suitable for use as the parish church and that the Archdeacon should seek legal advice from the Church Commissioners. This the Archdeacon duly did and the response was characteristically inconclusive, the sticking points being, firstly, the proprietary constitution and whether the Trustees could transfer the building to the benefice and hand over their funds; and, secondly, whether under current law St John's could legally be made the parish church. From pondering such problems are lawyers' fortunes made and it was decided to approach the Charity Commissioners regarding authorising a conveyance of the trust. The Trustees naturally agreed to adopt the option of St John's becoming the parish church but Tyler's report revealed that £3,500 would be needed to carry out the necessary repairs and alterations to the Chapel.* Meanwhile the Diocesan Board of Finance turned down the application for a loan to finance the works but, as the bank would advance a loan on the security of 68 North Street, the Trustees again proposed that St John's become the parish church and put it to the vote at the PCC[22] on 18 July 1969. The outcome of the PCC is not recorded, the whole process was dragging along and cracks appeared in the relationship with the rector when, in October 1969, he proposed suspending services at St John's during the winter owing to the inadequate heating arrangements. Obviously the rector was becoming impatient with slow progress but the Trustees were having none of it and resolved that the Archdeacon should write to the rector reminding him that he could not suspend services without the Bishop's sanction and that '... it was considered that the Trustees should have been consulted and their approval first obtained'. It appears that the winter closure went ahead and the rector failed to respond to the letter. Meanwhile the wheels of the legal profession continued to grind exceedingly slow and in April 1970 it was announced that the Pastoral Committee would make their verdict on 3 May, a sub-committee thereof having been set up to consider the various reports on the structure and the alternatives. The Law of Delay set in again and by December no decision had been made but it was widely believed that the Pastoral Committee's proposal would involve making St John's redundant, against which the Trustees firmly resolved to make formal objections. However, they resolved not to challenge a temporary winter closure 'to avoid friction' provided St John's reopened in April 1971.[23]

At the April 1971 Trustees' meeting the Archdeacon confirmed that the Pastoral Committee's draft scheme would contain a declaration of redundancy in respect of St John's and that formal objections would have to be made. Meanwhile the chapel had not reopened in April as requested but the Trustees agreed to the rector's proposal to hold, from the first Sunday in May, two morning services, 10.00 at St Pancras and 11.15 at St John's. This arrangement continued until October when the Bishop agreed to a further winter closure. On 7 October the draft scheme was considered which provided for St John's to be declared redundant and vested in the Diocesan Board of Finance and the assistant curate's position to be revoked. This left the Trustees questioning their future position[24] with their principal *raison d'être* taken away from them while still being in possession of the schoolroom and 68 North Street.

This meeting marked the end of the Minute Book started in 1902 but as only the left-hand pages had been used it was turned upside-down and

---

* The nature of the alterations is not specified but one can be fairly certain that removal of the three-decker would have featured among them.

44   *View from the gallery looking east in 1971. The gallery accommodation was by then out of use and some of the brass rails are missing. The organ case had been discarded in the 1940s owing to the ravages of woodworm.*

re-started, very economically, from the back. By January nothing further had developed but the clerk was instructed to write to the Bishop stating the Trustees' wish that St John's be reopened on Easter Day and that the rector be asked to make the necessary arrangements. Once again this wish was not fulfilled and at the meeting of 4 April 1972 it was resolved that the rector be approached again to reopen the chapel every Sunday. This meeting was on Easter Tuesday when, traditionally, chapel wardens were elected but no nomination for minister's warden had been received from the rector so, for the first time in the 159-year history of the Chapel, no wardens were elected. This did not augur well. The draft declaration of redundancy was presented to the Trustees in October 1972 but a motion to accept it found no seconder and Mrs Curry, a recent recruit to the Trustees, gave 'at some length' her opinions on why St John's should be retained, so it was agreed to put forward another objection. This was submitted but not without a dispute amongst the Trustees about the fact that the clerk's wording of the

> ### SCHEDULE
>
> #### PASTORAL SCHEME
>
> This Scheme is made by the Church Commissioners this 17th day of April 1973 in pursuance of the Pastoral Measure 1968, the Right Reverend Roger, Bishop of Chichester, having consented thereto.
>
> *Declaration of redundancy*
>
> 1. The chapel of Saint John the Evangelist within the parish of Saint Pancras, Chichester (hereinafter referred to as "the chapel") shall be declared redundant by this Scheme.
>
> 2. Upon the declaration of redundancy coming into operation, and notwithstanding any provision contained in the Act of the 52nd year of the Reign of His late Majesty King George the Third, Chapter 71, entitled "An Act for building a Chapel in the City of Chichester in the County of Sussex" (hereinafter referred to as 'the Act') the chapel shall vest in the diocesan board of finance of the diocese of Chichester as a redundant building in accordance with the provisions of section 49 of the Pastoral Measure 1968, and the provisions of section 28 and of Part III of the said Measure shall apply to the chapel and the contents thereof.
>
> 3. The provisions of paragraph 6 of the Scheme of the Church Commissioners which was confirmed by Order of Her Majesty in Council dated the 1st February 1955 and published in the London Gazette on the 4th February 1955 (which relate to the employment by the incumbent of the benefice of Saint Pancras and St. John, Chichester, of an assistant curate, or other clerical or lay assistance, and to the performance of services in the chapel) shall be revoked.
>
> 4. Nothing in this Scheme shall prejudice the power of the trustees for the time being being appointed pursuant to the Act to apply monies arising thereunder as therein provided and in particular to make such payments as they may from time to time approve towards the stipend, expenses or other emoluments of the incumbent of the said benefice.
>
> *Coming into operation of this Scheme*
>
> 5. This Scheme shall come into operation upon the date on which notice of the making of any Order of Her Majesty in Council confirming this Scheme is published in the London Gazette.

45 *The Pastoral Scheme for the redundancy as signed by HM the Queen. Note that Clause 4 allowed the Trustees to make contributions to the Benefice.*

document had been altered.* The following April, on Easter Tuesday, after having spent over £600 on treating an outbreak of dry rot in the vestry, the Trustees were dealt a final blow: a letter from the Church Commissioners was read out announcing that the redundancy scheme would be put forward for confirmation by the Queen with 28 days being allowed for appeal. For the first time the Trustees seemed to have lost the will to fight and agreed to take no further action but await the outcome. The scheme[25] was published in the *London Gazette* on 22 June 1973 and, with no objections having been received, it came into effect on that day. St John's had had an incredible innings as a proprietary chapel; of the six that had opened in Bath four had closed before 1900, having fulfilled their intended purpose, but the last, All Saints, managed to struggle on to 1937.

Just two months short of its 160th anniversary St John's closed its doors on the public, apparently for good. Fortunately in August 1950[26] the Chapel had been added to the list of buildings of special architectural and historic interest under Section 30 of the Town and Country Planning Act 1947, so at least it was protected against the depredations of developers who might seek to demolish it.

---

* As we are getting into more recent history the names and details of this are best left unsaid!

Ten

COMPLETING NEWTOWN 1831-2000

As we saw at the end of Chapter One, the close of the Georgian era saw the New Town development nowhere near completion and the dream of Major General John Gustavus Crosbie largely unfulfilled. In 1830 most of the west side of St John's Street north of its junction with New Town (New Town the street, that is) was vacant and laid out as gardens whilst on the east side, south of the Chapel, only the houses currently numbered 5 to 7 had been built and there were vacant plots beyond. In Friary Lane only the first two houses (Nos 1 & 2) on the east side and St John's House (Friary Close) at the far end were in existence; on the west side nothing had been, or was to be, built as all the plots had been sold to enlarge the garden of East Pallant House. It was left to later generations to complete the development.

The first development of the post-Georgian era was in fact a redevelopment for the Mansion House (lot 1 of the 1808 sale) and its substantial garden was sold to create the new Corn Exchange for the city, which was completed in 1832. This will be dealt with in Chapter Eleven as part of Newtown's commercial history.

A few new houses were added to Newtown in the 1830s – that awkward stylistic period which sits so uncomfortably between the Georgian and the Victorian – and an early example was that which is now No 2 New Town. This two-bay house was built at the west end of Lot 22 of the 1808 sale, thus robbing the garden space of the two houses already on the plot, and it abutted the hitherto-detached house (No 3) which had been built on adjacent Lot 30. It was three-storey and its front-elevation brickwork and upper-floor fenestration matched its neighbour exactly, but the stuccoed ground floor was given a wider proportioned window and a recessed front door. The rear and side elevations were of flint with bands of Mixon rock whilst the basement is entirely of flint. In its typical Regency front door can be seen a spy-hole protected by a grille which is a relic of its use by the Sisters of St Margaret[1] in the early years of the 20th century – an interesting, albeit brief, return of religious-community life to the Black Friars site!

The house which is now No 8 St John's Street was given a decidedly mid-Georgian appearance by its builder, but owing to gaps in the title deeds as well as in the town plans its precise date of construction cannot be deduced.

It was built on Lots 16 and 17 of the 1808* sale which had been sold, along with Lots 18 to 21and 38 to 40, to William Dearling in the name of John Fookes, the deeds for the sale of all these lots being included with those for Friary Close.[2] As we saw in Chapter One, Dearling had moved to France† in 1817 leaving his affairs in the hands of a trust and after these two lots had failed to sell in the 1816/17 auction, they were sold on by the trustees to Susanna Ferris in December 1817. The earliest document in the title deeds for No 8 itself is a conveyance dated 1885 which recites back only to 24 July 1832 when the land was conveyed to the trustees for William Frazer. The 1832 recital shows that the house was then in existence but as there is no recital of earlier conveyances we do not know what happened between 1817 and 1832. No house is shown on this plot on the 1822 town plan so we can only deduce that it was built at some time between 1822 and 1832.‡ The handsome red-brick, three-bay house, which was rather old-fashioned for its date, was of three-storey construction under a hipped slate roof and possessed the best doorcase in Newtown but only occupied the northern part of the 60-foot-wide frontage, the remainder

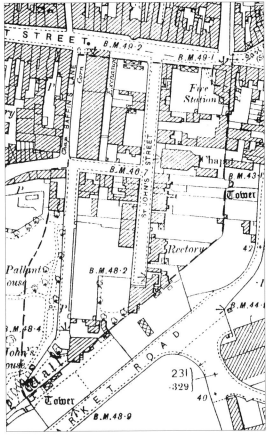

46   *Newtown in 1896 from the 1;2500 Ordnance Survey map. St John's Street is still a cul-de-sac and Friary Lane (unnamed) has not changed since the 1822 town plan, being still largely undeveloped. The boundary of the Newtown site has been added as a dotted line.*

being laid out as part of the gardens. It has a particularly impressive entrance hall which occupies over a third of the width of the original house but at the expense of the size of the adjacent rooms. The house was later extended to the south in a manner which, whilst carefully matching the existing brick colour and window style, was completely oblivious to the proportions of the house. Instead of making the extension three storeys and extending the hipped roof to suit, it was made of only two and the southern slope of the main roof was extended down in a cat-slide to encompass it. This resulted in an awkward blank triangular section of wall below the roof line which

---

* See Fig 3.
† See page 19.
‡ As such this house could have been covered in Chapter One but in view of its later alterations it is more conveniently dealt with here.

47 *No 8 St John's Street. The portion of the house below the cat-slide roof is an early 20th-century extension.*

gives the upper reaches of the building a lop-sided air and, now being of five bays with the front door in the first, was decidedly asymmetrical at street level as well. The extension did, however, make No 8 the largest house in St John's Street after Ivy Bank.

The date of the extension is post-1896.* Messrs Wyatt's particulars for the house when it was sold on 11 March[3] that year describe it as having the same number of bedrooms (three) on both the first and second floors whilst the ground floor consisted of '... dining and drawing rooms communicating with doors' all of which points to the house as still being of only three bays. The same sale particulars describe the outbuildings as consisting of 'a knife house, tool house, WC and a large aviary or Dove House'. The garden contained 'a summer house with fireplace and veranda at the front having a room under with a copper, ironing stove and pump. Also a boarded and wire Fowl House with Run, a small pheasantry [*sic*] and wire enclosed Fowl Run'. The sale was made on behalf of a trust set up to execute the will of Mrs Anne Hayllar[4] whose husband Charles had been a butcher and a trustee of St John's and, to judge by the facilities in his garden and the game larder in the basement, obviously had a taste for game unless the birds were destined for the shop! Charles Hayllar is first recorded in the Trustees' Minute Book[5] at the meeting of 10 April 1860 when he was sworn in as a trustee and he was chapel warden from 1863 to 1876. He was obviously a wealthy man as the same sale (all on behalf of Ann Hayllar's trustees) included a slaughter house in Chapel Street, a cottage at No 1 South Pallant and two meadows in Watery Lane, Rumboldswhyke. The purchaser of No 8 was Reginald Humphrey, a physician of 7 North Pallant, and it was most likely he who made the extension to the house. This sale started a long association of No 8 with the medical profession as we shall see in the next chapter.

Of a late 1830s date is No 4 St John's Street, just to the north of the Chapel, built on part of the site of Mr Cooper's timber yard which occupied

---

* The 1896 1:2500-scale Ordnance Survey map still shows the house to its as-built plan.

48 *The rear of 8 St John's Street in the 1930s. The single-storey wing was later given another floor. Through the gap in the houses No 12 St John's Street can be glimpsed.*

Lots 12 to 14 of the 1811 sale. As we saw in Chapter One, Cooper had made over the timber yard and the buildings on it in 1827 to Charles Ridge in order to address his debt of £1,100 and in May 1829 Ridge drew up an indenture[6] with Edward Martin for the latter to sell Cooper's property by public auction. There is no record of the result of this but when Cooper died on 7 July 1830 Benjamin Binstead was appointed devisee-in-trust to the will and an indenture dated 10 January 1831[7] provided for the other parties to Cooper's properties (Messrs Farhill, Bennet and Freeland) to sell everything to Binstead. However, although the properties in Cooper Street* are mentioned in the indenture, that in St John's Street is not, suggesting that it had already been sold. No 4, which was known as 'Cambridge House' in the early 20th century, is a three-bay double-fronted house much more in keeping with its date, being of a typical 'transitional' design but unusually for St John's Street was only of two storeys. It is built hard against the southern boundary of the site and abuts Cooper's flint boundary wall to the Chapel. The front has been stuccoed as has the front half of the south wall and the rest of the brickwork has been painted over, so whether the tradition of white/yellow brick was continued cannot be seen. The downstairs windows have plate-glass sashes with margin lights outside the sash boxes but the narrower upper windows have six-over-six barred sashes. The remainder of the timberyard site remained in industrial usage and was occupied by Johnsons the builders up to 1907, as we shall see in the next chapter.

Across the street from No 8 the four large houses, Nos 11 to 14 St John's Street, had by 1848 all passed into the ownership of Thomas Brooks of Maudlin who conveyed them on 22 February 1848[8] to Wm Gruggen Jnr,† George Rusbridger of Goodwood and Robert Raper of Chichester, the latter two being described as 'gent'. The conveyance of the freehold of the four houses included gardens, coachhouse and stables, and also the freehold of 'a pew or seat in St John's Chapel'. The conveyance states that three of

* Cooper Street was named after Charles Cooper who built it, see page 13.
† See pages 17-18 for more details of the Gruggen family.

the houses were occupied whilst the fourth was vacant. On 13 August 1850 the four houses and two separate gardens were included as Lots 21 to 26 in a property sale held at the *Anchor Hotel* and the sale particulars,[9] some of which have been annotated with the names of the buyers, are particularly interesting as they give the names of the tenants and their rents as well as illustrating the misleading commercial practices which took place in the days when there was no Trades Descriptions Act. Lot 21 was house No 14 which was described as 'new within a few years' which, considering it was built before 1812 – 38 years previously, was stretching the truth a bit! It was 'well supplied with pure spring water' and said to be in the occupation of Mr Elliott, a surgeon, at a yearly rent of £40. The sale notice is annotated that the house was sold to Mr Raper for £700. Lot 22 was house No 13 which is described as 'newly built' – another stretch of the imagination – and the compiler of the sale notice eulogises about the 'veranda' (meaning the balcony) onto which the drawing-room windows opened. It was said to be in the occupation of the Rev. Henry Browne, who was Principal of Chichester Theological College from 1842 and Bishop's Chaplain from 1843,[10] at a yearly rent of £45. The house was sold to Mr William Stick for £665.

Sale Lot 23 was a separate garden at the rear of No 13 (i.e., it was a Friary Lane plot) which was sold to Mr Titchener for £665. Lot 24, house no 12, was also described as 'newly built' and 'corresponding in every respect with Lot 22' (i.e. house no 13) and was sold to a Mr B. Noton for £680 who happened, conveniently, to be the sitting tenant which obviously saved him having to move. Lot 25, house No 11, was sold to a Miss Titchenor for £610 but had been let to Mrs Fanny Humphry until 1852 at a yearly rate of £40. It is interesting to note the variation in the prices reached by these three apparently identical houses; although the difference between highest and lowest was only £70, negligible in today's values, it represents a range of 11 per cent which puts the differences into perspective. No doubt the terms of the sitting tenancies influenced the bidders.

The final Lot in this sale, Lot 26, also sold to Mr B. Noton, was described as 'A large freehold yard' containing two stables and double coach-houses measuring 28 feet in front and 80 feet 4 inches deep, adjoining Lot 25. This was the area south of house No 11 now occupied by the modern Martlett House and was on Lots 27 and 28 of the 1808 sale. From the description we can infer that this yard provided stabling and coach accommodation for the three adjoining houses and maybe No 14 as well. In the will of William Gruggen Senior dated 1827 his estate is listed as including 'a 12-stalled stable with yard and sheds in occupation of John Hayllar'. The location of that yard is not given but as Gruggen had come to own the four houses it is quite likely that it refers to this one which he had also acquired. The common ownership of these four houses in Victorian times can be read in the changes which had been made to the windows. All the sashes in No 14 had had their glazing bars replaced by plate glass with vertical margin lights, which could easily mislead one to assume, from a first glance, that it is the more recent of the four rather than the other way around. The ground-floor windows of Nos 11 to 13 have been fitted with identical plate glass sashes but fortunately have retained their glazing bars on the upper floors. At some time the balcony of No 13, whose virtues were so extolled in the 1850 sale particulars, was removed which has spoilt the balance of the terrace. One day it may be restored.

In 1851 James Atkey Junior, son of the brewer James Atkey we met in Chapter One, died and in his will[11] he left an impressive array of properties in the area. These were mostly licensed premises but the list included 'the four houses in St John's Street'. Unfortunately the Atkey family cannot shed any light upon which houses these were but as we have seen in Chapter One James Atkey Senior, who had died in 1837, was a 'proprietor' of Newtown by 1825 even though he was not resident there. In searching for the Atkey houses amongst those which were in existence by 1851 we can eliminate 11 to 14 along with Nos 5 to 9, so the most likely candidates would seem to be Nos 1 to 4. By 1892 the terrace comprising Nos 1 to 3 were all in single ownership and may well have been so before. The detached No 4 had been built on the same former Cooper plot as No 3 and hence these two houses had a common link at the start; it is possible that in 1851 they may still have been in the same ownership. The proximity of No 1 St John's Street to the site of the chains put up in 1825 to keep cattle out of the New Town, to the agreement for which Atkey Senior was a signatory,[*] suggests that he might perhaps have owned Nos 1 to 3 at that stage and that later he, or his son, acquired No 4 when it was built in the early 1830s. Maybe one day a vital piece of evidence will surface and the mystery will be solved, but until then this can only be taken as pure conjecture.

As the 19th century progressed photography came into vogue and Chichester has in the main been well recorded by this medium – sufficient for several volumes of old Chichester photographs to be published. Frustratingly though, Newtown proves to have been rather camera-shy and it has been impossible to track down many early photographs – a great shame since they can provide so much incidental evidence. The photograph of the exterior of St John's (Fig 49) shows that in the early 1870s St John's Street was still unmade, necessitating a pitched foot-crossing to reach the chapel dry-shod.

On the whole Chichester did not suffer as badly at the hands of vulgar Victorian builders as did many historic cities and Newtown got off quite lightly with its Victorian additions. The only bit of really camp Victorian architecture in Newtown was the St Pancras Rectory, No 9 St John's Street. It was built in 1840 on Lots 18 and 19 for the Rev. George Ranking,[12] newly appointed as rector of St Pancras, and the 1841 Census Return shows that he and his wife Eliza were then in occupation. It is in a confused mock-Tudor style in flint with brick quoins and the gables, springing from carved stone kneelers, have stone-capped parapets. Pevsner[13] describes it as

---

[*] See page 21.

49 *The exterior of St John's Chapel, c.1871, still in its as-built condition. In the left foreground can be seen the wall of No 18 St John's Street . To the right of the Chapel is house No 5 whilst No 4 is to the left. Note the partial rendering to the south wall of No 4 and the pitched crossing of the still-unmade street. The Trustees contributed £3 towards the repair of the crossing in 1849.*

'seasidey' but does not specify which particular seaside he had in mind. It is still in use as St Pancras Rectory but when built it must have been a rare example of a new clergy house situated on extra-parochial ground rather than in the heart of the associated parish.

In 1862 the undeveloped area of land between the Corn Exchange and St John's Street, bounded on the north by East Street, was put up for sale in 10 lots[14] of valuable freehold building land. From Fig 4 we can see that this area of land was formed of Lots 2 to 6 inclusive of the 1808 sale measuring 207 feet along St John's Street and an average of 80 feet deep. These had originally been bought by the banker William Ridge and his cohorts[15] and, like the rest of their investments, was conveyed in trust to Richard Dally in January 1809.[*] They were left fallow and the 1820s town plans indicate that they were being used as gardens. In 1830 William Ridge died leaving his interest in the plots to his sons William and Charles who were also partners in the Ridge and Newland Bank.[16] Unfortunately for William and Charles, the Ridge and Newland Bank failed in 1841 and their Newtown lands passed to assignees in bankruptcy who then conveyed it to the Misses Esther, Elizabeth and Mary Johnston[17] who used it as a garden, screened from the public gaze by a high wall. Their house was on the north side of the East Street, thus providing the interesting concept of an over-the-road rather than a 'back' garden.

The 1862 sale particulars are not available[†] but the overall size of the site suggests that they were each 20 feet by 80 feet since a parcel of land 40

[*] See page 7.
[†] There was a copy attached to Add MS 6155 but these documents have been withdrawn from the West Sussex Record Office and are no longer available for consultation.

50   *A view of the corner of St John's Street and East Street in 1919. The photographer was interested in the WW1 tank which was being presented to the City (after all, it is not every day you come across one of those) but he has captured parts of Newtown now gone. Behind the high wall in the foreground are the still-undeveloped 1862 sale lots which were being used as a garden. The wall has since gone and Stocklund House (1966) occupies this site. Through the trees can be glimpsed part of the upper storeys of Nos 1 to 3 St John's Street which were demolished and replaced by Blackfriars House, whilst on the corner No 56a East Street (the only building in this view which still exists) is a small tobacconist's shop. Note the post box set in its wall.*

feet wide, and hence possibly two lots, was bought from Benjamin Binstead (and others), who had been involved with the sale of Charles Cooper's property in St John's Street. They were bought by a builder, James Kerwood the Younger, for £170[18] for the construction of two semi-detached houses, now Nos 19 and 20 St John's Street. These were built between 1862 and 1864 when Kerwood mortgaged the land and 'other buildings now erected' to William Churchman. In 1894 when Kerwood died he left No 20 to his son Alfred and it remained in the ownership of the family until 1947 when it was bought by West Sussex County Council.[19] It carries the name 'Kerwood House' but curiously the *Chichester Directories* show that the Kerwoods were living at No 7 St John's Street from the late 19th century to the mid-1930s. The two houses are substantial with 20-foot frontages, which would have pleased Major General John Gustavus Crosbie, and as Victorian buildings

51 *Nos 19 and 20 St John's Street in 2003.*

go are fairly well mannered. Built of yellow brick in the best Newtown tradition, they are of three storeys with basements and attics, their ground floors stuccoed with steps up to the front door contained within a recessed porch. The end walls were left blank and unfenestrated as though it was expected that they would later form part of a terrace; but this was not to be. In December 1909 Mr Kerwood applied to the Chichester Corn Exchange Company for a right of way over their roadway alongside the Exchange to an access he was proposing to make at the bottom of his garden. This was declined, but in 1913, having granted such a right to the next-door house, the Directors relented and resolved to write to Mr Kerwood[20] to give him '... the same privilege on behalf of his tenant Mr Steiniz'. This Mr Steinitz was, of course, the minister of St John's who rented No 20 from 1912 to 1914.

Another Victorian house in St John's Street is No 7. As we saw in Chapter One, a 24-foot-wide house had already been built on the north side of this 48-foot-wide site in 1818 for William Gruggen Senior. In 1867 William Gruggen Junior, who had inherited the house and was described in his will[21] as 'a surgeon and apothecary', died and the interest in the estate passed to his three sons William John MD, Rev. Frederick James, Rev. George Septimus and also to Mathias James Sowton of Chichester. The Georgian house was subsequently demolished and replaced with the present one, a wider three-bay two-storey building of red brick under a tiled, hipped roof. It was later extended so as to fill most of the 48-foot frontage but in a most curious manner which made the extension look like a separate house – albeit one with no front door! The extension is built in flint with brick quoins with a single-pitched roof which runs east-west contrary to the north-south orientation of the main house. A narrow passageway was left at the south end to provide a rear entrance. The 1896 O.S. map indicates that all the rebuilding of No 7 had been completed by then.

Before we leave the Gruggens and their last involvement with Newtown it is worth continuing the story of their curious mixed profession of surgery and banking. When William Senior died in 1828 William Junior went into partnership with his younger brother John Price Gruggen, running a surgery

52 *No 7 St John's Street rebuilt in Victorian times. The two stuccoed houses beyond, next to the Chapel, are Nos 6 and 5.*

in West Pallant and sharing equally the profits from the practice. However, William had also inherited his father's banking interests which seemed to be of greater interest to him and this put more of the surgical workload onto John. Accordingly in 1841 the two partners drew up an agreement[22] to make John's reward more equitable. The agreements starts:

> Whereas the said William Gruggen and John Price Gruggen have for some years carried on and exercised the Profession and business of a Surgeon Apothecary and Man Midwife in the said City of Chichester ... and whereas William Gruggen in addition ... carries on the business of a Banker – and to which said last-mentioned business devotes a considerable portion of his time and attention ...

The agreement sets out the mechanism for John being rewarded for his extra effort and states that the surgery shall be at the dwelling house of John Price Gruggen, the address of which (West Pallant) is not given. Another of William Gruggen Junior's sons, George Septimus Gruggen, became vicar of the new church of St Peter the Great in 1868.[23] Both the William Gruggens and also Robert Elliott from St John's Street were listed as 'Honorary Surgeons' to the West Sussex, East Hampshire and Chichester General Infirmary.[24] William Gruggen Junior became Mayor on two more occasions, in 1843 and 1851, before his death in 1867. Owing to burials in the grounds of St John's being proscribed by the Act the Gruggens, as with the Marshes before them, were all buried at All Saints in West Pallant. William Junior was commemorated in a stained glass window in this church which has since been removed, and in 1909 a huge marble memorial tablet was put up inside which commemorated all the departed Gruggens from 1796 to 1909. This does survive, but is partially obscured by a fixed heater. However, the entries for Williams Senior and Junior and John Price are visible.

The census returns for the 19th century[25] were presented by parish and Newtown was listed separately as an 'extra parochial' and hence gives an interesting indication of the rate at which its population grew – and fell.

1811	1821	1831	1841	1851	1861	1871	1881	1891	1901
✦	82	112	123	135	143	127	157	138	132

✦ In 1811 the extra-parochial population was included in the figure for St Martin's parish, so the combined entry is meaningless as far as Newtown is concerned.

The fluctuation in 1871 is curious but the decline after the 1881 peak probably reflects the turning over of some of the houses in St John's Street to business usage, as we shall see in the next chapter.

The early 20th century made only one addition to Newtown in the form of a terrace of three cottages in Friary Lane, now numbered 3 to 5. As we have seen in Chapter One, Friary Lane was not so named until 1918, prior to which the postal addresses of the three Georgian houses had been New Town; perhaps the arrival of more housing sparked the desirability of a separate identity. Typically Edwardian in style, the new houses are built with cavity walls in a hard, orange engineering brick. Although some 100 years later than Nos 1 and 2 adjacent, they have the same 15-foot frontages and the same layout, with a scullery at the rear and a steep staircase rising between the two downstairs rooms. No 1 Friary Lane suffered a serious fire in the early 20th century after which it was largely rebuilt in orange engineering brick similar to that used on Nos 3 to 5. As a result of the rebuilding (which also included the infilling of its cellar) the modern brickwork and different window sizes meant that it no longer matched its neighbour. Next door, No 2 Friary Lane in the early years of the 20th century was also used by the Sisters of St Margaret who lived around the corner at 2 New Town.[26]

At the bottom of Friary Lane the coach house and stables of St John's House had been converted into a separate house by 1890 and named 'St John's Mews',[27] although both dwellings remained in the same ownership. Now known as 'Friary Cottage', it continues in separate occupation. Between 1943 and 1970 St John's House, by now renamed 'Friary Close', was owned and lived-in by Miss B.M. Scott,[28] a well-known and very philanthropic lady* who hosted lavish garden parties in the grounds in aid of local churches and charities. St John's was one of these beneficiaries as was announced in the St Pancras and St John notes in *The Chichester Observer* for 8 July 1966:

> Tomorrow (Saturday) the annual garden fete is to be held in Friary Close, Market Avenue [*sic*] by permission of Miss Scott. The fete will be opened at 2.30 pm and there will be stalls of all kinds to appeal to the tastes of all ...

Miss Scott lived in this vast house with her companion Miss Campbell and kept a full retinue of staff, including Miss Bridger who was the live-in cook. Her

* In the 1950s we had no family car and Miss Scott one day loaned my father her Austin Seven in return for his cleaning it. The day sticks in my mind as the car stalled going up the hill in Arundel and rolled back, alarmingly, to the bottom. Fortunately there was little traffic around in those days.

53 *Nos 1 to 5 Friary Lane in 2003. Nos 1 and 2 date from 1810 whilst Nos 3 to 5 beyond are 100 years later. No 1 was rebuilt following a fire in a similar engineering brick to that used for the later houses.*

maids at this stage were still traditionally dressed in black and white.

St John's Street was originally set out as a cul-de-sac which ensured that it remained quiet and relatively free from traffic but this was not to last. By the 1930s motorcar usage was increasing rapidly and the narrow confines of Chichester became clogged with vehicles, the only usable entrances to the city being at the four gates. One solution to this was to connect St John's Street with Market Avenue, which was itself being widened and provided with car parks, and this was done in 1938. Unpopular with residents, it entailed the compulsory purchase and demolition of part of No 10 St John's Street (Southdown House) and taking part of the Rectory Garden. There was a considerable difference in levels between St John's Street and Market Avenue and this, allied to the need to minimise the land-take, accounts for the clumsy alignment of this link-road. Prior to this an alleyway served those who wished to make this particular journey on foot.

Whilst Newtown may have got off lightly at the hands of Victorian builders, it did not escape the worst depredations of the 1960s and '70s developers. Of the later 20th-century additions the least said the better as they are neither sympathetic to their neighbours nor outstanding edifices in their own right. The first of these was Stocklund House, a commercial development of shops and offices which filled the last remaining Lots of the 1862 sale, lying to the north of Nos 19 and 20 St John's Street. In the 1950s this land had ceased to be a garden, the high wall (see Fig 50) was taken down and the site used as a car park. An archaeological excavation was carried out here in 1966 by Alec Down[29] which revealed that this area had been the Black Friars' burial ground and scores of skeletons were unearthed and removed for re-interment at the cemetery. When the dig was completed the present typically-bland 1960s building, most of which fronts onto East Street, was erected. It does have one interesting feature, though, in the form of a turntable for cars in its courtyard car-park which is reminiscent of the one which once existed for turning Bournemouth Corporation trolleybuses in a pub yard in Christchurch. On the opposite side of the road Nos 1 to 3 St John's Street were demolished in the early 1970s to be replaced by a brutalist modern housing block containing five maisonettes. The building is raised on columns over the obligatory car-park, the latter surrounded

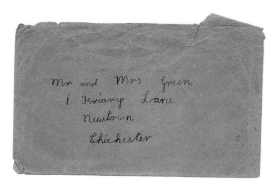

54 *A letter addressed to No 1 Friary Lane showing the use of the term 'Newtown'.*

by a blank brick screen-wall. It does, however, carry an appropriate name in 'Blackfriars House' and it too has a turntable in its rear courtyard in another (probably unintentional) homage to the much-lamented Bournemouth trolleybus network. At the south end of St John's Street a new link road was cut through to Friary Lane in 1970 which finally provided the street intended in 1809 to be called 'Cross Street'. Built to give access to the car-park, the new road allowed the construction of two more uninspiring office buildings: Martlet House, which was built on the site of the stable yard adjoining No 11, and Dominican House on the opposite side, whose only interest is in its appropriate name. At the other end of the new road two modern houses were built as Nos 6 and 7 Friary Lane and these, at long last, marked the completion of the Newtown development.

The majority of the older buildings in Newtown are now afforded the statutory protection of listed status under the Town and Country Planning Act. Whilst unfortunately this came too late to prevent Nos 1-3 St John's Street being destroyed, at least a similar thing should not happen again. St John's Chapel is listed Grade I but Grade II status has been applied to the following:[30]

> St John's Street: 4, 5, 6, 8, 9, Southdown House, 11-17, 18 and the
> New Corn Store.[*]
> New Town: 1, 2 and 3
> Friary Lane: 1, 2 and Friary Close (the gate posts and wall to
> Friary Close are listed separately)

Today it is not immediately apparent that Newtown had been developed as a separate area within Chichester; visitors and even most of the City's residents see it as just a group of three city-centre streets not segregated in any way from those around it. As such, the concept of a distinct community called Newtown has largely died out and only older Cicestrians now recognise the term. However 'Newtown' was still part of the postal address well into the 20th century as the envelope (Fig 54), addressed to my parents in Friary Lane and dating from the early 1950s, demonstrates.[†]

Despite this loss of identity Newtown remains an attractive area of the city and St John's Street in particular has become what estate agents term 'a most sought-after address' and the properties, when they do come onto the market, achieve prices which match to this expectation.

---

[*] See pages 136-8 and 141 for details of the construction and use of this building, at one time known as The Booth Rooms.
[†] Your author's birth certificate of 1950 carries exactly the same form of address.

Eleven

COMMERCIAL NEWTOWN

Crosbie intended his New Town to be an area of high-quality housing for the professional classes and saw to it that all the leases included a restrictive covenant to prevent inappropriate uses. However, despite his best efforts, businesses, albeit not all industrial, did creep in from fairly early on. Indeed, for much of the 20th century more commercial than residential use was made of the houses in St John's Street. Charles Cooper's use of the land north of the Chapel as a timberyard has already been noted in Chapter One and after he came to grief the yard was taken over by William Johnson, who carried out his building and funeral-furnishing business there. The range of his services can be seen from the invoice in Fig 55 below, which was for work he had done to the Chapel. Johnson was a pew-holder at St John's and derived much business from the Trustees around this time. In the 1875 *Chichester Directory* the premises were described as 'The City Steam Saw Mills'.

The biggest commercial venture undertaken in Newtown was the Corn Exchange which opened in 1832 on the site of the Mansion House and its gardens. The Corn Exchange, like the Mansion House before it, faced onto East Street and thus did not have a Newtown address, but as it was part of the history of the Black Friars site it has a rightful place in this story. The Mansion House and its garden was sold in 1831 to the newly-formed Chichester Corn Exchange Company (of which William Gruggen Junior was, perhaps unsurprisingly, a shareholder), who demolished the house and in its place built the main trading building of the Corn Exchange.[1] Opinion over the building's designer is divided, the two candidates, both local men, being John Elliott and George Draper. Howard Colvin[2] is of the opinion that the architect was Elliott, quoting as his

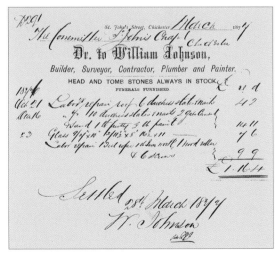

55 *Invoice heading for William Johnson of St John's Street for work done at the Chapel which was next door to his yard.*

133

source a Victorian *Dictionary of Architecture* published by the Architectural Publication Society. Pevsner[3] gives the same attribution. John Elliott, who was both architect and builder, had completed the east wing of Goodwood House in 1838-9 but was declared bankrupt in 1843 as a result of claims arising from his building of the Gothic Christchurch Worthing.[4] George Draper's local architectural works include the Chichester Infirmary and the rebuilding of St Bartholomew's church.[5] He had also been appointed by the St John's Trustees as architect to the Chapel after Elmes was dismissed (see page 71).

The minute books of the Chichester Corn Exchange Company[6] do not mention the appointment of either architect or contractor for their new building, but they do record in August 1835 the serious problems which had emerged with both the roof and floors, estimated as requiring expenditure of £400-500 to put right. Bearing in mind that the Corn Exchange had only cost £1,000 to build, the magnitude of these problems was serious indeed. The shareholders' meeting resolved to take legal action as the minute records:

> ... it is the opinion of this meeting that Mr Draper the Architect be held responsible for any loss or damage which may be sustained in consequence of any effects arising from want of judgement or otherwise on his part – if in the opinion of Counsel on a statement of circumstances should be liable to indemnify the shareholders.

This quite firmly points to Draper as being the architect whose judgement in design matters is being questioned. So how did Elliott come to be attributed in the Victorian *Dictionary of Architecture*? Elliott, as we have seen, traded as both architect 'and builder' so it is possible that he was the 'contractor' for the construction of the building and the compilers of the dictionary sprang to the wrong conclusion, assuming that with his dual trading role he had designed it as well.

The shareholders sought the independent opinion of the London architect James Savage[7] who had made something of a name for himself as an advisor in architectural and engineering legal cases. He opined that the timber was 'much to [*sic*] weak and injudiciously constructed ...' and that the roof should be taken off and rebuilt and the floors strengthened. A copy of Savage's report was sent to Draper and the shareholders instructed Savage to proceed with procuring the re-roofing work. They also resolved to seek Counsel's opinion, but thereafter there is no mention either of that opinion or of any action being taken against Draper. Perhaps Counsel's opinion did not provide the hoped-for robust footing for a case, having revealed some contractual loophole through which Draper might be able to wriggle.

Draper had stuck to his favoured classicism for the Corn Exchange and produced an impressive stuccoed Greek-Revival temple which was to dominate (and still does) the East Street scene. The massive portico has six fluted Doric columns made of cast iron seated on pedestals right on the edge of the carriageway so that the pavement passes beneath. The *Hampshire Telegraph* reported[8] that the columns were three feet in diameter, 19 feet high and weighed 18 tons 9 cwt. but unfortunately, despite this close attention to detail, the identity and location of the maker is not given, so this remains a mystery. The red-brick grain-storage buildings behind, which occupy the entire Mansion House garden area and stretch the full length of Baffins Lane, have a distinctly industrial air about them. Baffins Lane was very narrow so the Corn Exchange was set out well to the east of the edge of the carriageway to allow an access road to be built alongside. A brick wall marked the boundary between the access road and the public highway but in 1928, after part of it collapsed, it was replaced with an iron fence.[9] Each Christmas Day the private road was chained off so as to prevent its becoming a public right of way.[10] The 1896 1.2500 O.S. map (Fig 46) quite clearly shows the demarcation between the two roads. This arrangement lasted until the fence and chains were removed before the War when the private access road was adopted by the Corporation in order to widen Baffins Lane.

Pigot & Co's *Royal National and Commercial Directory* of 1839[11] lists some smaller artisan businesses in St John's Street, carried on from the houses, namely:

> William Jenner – Bricklayer and Plasterer
> William King – Carpenter
> James Rogers – Painter, plumber and glazier

However, there were some professional businesses as well which would have been more acceptable to Crosbie:

> Mary Ann Boimaison – Boarding-School Proprietor
> John Nott – Surgeon
> Sawton & Fuller – Attorneys

The list also reveals that the Surgeon Robert Elliott who lived at No 14 had his surgery in West Street and Charles Hayllar who lived at No 8 had his butcher's shop in East Street.

An indenture dated 20 May 1862[12] conveying the site of Nos 19 and 20 St John's Street from Margaret Johnston to Benjamin Binstead (and others) states that the parcel of land to the south was also '... now belonging to, or about to be conveyed to, Benjamin Binstead' and a number of other speculators. This suggests an intention to extend 19 and 20 to form a terrace but instead, in 1871, the land south of No 19 was developed for commercial purposes. The sale conditions of these plots included Crosbie's covenant banning noxious industrial activities but this did not seem to stop the building here of an annexe to the Corn Exchange, a building not strictly in the spirit of the New Town ethos. Indeed, it could be argued that the Corn Exchange itself wasn't either, but as it faced onto East Street and bordered onto Baffins Lane – both existing streets – it was probably acceptable. Anyway, the Corn Exchange Company, whose business was booming, needed to build a new corn store and let a contract to a Mr Gammon for its construction in May 1871 in the sum of £880.[13] The foundation stone was laid on 17 June and can be seen low down on the north-west corner, bearing the inscription:

> Laid by C.T.Dendy Esq
> Chairman of CCEC
> June 17 1871
> Geo Elkington – Arch

Of the architect George Elkington nothing is known. His two-storey building was less industrial in appearance than the rear of the Corn Exchange proper, being of flint with red-brick dressings under a slate roof. It fronted onto the Corn Exchange's eastern access road and was linked into the main building by a bridge at first-floor level which can just be made out on the 1896 OS map (see Fig 46). The St John's Street façade was thus the rear of the building and the space between it and the street was made into gardens and rented out by the company. Together they filled completely the gap between houses Nos 18 and 19. The New Corn Store, however, had a limited life fulfilling its original purpose, for in August 1905 the directors decided to lease the building, on a full-repairing and insuring basis, to a Mr Nieville. Mr Nieville, who had rights of access over the Corn Exchange roadway and also the option to rent the St John's Street garden should he so wish,[14] used the building as a 'motor-store and garage', one of the first garages to be opened in Chichester. He was given permission by the directors to hang a sign from the portico of the Corn Exchange to advertise his business and in April 1907 he took up the option of renting the garden, then occupied by a Mr Chives, having been granted permission to make a doorway into it from the building 'at his own expense'. He then applied in September 1908 to transfer his lease to T.S. Adcock, which application was accepted by the directors. Adcock continued with the motor trade usage but later that year turned the building around by making its entrance onto St John's Street and at the same time sub-let the upper floor to Ben's Gas Company. This sub-letting was approved by the Corn Exchange Company but only subject to Mr Ben's men not using their urinal![15] Quite how Mr Ben overcame this restriction is not recorded but one can imagine that the adjacent garden might have proved to be quite a convenient asset in this respect.

That same year more industry crept into Newtown in the form of another garage which opened on the northern part of the old timber yard vacated by Johnson the builder. This garage, known as 'The Chichester Motor Works', was owned by Mr Alfred Humphry[16] who also traded as a plumber and gas-fitter from 61 East Street. The two rival garages of Adcock and Humphry thus faced each other across the street – both physically and no doubt competitively.

56 *A view of East Street c.1908. Hanging from the portico of the Corn Exchange can be seen the sign for Adcock's Garage then housed in the New Corn Store. J.W. Moore's printing shop is opposite.*

Adcock managed to get himself elected as a director of the Corn Exchange Company in May 1911,[17] which no doubt aided his being granted permission to enlarge the windows of the building and erect lock-up garages in the garden. By 1923 he had bought out his rival, A.T. Humphry,[18] and was trading from both sides of St John's Street. He renewed his lease on the New Corn Store in June 1925 but unfortunately died the following month. The Adcock family continued the business but in 1930 applied to have the lease on the New Corn Store transferred to J. Sadler, the corn merchant and miller, who seems to have used it as a garage[19] for maintaining his fleet of lorries. Sadlers also occupied the grain stores of the Corn Exchange until it was sold in 1966.

CHICHESTER
MOTOR WORKS,

61, East Street,
and
St. John's Street,
CHICHESTER.

᠃᠃

A. T. HUMPHRY, Engineer Proprietor.

᠃᠃

Tyres Vulcanised and Accumulators Charged on the
Premises.

———

All kinds of Repairs done on the Premises by
Competent Workmen.

———

Competent Engineer always at the Works Day and
Night.

———

EVERY MAKE OF MOTOR VEHICLE
SUPPLIED.

A Large Stock of Accessories and Tyres.

57 *An advertisement for A.T. Humphry's Chichester Motor Works from the 1908* Chichester Directory.

The longest-surviving Newtown business was Moore and Tillyer's 'Regnum Press' printing works. The firm was established in 1875[20] by Mr J.W. Moore when he took over a small printing company in Eastgate. He moved to larger premises at 39 East Street behind which he set up a small printing works and one of the many publications to flow from his press there was the annual *Chichester Directory*. As business grew, the printing operations were transferred to St John's Street in 1908* in a works set up on the south side of site of Charles Cooper's former timber yard. Cooper's buildings, including the sawpit shop, were re-used and extended, the southern range being built onto the flint boundary wall adjoining the Chapel. J.W. Moore died in the early 1900s and was succeeded by his son H.W. Moore (a deaf mute) and his son-in-law Percy T. Wingham, the business continuing to be known as J.W. Moore until 1925 when it was renamed as Moore and Wingham.

Arthur William Tillyer had purchased the bombed-out contents of Thomas Triggs' printing works in North Street† in 1944 and moved its operations firstly to Northgate and then to the Hornet. However, whilst Arthur Tillyer's business was thriving that of Moore and Wingham was in decline so in 1945 the two merged and became known by the present name of Moore and Tillyer. H.W. Moore retired at the merger and Arthur Tillyer then ran the company, all the printing being carried out in St John's Street with the East Street premises used as the stationery shop. Arthur Tillyer was joined by three of his five sons, Stanley, Sidney and Derek, who continued to expand the business and when Arthur died in 1948 the company passed into the hands of the three brothers.

* The Tillyer family are uncertain of the precise date but the first entry for the St John's Street works in the *Chichester Directory* was in the 1908 edition.
† The 1937 St John's Chapel accounts were printed by Mr Triggs whose business address is given as Adcock (T.R. Triggs) Printer, 18 North Street, Chichester.

58 *The Corn Exchange New Corn Store, later to become the Booth Rooms and now in use as offices. The stuccoed end wall of 19 St John's Street can be seen to the right of the picture.*

In 1950, in order to get more light into the printing works, Moore and Tillyer applied to the St John's Trustees[21] for permission to insert two windows into the flint boundary wall. This was duly granted but in a letter dated 11 October that year the company wrote to the Trustees advising that 'the work is likely to take longer than hitherto expected due to difficulties with dust and the builders cannot work whilst machines are operating'. One can understand the problems, especially when seen in the light of today's more health-and-safety conscious climate, but the work was eventually carried out and the company continued to pay the annual 19s. 11d. (98p)

59 *A panoramic view of Moore and Tillyer's printing works from the north in 1974 when Adcock's garage was being demolished. The left-hand building was converted from the sawpit shop of the former timber yard; a hoist can still be seen below the eaves.*

60 *An interior view of Moore & Tillyer's printing works prior to the arrival of the new technology.*

wayleave for the privilege. Curiously the printing works was never accorded a street number, ending up sandwiched between Nos 3 and 4 (neither of which were owned by the company) so it was named 'The Regnum Press' in order to give it an identifiable address. It should be pointed out that the Chichester Papers, including appropriately that on St John's Chapel, were all printed there. The printing industry's new technology, which ousted the traditional type, was embraced ensuring the company's survival and it is still run by the Tillyer family; Clare Holder, Derek's youngest daughter, took over the reigns in 1997 when her father retired. However, the firm's 128 years of trading in Chichester and long association with St John's Street ended in September 2003 when the firm relocated to Fernhurst and at the time of writing the site, with its fascinating industrial buildings, was awaiting a new use.

North of the printing works, Nos 1 to 3 St John's Street in 1892 belonged to a Mr Arnold. A valuation[22] carried out in July that year shows that No 1 had a front shop and selling room and was let to Mr J. Moore (who was probably the printer J.W. Moore) whilst No 2, which was occupied by a Miss Jane Wilson, included a 'workroom' over the scullery, suggesting that perhaps Miss Wilson was a seamstress. No 3, in the early years of the 20th century, was let as apartments by a Mrs Peay.

The north-east section of the Blackfriars site facing onto East Street, which was sold at the first 1808 sale, was never developed for housing; the 1875 OS map shows the land east of 56/56a East Street as the yard for the fire station. When the fire station was moved to Market Avenue in 1929 Adcocks spread onto the site from their St John's Street premises and remained there until the early 1970s when the site was redeveloped, providing the commercial premises, now numbered 51 to 55 East Street. The goods access to this development was from St John's Street adjacent to the Regnum Press and it was for this that the turntable was needed.

The New Corn Store was taken over in 1951 by George Booth, a wealthy philanthropist, who proposed to turn it into an arts centre in conjunction with local artist and dealer David Goodman.[23] Unfortunately the venture folded when insufficient capital was forthcoming and so George Booth converted the building into a suite of meeting rooms known as 'The Booth Rooms', adding a porch and entrance hall to the St John's Street frontage. Its most famous use was as home to the Chichester Ballet School, or 'The Lombard School of Dancing' named after its founder, Miss Marian Lombard. With her companion, Miss Mollie Child,* she also ran the Chichester Ballet Club which was founded in 1944[24] and transferred to the Booth Rooms when they opened. Both ballet organisations flourished under the Misses Lombard and Child until they retired in 1976. Both ladies were loyal members of the Church of St Peter the Great rather than St John's (Mollie Child being a St Peter's churchwarden for a time) but they were obviously on good terms with the Chapel for in December 1958 the Trustees decided[25] to

> allow Miss Lombard to have use of the chairs as usual in connection with the Inter-church Aid and Refugee Service for a nominal payment of 10/-, she to collect the chairs and return them and be responsible for any breakages.

George Booth was obviously held in high esteem by Chichester's ballet set for in 1970 a large hand-drawn 'certificate of appreciation', signed by all the girls and teachers,[26] was presented to him. It was headed:

An appreciation from all those who enjoy the lovely
BOOTH ROOMS
This spring term 1970.

After the Booth Rooms closed the building was converted to office use. Wiley's, the American publishers, had moved to Chichester from London in May 1967, taking over the then semi-derelict rear part of the Corn Exchange itself. In 1982 they expanded into the Booth Rooms,[27] enlarging

---

* Miss Child was a teacher at Chichester High School for Girls.

61   *Walter O. Stride (centre) pictured on 13 May 1937 at a donkey derby on the New Park recreation ground with J.G. Johnstone (left) and E.W. Garry (right). He moved the family firm from East Street to Southdown House, 10 St John's Street, in 1937.*

the windows and extending the porch, and they remained in occupation of both buildings until 2002 when they relocated to their newly built headquarters in Stockbridge Road. Thomas Eggar & Sons the solicitors, who had long occupied three houses in East Pallant, then moved into the Corn Exchange main building in 2003, whilst the New Corn Store became an independent suite of offices.

The inscrutable 10 St John's Street, 'Ivy Bank', remained in domestic use well into the 20th century before becoming commercial premises. Between 1895 and 1908 it was lived in by the Quaker William Smith[28] who had been the last worshipper at the Friends Meeting House in Priory Road prior to its temporary closure in 1908. William Smith was a major contributor to Chichester civic life holding the office of Mayor for two three-year stretches between 1886 and 1888 and again from 1892 to 1894; his tenure of 10 St John's Street is commemorated by a plaque fixed to the front of the building. William Smith was followed at No 10 by another civic dignitary, Sir Sharp Archibald Garland,[29] the son of Sharp Garland who owned the celebrated grocery shop in Eastgate Square.* Sir Sharp was also a long-serving Mayor of Chichester between 1911 and 1918 and died in 1937.

The Chichester auctioneers and estate agents Stride and Son was established in 1890 in East Street[30] and the business was moved into Ivy

---

* This much-lamented shop, reputedly the oldest grocery business in the country, was demolished in an act of civic vandalism in 1964.

Bank in 1937 when Walter O. Stride bought the house from Sir Sharp Archibald Garland. This gave Stride's premises conveniently close to the cattle market at which they were the auctioneers. The name of the house was changed to 'Southdown House' which commemorated the family's association with Southdown sheep rather than the local bus company! W.O. Stride was the secretary of both the Sussex Agricultural Society and the Southdown Sheep Society and Southdown House was listed as being the headquarters of both.[31] When Market Road was widened and the road connection from St John's Street was put through not only did Mr Stride lose part of his house he also lost the garden to the south which was compulsorily purchased to construct the present car park.

St John's Street also sported three small private schools all accommodated in houses, the first to open being at No 20 which was listed in the 1890 *Chichester Directory* as being a 'school for young ladies' run by Miss Wilson. By 1894 it had been taken over by Mrs Garrett and Miss Ostler and named 'Clydesdale House School'; its lofty claims for excellence can be seen from

CLYDESDALE HOUSE SCHOOL,

ST. JOHN'S STREET, CHICHESTER.

IN CONNECTION WITH THE LONDON COLLEGE OF MUSIC.

PRINCIPALS:

Mrs. E. GARRETT & Miss OSLER,

Trained Certificated Teacher,

Assisted by Resident Governess, and Visiting Music Master —
MR. A. W. LAMBERT, L.Mus., L.C.M.

General Course of Instruction.

For Senior Pupils (over 10).

Reading, Writing, Mathematics, History, Geography, English, (including Composition, Literature, Analysis and Parsing) Plain Needlework, and Cutting out (for Girls) Elementary Science, French and Drawing.
Day Pupils 4 guineas per annum.

For Junior Pupils (under 10).

Kindergarten receives special attention, Reading, Writing, Arithmetic, English Needle-work, and Object Lessons on Common things, &c.
Day Pupils 3 guineas per aunum.

The Pupils enjoy the full privileges of the family circle, and all matters of health, recreation and care, receives the personal attention of the Principals.

REFERENCES ON APPLICATION.

Pupils are prepared for Teachers' Government Certificate Examinations, College of Preceptors, Oxford, and Cambridge Local Examinations.

62 *An 1894 advertisement for the Clydesdale House School at 20 St John's Street which seems to offer all a Victorian parent could possibly wish for – for four guineas per annum.*

the advertisement in Fig 62. The directories show that in 1900 the school had changed hands again and was now being run by the Misses Inkston. However, this was to be short-lived as it had closed by 1903 when the house went back into private occupation for a time.

Miss Maria Apedaile established a small dame school in St John's Street in the early years of the 20th century which she ran with her sister Kit who acted as housekeeper.[32] The name Apedaile is first listed in St John's Street in 1903[33] when Mrs S.A. Apedaile moved to No 17 with her daughters. However, by 1908 the mother must have died as the residents were now cited as 'The Misses Apedaile'. In 1910 they moved to No 15, a house rented from Teddie Game who ran a bakery in Broyle Road and lived at 1 New Town. Miss Apedaile did not advertise her school nor did she list her business in the *Chichester Directories* so the date that it opened is uncertain.

63 *Maria Apedaile who ran a dame school at 15 St John's Street. She is pictured here on 25 May 1954, about to be taken out by Tom Kimble to mark her 86th birthday.*

However, Thomas Kimble, who was born in 1897, was one of her pupils[34] so, assuming that he started at the age of five or six, the school must have been in existence in 1903. Furthermore, the school must have been started at No 17 since at that time No 15 was occupied by a Mr Millyard. Born in 1868, Maria Apedaile was affectionately known as 'Collie' as she was deemed by her pupils to resemble a dog of that breed. After she retired and closed the school she continued to live at No 15, and was looked after by the Kimble family, her erstwhile pupil Tom Kimble taking regular meals to her. Every Monday evening Tom would take her out in his car, usually to the *George* at Eartham, until in the early 1960s when she died. At that time the house had not been modernised and still had gas lighting and only one tap in the yard.[35] No 15 St John's Street is now named 'The Old School House', providing a fitting memorial to 'Collie'.

The last and biggest of these educational establishments was St John's School at No 13 which provided a very popular alternative to the Prebendal School from the early 1930s. It was a mixed kindergarten and preparatory establishment run by Mrs Munro and Miss Evans, the latter being responsible for the kindergarten. A concert programme in aid of Dr Barnardo's held in 1936[36] lists many famous Chichester names in a performance of the play *The old woman who lived in a shoe* such as Sadler, Gough, Bartholomew and Goodger. It also included Maurice Voke who became a musician and held the post of organist at St John's in its final years. The school was the most successful of the three and soon outgrew 13 St John's Street. It relocated to larger premises in 1937, much to the dismay of Dr J.H.H. Gough who had moved to St John's Street earlier that year and whose three children already attended the school which was so conveniently opposite his new house.[37] St John's School was still in operation at its new premises at 88 The Hornet[38] in 1957.

In the first half of the 20th century St John's Street attracted various branches of the medical profession to set up their practices and it became very much a street of brass plates. No 8 was the house longest in medical usage; between 1896 and 1918 Dr Humphry[39] had his surgery there but in 1930 it had been bought by Dr Arthur Barford, a physician who was also Medical Officer for Health for the City of Chichester and an active supporter of the St John Ambulance Brigade. At the same time part of the building was also used as a surgery by Doctor John Henry Harley Gough who quickly became one of, if not the, most respected doctors of the time in Chichester. The surgery and waiting rooms occupied part of the ground floor with the patients using the side entrance adjacent to the garage, while the Gough family lived "over the shop' in this very spacious house.[40] Dr Gough was kept very busy during the war as Medical Officer to all the local

64   *Advertisement for St John's School in the 1936 Chichester City Guide.*

Army and RAF camps and in 1940 he delivered a daughter to the Duchess of Norfolk in a turret in Arundel Castle! He was also Medical Officer to numerous Chichester institutions and heavily involved with the work of the Royal West Sussex Hospital as a surgeon. The medical profession is renowned for its dry sense of humour and typical of such wit is this poem[41] which was attached to a Christmas present given to him at the Royal West. Judging from the subject matter – tonsillectomies – it was probably written in the 1950s when such operations were performed on children almost as a matter of course:

MR GOUGH
The patient stood in out patients
Whence all but he had fled,
He heard Mr* Gough's low gentle voice
'I'll have his tonsils or his head'

The scene is changed. The trolley's laid
The surgeon wears a grin,
For there before him are a row
of tonsils, neat and trim.

The Streptococcis foiled again
In vain it seeks its host
For Mr Gough has pinched the pair
of tonsils it loved the most!

---

* As a surgeon he would have been referred to as Mr rather than Dr at the RWSH.

65 *Dr J.H.H. Gough in the garden of 8 St John's Street with his dog Bracken. The garden extends back to the City Wall which can be seen in the background.*

He was later granted title of Surgeon Emeritus and a seat dedicated to his memory was installed in front of the Royal West and, although the building is a hospital no more, the seat remains as part of the landscaping of the housing development that replaced it. In June 1943 Dr Barford died and in his will he left No 8 St John's Street to The Order of St John of Jerusalem with the intention of its becoming the headquarters of the St John Ambulance Brigade.[42] St John's Street would have provided a particularly apposite address for the Brigade but this was not to be as there was no suitable parking for their ambulances and (fortunately for posterity) alteration of the house to incorporate more garaging was seen as too difficult. The Order of St John sold the house to Dr J.H.H.Gough[43] in October 1951 and used the proceeds to fund their new headquarters in The Hornet[44] which they named, appropriately, 'Barford House'. Dr Gough remained at No 8 until he retired in 1968 when he sold it. Then, after a long medical association, No 8 reverted to being a private house.

Another successful general practice surgery was founded in the 1920s at No 20 St John's Street. In the 1929 *Chichester Directory*[45] the practice was listed as being run by Drs Arthur Bostock and Frank Heckford. By 1933 they had been joined by Dr Douglas Langhorn and in 1939 by Drs Wilson and Guy Emmerson.[46] No 20 was now too small for the growing practice (patients had to wait in the entrance hall) so in 1939 they all moved to West Street, where it became the Langley House practice which is still very much alive today. Dr Bostock ('Old Bossy') was also heavily involved with the work of the Royal West Sussex Hospital[47] and a new ward, one of a block constructed there during the Second World War, was named after him.

No 14 St John's Street had some interesting medical uses. As we have seen, in the early 19th century it had been occupied by the surgeon Robert Elliott but he does not seem to have carried out his practice there. Between 1923 and 1927 it was occupied by one G. Lansdowne CSMMG* who was

* Chartered Society of Massage and Medical Gymnastics.

offering the services of 'massage and medical electricity', services which sound a little ambiguous today but were doubtless completely innocent. In 1934 the practice had been taken over by a Miss Peters, described as a masseuse, and she shared the premises with a Miss Insley who was a chiropodist. However, by 1950 Miss Peters was the only person listed at No 14 and was described as a physiotherapist. Not far away No 18, Hasted House, was in the 1950s the dental practice of Mr Douglas Robertson Richie whilst No 4 opposite was used as a County Council dispensary and clinic in the 1920s.[48]

Several other smaller businesses and other non-residential uses were also established in Newtown in the second half of the 20th century. The 1957 *City Guide* lists No 11 St John's Street as being both the Chichester Labour Party Headquarters and the Spiritualist Church; both organisations have long since moved on but No 11 remains in commercial use as offices. No 13 was long in office use, occupants including Farr's Depository, Eagle Star Insurance Company and the Ministry of Transport. Happily it has recently been converted back most successfully to domestic use. In 1962 Mrs Iseult Beaumont-Thomas was trading in antiques and decoration from No 14 St John's Street, whilst on the other side of the road 56a East Street was in use as the David Paul Gallery founded by Chichester artist and art-dealer David Goodman;[49] its small rear extension is now a take-away food outlet. On the corner of Friary Lane, No 4 New Town, the former stables to No 3, has had a variety of commercial uses including an art gallery, The Canon Gallery, and subsequently two different estate agents. Currently 11 and 19 St John's Street are in use as offices as are three of the modern additions to Newtown, Stocklund House, Martlet House and Dominican House, the first named also having shops fronting onto East Street. Also in office use is 2 New Town but, following a refurbishment in 2003, the ground floor and basement was taken over by Chichester Chiropractors who relocated from The Hornet, thus reintroducing medical practice to Newtown. In 1990 a planning application was made by the then owners of No 8 St John's Street to convert the house into an hotel but this was rejected by the District Council Planning Committee[50] on the grounds of its 'introducing commercial use into a part of St John's Street which is predominantly residential in character' (!). The wheel seemed to have turned its full circle from the extensive commercial usage of not very long before.

Major General John Gustavus Crosbie would certainly not have been impressed with some of the uses to which his development had been put, especially those relating to the repair of horseless carriages which would have given rise to noise and smells, but by then he was long gone and hence had no say in the matter – it was left to the lease holders to reconcile their activities with the restrictions imposed by his covenant.

Twelve

St John's – Recession and Restoration

Although the congregation had withdrawn from St John's and settled in their now-permanent home at St Pancras, the Trustees' involvement with the Chapel was by no means over. There was still the tricky problem of their legal role in the building, its contents, the surrounding land and the schoolroom to be resolved. At the meeting on 9 November 1973[1] it was reported that although responsibility for the Chapel building was to pass to the Redundant Churches Fund the contents remained vested in the Trustees. The Diocesan Board of Finance agreed to insure the organ for £6,000 and the remainder of the contents for £5,000. The vestry, which also adjoined and served the schoolroom, had been treated for a severe outbreak of dry rot in the April prior to the closure but, as further repairs and modifications were needed to it, the Trustees were faced with a conundrum – whether to spend money on a building they no longer owned in order to keep another one, which they did own, going! It was agreed not to proceed until the advice of the Diocesan Board of Finance could be obtained. All was resolved in October 1974 (wheels were still grinding exceedingly slow) when the Church Commissioners proposed to vest the Chapel and the land on which it stood* in the Redundant Churches Fund and to make a gift of the vestry and kitchen to the Trustees, a gift which was accepted.[2] In addition to the gifted vestry, the Trustees were left owning the schoolroom, the forecourt and all the land surrounding the Chapel – but not the Chapel itself. This important principle being agreed, work went ahead to make the vestry more suitable for its new purpose as an annexe to the schoolroom. The transfer of the Chapel to the Redundant Churches Fund† was finally completed in August 1976[3] and this also allowed for certain of the furnishings to be transferred to local churches, if so requested, but the Communion Table (fortunately) had to remain in St John's. From now on, though, and for the

---

* What would be termed the building's footprint in today's jargon.
† Renamed The Churches Conservation Trust in April 1994 – See Postscript II, p.156.

---

66 *The west front of St John's in 1971 showing the trees which were felled 11 years later and also the hedge which had been planted to replace the iron railings. In front of the left-hand tree can be seen the wayside pulpit.*

next twenty years, St John's was to become impregnable for visitors who could only glimpse the three-decker through the grimy and now be-grilled windows. St John's had entered its wilderness years.

In February 1977 Elmes' ghost returned once more to the roof which again had to be re-slated, but this time it was not the Trustees' worry to find the money – indeed, without the liability of the Chapel and its minister their financial position was better than it had ever been. However, troubles continued to beset the Trustees in connection with the bits they still owned, the principal one of which was the battle over the trees in the forecourt. Complaints were received in July 1977 from the (then) Chichester Civic Society that the trees 'had outgrown their usefulness and detract from the street scene' whilst a further complaint from a resident claimed that they were dangerous. The Trustees' decision to fell the trees failed when their planning application was turned down, consent only being given for lopping as the trees were subject to a Tree Preservation Order. An appeal was made in 1979 and was also turned down, so selective lopping continued until planning permission was finally granted[4] in April 1982 to remove them completely. Their removal, it has to be admitted, did improve the view of the Chapel from the street.

The fact that the gifted vestry building shared a party wall with the Chapel was to prove a recipe for two disasters, the first of which surfaced when the organ gallery, which was supported on a heavy timber frame overtop the vestry, became unsafe owing to another outbreak of dry rot. The Redundant Churches Fund decided to apply for listed building consent to demolish it rather than rebuild. This took place in 1980 but in order to facilitate it the organ had to be dismantled and the best of the pipework was packed into cases under the watchful eye of Kenneth Wiltshire of Brandt Potter and Partners.[5] When the demolition was complete the Trustees carried out major internal alterations to the vestry but two years later another outbreak of dry rot in the Chapel spread through the party wall and into the floor. The Redundant Churches Fund were faced with major works to eradicate the rot in the Chapel which involved replacing much of the floor at the east end and rebuilding the dais as well as blocking up the doors leading to the vestry. This was completed in 1983 but despite this major expenditure, and further works to stabilise the walls and campanile, public access to this fascinating building continued to be denied to the great frustration of visiting architectural historians. On completion of these works the Chapel returned to its slumbers.

However, in September 1981 it had nearly been rudely awakened when the rector of St Pancras applied for planning permission to build a new church on the Trustees' land at St John's. Once again the Trustees felt that they were being challenged and advised the rector[6] that the land was not for sale. At a Trustees' meeting on 20 April 1982 the rector questioned the Trustees' *raison d'être* alongside the PCC and asked them how they saw their future. The rector proposed that an open forum be staged in June which would include giving consideration a possible reopening of the Chapel. This duly took place but no unanimous decisions emerged from any of the votes taken on these visions for the future. Subsequently, the Trustees resolved that they had no plans either to sell the land or wind up the trust but might agree to the parish using the schoolroom if suitably enlarged. In October 1982 a change of rector delayed the decision-making process again but in December the PCC requested the Trustees to consider selling the land in conjunction with a sale of the Chapel itself, the proceeds being put into building a new church. The implications of selling a listed building held in trust by another body almost speak for themselves and, when the Church Commissioners advised that Parliamentary Powers would probably be required, enthusiasm seems to have waned. In July 1984 the PCC decided to pursue an alternative option of building a new church in New Park* after selling off their other premises. The Pastoral Sub-committee set up to look into the implications for St John's finally reported[7] in October 1985 and it was read out at the Trustees' meeting. It is worth quoting since it illustrates not only the historical value of St John's but also the perils of trying to tinker with Grade 1 listed buildings.

> The repossessing and extensions of St John's Church [*sic*] would appear to present formidable difficulties of both a structural and financial nature bearing in mind its status as a Grade 1 listed building. A re-ordering scheme for St John's would seem to be hardly feasible in that it is the interior plan, closely following the original of 1813, which contributes to its listed status and the desired liturgical arrangement and seating capacity is unlikely to be achieved within that constraint; in addition there is limited car-parking space on the site.

Back in 1975 a three-week festival had been staged to mark the 900th anniversary of Chichester Cathedral. Although it was intended to be a one-off event the popularity of an arts festival in Chichester was to ensure a repeat and it grew into an annual event known as 'The Chichester Festivities'. One of the problems an arts festival faces is finding venues with both seating capacity and suitable acoustics for classical concerts. One potential venue existed, albeit run-down and inaccessible – St John's Chapel. In 1990 The Festivities Committee, following an initiative of the Duke of Richmond, commissioned a report into the feasibility of using St John's as a concert venue.[8] This would obviously have to be limited as there was no lighting or heating in the building, thus restricting events to daylight hours in the summer months, but this initiative was to be the beginning of a new life for St John's.

The impetus was provided by the St John's Chapel Group; set up on 22 July 1991 under the chairmanship of the Duke of Richmond and with Noel Osborne as secretary, it campaigned vigorously for the restoration of the building. One of the group members was the late Harry Axton who, as

---

* This did not happen either.

chairman of the Chichester Festivities, was able to guarantee that a restored St John's would be extensively used as a concert venue during the festival. Harry Axton succeeded the Duke of Richmond as chairman and proved a tireless campaigner for the cause.

The Redundant Churches Fund agreed to the proposal and put in place further repair and redecoration works so as to make the Chapel presentable to the public once more. These works, which were completed in 1992 in time for that year's festival,* included an improvement to the ceiling – the match-boarding being covered over with canvas and painted white so that it resembled plaster† – and painting the main body of the Chapel with white distemper. The staircases, however, were left untouched as the gallery was not put back into commission owing to fears about its structural safety.

The first public event was a commemorative service,‡ the first for nineteen years, held on 7 June at which the Dean preached and the St Richard Singers provided the music. During the festival a concert was held on Tuesday 14 July, given by the Consort of Twelve, entitled 'Handel at St Johns' whilst the following week, on the 21st, the Local History Society staged presentations by some of its members on the history of the Chapel. One of the speakers was Maurice Wilson-Voke who had been the last organist at St John's and who told of the gasps of horror which arose from the congregation when he played for the first time arrayed in cassock and surplice! The interest in the Chapel from the public was immense and those who had not been inside it before cannot have failed to be impressed by the acoustic. At the end of the festival the doors were closed again but St John's was back – and in April 1993 The St Richard Singers, under the direction of Noel Osborne, gave the first of a series of choral concerts in the Chapel. This first concert included Vaughan Williams' ethereal *Mass in G minor*, for unaccompanied double-choir and soloists, which showed off the Chapel's acoustic admirably and, in a subsequent concert, the three-decker pulpit was put to good use when the top deck was occupied by the soloist in Carissimi's oratorio *Jepthe*.

In addition to the St Richard Singers' concerts, which lasted until October 1996, St John's reopened for every festival after 1992, its use increasing each time. However, such was the public interest in the building there was a real need for better access, so the St John's Chapel Group organised limited openings until The Churches Conservation Trust (as the Redundant Churches Fund had now become) appointed a custodian, Nigel Bowers, enabling the Chapel to be open all day and every day. To mark the Millennium Nigel Bowers put the bell back into commission, having obtained a rope from the Cathedral, and at midnight St John's added its voice to those of the other Chichester churches, the sound of its bell floating

---

* 1992 was a good year for new concert venues as Edes House in West Street had been newly restored by West Sussex County Council and was also used for the first time by the Festivities.
† Unfortunately this feature was short-lived as the canvas soon began to part company with the underlying matchboarding and had to be removed. The match-boarding was then painted white.
‡ Despite its redundancy St John's remained, and remains, a consecrated building.

out over Newtown for the first time in over 30 years.

The St John's Chapel Group had also opened St John's for the first national Heritage Open Day and, from September 2002, it became a regular feature of the Heritage Open Days programme. In this it takes its place alongside other historic Chichester buildings and structures such as Edes' House, the Council House and Poyntz Bridge, with your author staging hourly guided tours giving a potted* history of the Chapel. It is quite surprising how many visitors are local people who simply had not realised what was on their doorstep. Weddings and funerals are also permitted at St John's and this is much appreciated by those who have had a connection with the Chapel or who are looking for somewhere which is different yet still a place of worship.

One thing upon which all visitors commented was the Chapel's tatty appearance and its need for a little 'tender loving care'. This was not surprising since the paint was flaking in large patches from the walls and ceiling and the latter was developing an unsightly culture of mould. The neglected appearance was not helped by the spectre of the gaunt framework

67   *Restoration work in progress, March 2003. The scaffolding was needed to gain access to the ceiling. The walls have been stripped back to the bare plaster.*

of the dismantled organ with its larger pipes stacked untidily against the back wall. The Chichester Festivities Committee were keen to have the facilities improved with lighting and power circuits suitable for their staging equipment and so the Trust embarked upon a major restoration scheme for the interior which commenced on site in January 2003. Paint scrapes had been taken on the walls and joinery and a redecoration scheme based upon them was designed by Louise Bainbridge who also supervised the restoration works. A new power supply was installed and the 1948 ceiling lights under the galleries were re-wired and brought back into use complemented by new wall-mounted up-lighters in the gallery. During these works the Chapel yielded up many of its secrets including the curious timbering of the gallery, the fact that the brass handrails to the gallery had

* As each tour was only 45 minutes long the 'pots' were of necessity very small!

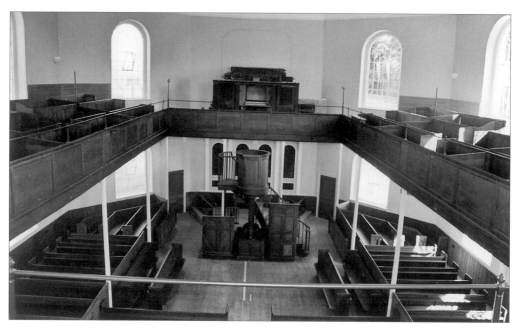

68   *The interior following the 2003 restoration. The colours used have been based on paint-scrapes.*

been replaced with steel and the signature to the graining on the gallery plasterwork mentioned in Chapter Five.

This time the redecoration included the stairwells and the internal doors were recovered in crimson baize, the existing material having rotted in the ultra-violet light. The restoration work was completed for the 2003 Festivities and was a fitting way of marking the Chapel's 190th anniversary.

Much as one must regret the fact that St John's is no longer used for its intended purpose its destiny was, from an historical point of view, the best there could possibly have been. Having seen off the Oxford Movement and the Victorian improvers, its twenty years in the wilderness saved it in turn from late 20th-century trendy modernisers. Their attentions would have seen the pews replaced by comfy chairs and the three-decker pulpit ousted in favour of a console from which a sound system would amplify the raucous strains of the electric guitars and drum kits which would have superseded the organ upon which John Marsh and Thomas Bennett once played. As it is now, beautifully restored, St John's can be appreciated for its architectural and ecclesiastical importance, a tribute to the tireless band of Trustees who had it built and kept it running and James Elmes who designed it. Its use as a concert venue is a tribute to John Marsh and Thomas Bennett who established its musical tradition and one hopes that one day the organ may be restored to a form that they would have recognised. But, above all, one must remember that it is still a consecrated building and one where it is possible outside the festival season to sit in stillness and add one's own prayers to the thousands that have been offered up here in the past.

Postscript I

THE ST JOHN'S TRUSTEES TODAY

Most proprietary chapels had closed by the early part of the 20th century having fulfilled the purpose for which they were built, their buildings were disposed of and the trusts wound up. By any standards St John's was remarkable in surviving as long as it did under its proprietary status. For even after the uniting of the benefices of St John and St Pancras, when St John's became a chapel-of-ease, the Trustees still continued to fund the maintenance of the building. Even more remarkable, despite the fact that the Chapel has closed and is now owned by the Churches Conservation Trust, the St John's Chapel Trust is still in existence.

As we saw in Chapter 9 when the Chapel was transferred to the Churches Conservation Trust, the St John's Trustees were still left owning the schoolroom (or hall as it had then become known) as well as the surrounding land and the chapel forecourt. They also still owned 68 North Street and other investments which, together with the hiring out of the hall, were still generating income to be directed towards new good causes. The Trust achieved charitable status in 1987 and is now in two parts: one, to maintain and run the hall for the purposes of religious and other charitable work of the Church of England in the Parish of St Pancras and St John; and the other, directing the Trust's income to furthering the work of the Church within the parish.

Despite earlier pressure to amalgamate with the PCC the Trust maintains its independence and membership of the Trustees still includes the Mayor, Archdeacon and the Dean of Chichester as prescribed by the Act. Although the Pastoral Scheme for Redundancy vested the Chapel in the Diocesan Board of Finance on a 'notwithstanding-the-provisions-of-the-Act' basis, the Act itself was never repealed. Similarly, under the terms of the measure which united the benefices, the St John's Trustees still share the advowson of St Pancras with the Simeon Trustees; St John's appoints rectors on a one-in-three basis.

What exists now must surely be highly unusual, if not unique, in the annals of ecclesiastical history – a proprietary chapel trust having no chapel but which is still generating income used for furthering the work of the Church of England. This is something of which John Marsh and the other founding fathers would have been very proud indeed.

The St John's Trustees have now been in existence for 190 years and, freed from the challenges of having to pay shareholders' dividends, collect pew rents and rates and pour money into the fabric of the Chapel (Elmes' building proved a very effective sponge in this respect), they continue to keep alive the spirit of the St John's ministry in Chichester.

Long may they continue to do so!

Postscript II

THE CHURCHES CONSERVATION TRUST

The Churches Conservation Trust, in whom St John's Chapel is now vested, was created in 1969 when it was known as the Redundant Churches Fund. It exists to take care of those Church of England buildings which, although no longer used for regular worship, are of sufficient historic or architectural importance to require preservation and hence be protected from conversion to other uses or, even worse, demolition. The Trust is a registered charity and its funding comes principally from The Church Commissioners and the Department for Culture, Media and Sport to which is added general donations, individual legacies and, where possible, grants available from appropriate bodies. The extensive refurbishment of the interior of St John's carried out in 2003 by craftsmen builders using traditional materials is typical of the Trust's conservation work and is a good illustration of how the funds are used.

St John's Chapel is just one of over 330 churches currently in the care of the Trust which are maintained for the enjoyment of the public and details of opening arrangements are given on the website and in their free publications. St John's, on account of the rare survival of most of its Georgian layout, features in the booklet *Your Starter for 50 English Churches* which describes the Trust's 'top 50' buildings.

The Churches Conservation Trust
1 West Smithfield, London EC1A 9EE

Tel 020 7213 0660
Email central@tcct.org.uk
Registered Charity No 258612
Website WWW.visitchurches.org.uk

THE CHURCHES CONSERVATION TRUST

Appendix A

THE ACT OF PARLIAMENT –
SUMMARY OF PROVISIONS

The building and subsequent use of the Chapel had to be authorised by Parliament and the Act, which was passed on 5 May 1812, is in 52 sections occupying no fewer than 26 pages. Whilst the reading of such Acts can be somewhat tedious it is most interesting to see what Parliament both empowered and required the Trustees to do, so the following gives a very brief summary of the principal provisions of each section.

I   Explains the need to build the Chapel and names the Trustees.

II   Requires all proceedings under the Act to be executed by any three or more of the Trustees.

III   Sets out the procedure for appointing new Trustees and gives the form of oath to be used.

IV   Gives the date (second Monday after the passing of the Act) and place (The *Swan Inn* Chichester) of the first meeting of the Trustees and requires at least nine Trustees to be present.

V   Requires seven days' notice to be given of Trustees' meetings and for the notice to be posted at the Chapel and on the south-east door of the Cathedral.

VI   No act or proceedings carried out under the Act is valid unless it is done at a Trustees' meeting.

VII   An order or appointment made at a Trustees' meeting can only be revoked at a special meeting.

VIII   Requires the proceedings of the Trustees to be entered into a proper book and signed by the chairman.

IX   Gives the procedure for appointment of Treasurer, clerk, chapel wardens and other officers, production of accounts and the conduct of such officers.

X   Empowers the Trustees to contract for purchase of the ground at a price not exceeding £1000 anywhere within the City of Chichester except the parish of All Saints.

XI   Empowers corporations in the conveyancing of the land.

XII – XIV   Compensation payments to affected landowners.

XV   Procedure for dealing with disputed titles (i.e. to the land).

XVI   The premises are to be vested in the Trustees.

XVII   Gives the form to be used for the conveyance of the land.

XVIII   Empowers the Trustees to erect the chapel and finish and furnish it for 'the celebration of Divine Service according to the Usage of the Church of England'.

XIX   Empowers the Trustees to contract for the building of the Chapel.

XX   Empowers the Trustees to take legal action in respect of breach or non-performance under the contract.

XXI   Chapel to be subject to Ecclesiastical Jurisdiction by Law established and The Bishop of Chichester is authorised to consecrate it as 'The Chapel of St John the Evangelist'. Proscribes the creation of a new parish and makes it unlawful for the minister to publish banns of marriage, solemnise marriages, administer baptisms, churching of women or carrying out of burials in the Chapel's grounds.

XXII   Contents of Chapel to be vested in the Trustees.

XXIII – XXIV Sets out the methods and powers to raise the money to build the Chapel.

XXV Requires at least 250 free seats to be provided for the use of the poor.

XXVI Requires a plan of the pews to be entered into a register, giving sizes and numbers etc.

XXVII Requires pew numbers to be painted on the doors and the values to be entered into the pew register.

XXVIII Pews are to be either let or sold and memoranda of each sale or lease to be drawn up. Uses the term 'Proprietor' for such owners.

XXIX Requires subscribers to the building of the Chapel to be given preference in the purchase of the pews in order of the size of their subscriptions.

XXX Requires memoranda of sales to be entered into a book 'for preventing Confusion or a Plurality of Claims'.

XXXI Forbids pews to be sub-let for a rent greater than that paid to the Trustees.

XXXII Forbids alterations to be made to the pews without the consent of the Trustees.

XXXIII The advowson is to be vested in the Trustees. Gives the procedure for the election of the minister.

XXXIV Gives the procedure for the election of subsequent ministers.

XXXV If the ministry remains vacant for six months the right of nomination passes to the Bishop.

XXXVI Sets out the duties of the minister, including using the Book of Common Prayer for services on every Sunday and on festival and fast-days.

XXXVII Requires the Trustees to arrange for clerical cover during vacancies.

XXXVIII Requires the Trustees to pay the minister's stipend of £80. The minister is given the power to take action in the event of default in payment.

XXXIX Minister to be allocated pews to the value of £40 p.a. which he can let and receive the rent monies therefrom.

XL Allows the Trustees to take gifts of land etc for the endowment of the chapel or augmentation of the minister's salary.

XLI Requires two chapel wardens to be appointed annually on the Tuesday of Easter week, one to be nominated by the minister the other by the Trustees. Sets out the duties of the chapel wardens which include collection of pew rents.

XLII Requires chapel wardens to have custody of the keys to the chapel and the books, plate etc.

XLIII Allows minister to appoint a chapel clerk at a salary not exceeding £20. Clerk given power to take action in the event of default in payment.

XLIV Requires all donations (i.e. collections) made at the Sacrament to be distributed by the minister to the poor of the City.

XLV Requires the Trustees to keep the Chapel in repair paid for out of chapel income. No repair over £5 to be carried out without an application being made to, and approved by, the Trustees.

XLVI Allows the Trustees to levy rates upon pew proprietors in cases where the rents do not yield sufficient income. Rate to be set by the Trustees and be no greater than two shillings in the pound. Sets out the remedial action to be taken against defaulting proprietors.

XLVII Sets out in order the priorities for application of the monies raised under the Act and from chapel revenue.

XLVIII Allows Trustees to sue and be sued in the name of the treasurer. Sets out the rules for such actions.

XLIX Gives a right of appeal against actions taken in pursuance of the Act.

L Parties making distress for monies levied under the Act are not deemed to be trespassers on account of any defect or want of form in the proceedings.

LI Actions against persons limited to six months after the committed act.

LII Deems The Act to be a Public Act.

Appendix B

LIST OF INCUMBENTS OF ST JOHN'S CHAPEL

1813-1858	Stephen Barbutt MA
1859-1871	Edward Whitehead MA
1871-1874	Chapel closed – no incumbent
1875-1876	George Blisset MA
1876-1878	Francis Gell MA
1878-1881	George Furness-Smith MA
1881-1893	William David Cowley DD. Died in office
1894-1898	William Bridger Ferris
1898-1901	Joseph Henry Monti. Died in office
1902-1948	Charles Edward Steinitz MA. Died in office
1949-1954	Maurice Grey Newton MA

February 1955 — Amalgamation with St Pancras to form United Benefice. St John's proprietary status effectively ends and is run as a chapel of ease to St Pancras. The following are the Rectors of St Pancras who had the care of St John's:

1955-1962	Jack Edward Marshall MA [following Newton's resignation most services were taken by Rev J Lowry Maxwell until January 1956]
1962-1967	John Gregg McKechnie MA
1967-1973*	Alan Lindsay MA
June 1973	Chapel closed and declared redundant

*Continued as Rector of St Pancras after the closure.

159

Appendix C

THE ORGAN SPECIFICATIONS

1.   The Organ as built by John Pyke England in 1813 and later modified by John Marsh

This specification was noted by Alexander Buckingham* in 1826[1]

GREAT ORGAN		SWELL ORGAN	
Open Diapason to G	46	Open Diapason	34
Stop Diapason	54	Stop Diapason	34
Dulciana to 4ft C	41	Principal	34
Principal	54	Hautboy	34
Fifteenth	54	Sexqualtra Bass 3 ranks	75
Cornet treble, 3 ranks	87	Trumpet bass and treble	54
Total No of pipes	465		136

The organ had two manuals, 12 speaking stops, a total of 601 pipes, but no pedal board. Its original appearance can be seen in the 1871 view of the interior at Fig 23.

2.   The organ as it was in 1898 following rebuilding by Hele & Co of Plymouth. The specification was given in the programme[2] for the opening concert on 8 December.

  The organ, now very Victorian, had a pedal board, 18 speaking stops and a total of 876 pipes.

GREAT ORGAN			SWELL ORGAN		
Open Diapason	8'	56	Double Diapason	16'	44
Stopped Diapason	8'	56	Open Diapason	8'	56
Dulciana (grooved bass)	8'	44	Gedact	8'	56
Gamba	8'	56	Keraulophon	8'	56
Octave	4'	56	Gemshorn	4'	56
Flute Harmonique	4'	56	Piccolo	2'	44
Super Octave	2'	56	Cornopean	8'	56
Total no. of pipes		380	Oboe	8'	56
			Total no pipes		424

PEDAL ORGAN			COUPLERS
Open Diapason	16'	30	Great to Pedals
Bourdon	16'	30	Swell to Pedals
Violincello (grooved)	8'	12	Swell to Great
Total no. of pipes		72	Swell to Octave

Three double-acting composition pedals.

---

* Alexander Buckingham was a London organ builder who compiled detailed descriptions of the organs he worked on. In Chichester, Buckingham had worked on St John's, the Cathedral and Marsh's own organs.

3. The organ as it was following the 1950ˣ rebuilding by Hele and Co.
    Specification as noted by the author in 1972 from the stop-knobs.

GREAT ORGAN		SWELL ORGAN	
Open Diapason	8'	Double Diapason	16'
Stopped Diapason	8'	Open Diapason	8'
Dulciana	8'	Keraulophon	8'
Gamba	8'	Piccolo	2'
Octave	4'	Cornopean	8'
Flute	4'	Oboe	8'
Super Octave	2'	Principal	4'

PEDAL ORGAN		COUPLERS	
Open Diapason	16'	Great to Pedals	
Bourdon	16'	Swell to Pedals	
Violincello	8'	Swell to Great	
		Swell to Octave.	

It can be seen that the specification is largely the same as it was in 1898 but two stops, Gedact and Gemshorn, have been removed and a Principal has been added giving a total of 17 speaking stops. The case had been discarded by 1944, being infested with woodworm.

The organ in this final form without its case can be seen in Fig 39. It was dismantled in 1980 when the recess had to be demolished. It is hoped that one day it may be restored to its 1813 form.

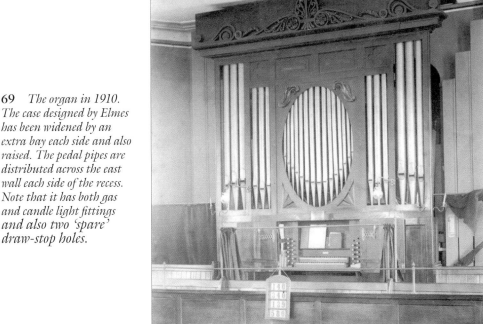

69 *The organ in 1910. The case designed by Elmes has been widened by an extra bay each side and also raised. The pedal pipes are distributed across the east wall each side of the recess. Note that it has both gas and candle light fittings and also two 'spare' draw-stop holes.*

ˣ The organ had also been rebuilt in 1928 by Hele & Co; an entry in the Service Book for 13 December records a musical service at which the organ was reopened. It had been fitted with an electric blower in 1948 prior to which it was hand-blown.

Appendix D

THE CHAPEL PLATE

70 *The two silver-gilt communion cups gifted to the Chapel in 1813 by Samuel Scudamore Heming.*

For the opening of the Chapel in 1813 a gift of two very fine communion cups was made by Samuel Heming. They are silver-gilt, six inches (168mm) high, with ovoid bowls on circular bases London hallmarked for 1813 with the maker's mark E.F., possibly Edward Fernell who was recorded as making church plate in 1780.[1] On the underside of each foot is engraved *The gift of Saml. Scudamore Heming Esq to St John Chapel Chichester 1813* and they are both engraved with oval designs around the lip of the bowl and the foot. One cup has engraved monograms of *TBH* and *SGH* for Thomas Bayley Howell and Samuel George Heming and the other has the monogram *SSH* for Samuel Scudamore Heming. Samuel George Heming, who died in 1813, was the only son of Samuel Scudamore Heming. Thomas Bayley Heming was the brother-in-law of Samuel Scudamore's wife.[2]

Following the closure of the Chapel the communion cups were loaned by the St John's Trustees to the Cathedral Treasury where they are on public display in the collection of plate from Sussex churches. Happily, on account of their practical design, they are used to augment the Cathedral plate at major Feasts which means that part of the St John's heritage is still fulfilling its intended purpose.

The rest of the plate is less exciting and is not on display. There is a silver flagon, 9¾ inches (248mm) high which was presented by Richard Merricks[3] in 1816. It has a maker's mark *WF* over *JF* (unidentified) and was described in a 1903 inventory[4] as:

> a plain flagon with an almost parallel body, it has a handle and an open thumb-piece to a somewhat flat hinged cover, the foot is formed by an ogee moulding.

There is a Sheffield plate stand-paten eight inches (203mm) diameter engraved with the *IHS* monogram set in rays and also a pair of Sheffield plate alms dishes bought in 1814 with similar monograms.

NOTES

CHAPTER ONE, NEW TOWN – NEW CHURCH, pp.1-23.

1. WSRO, Add MS 2920. This deed relates to the sale of the plot on which 7 St John's Street was built, but recites earlier indentures.
2. Bishop, Philippa, Holburne Museum of Art, Bath, *A Guide to the Collections*, 1999.
3. Elwes, G.C. and Robinson, Rev. C.J., *A History of the castles, mansions and manors of Western Sussex*, 1879.
4. WSRO, Add MS 2920, *op. cit.*
5. Thomas, Spencer, *West Sussex Events*, Phillimore, 2003.
6. Fleming, Lindsay, CP5, *The Little Churches of Chichester*, Chichester City Council, 1957.
7. Emerson-Semper, E.J., *Church History, Parish of St Pancras and St John*, 1958.
8. *Ibid.*
9. WSRO, MP1154, *A History of the Crosbie Family*.
10. *Ibid.*
11. WSRO, Add MS 2920, *op. cit.*
12. WSRO, GB1/2/2, *General Baptist Church Book 1763-1804* contains a listing of all members during this period. It includes both James and John Dearling.
13. Sparrow, Giles, *Kingsham Farm, Chichester*. Chichester Local History Society.
14. Steer, Francis, CP42, *The Corporation of St Pancras Chichester*, Chichester City Council, 1964.
15. WSRO, Add MS 19774, deeds to Friary Close. An indenture of 1809 gives Dearling's address as such.
16. WSRO, Add MS 2920, *op. cit.*
17. WSRO, Add MS 19775, *op. cit.*
18. WSRO, Add MS 19775. A copy of the sale particulars which includes a plan of the lots.
19. WSRO, Add MS 2920, *op. cit.*
20. Blakeney, Rita, *A History of Somerstown, Chichester*, 1987 (published privately).
21. WSRO, Add MS 2921, Deeds to 7 St John's Street.
22. WSRO, Add MS 2932, Deeds to 7 St John's Street.
23. WSRO, Par39/1, Rough minutes of the St John's Trustees, 1811.
24. Gadd, David, *Georgian Summer – Bath in the Eighteenth Century*, Adams & Dart, 1971.
25. WSRO, Add MS 2921, *op. cit.*
26. WSRO, Add MS 19776, Deeds to Friary Close.
27. WSRO, Add MS 7200. Indentures relating to Cooper's affairs.
28. Green, Kenneth, *The Street Names of Chichester*, Verdant Publications, 1996.
29. WSRO, Add MS 7201-7203. Indentures relating to the winding up of Cooper's affairs.
30. WSRO, Add MS 19788. Deeds to Friary Close.
31. WSRO, Add MS 19791, ditto.
32. WSRO, Add MS 19786 & 19788, ditto.
33. WSRO, Add MS 19791 & 19792, ditto.
34. WSRO, Add MS 19807 & 19808, ditto.
35. WSRO, Add MS 19810, ditto.
36. O'Neill, Hugh, 'Happy are we met', Chichester Freemasons (u/p).
37. WSRO, SP2068. Sale particulars for 5 & 6 St John's Street of 1989, describes the former linking of the two houses.
38. WSRO, Add MS 2931. Deeds to 7 St John's Street.
39. WSRO, Add MS 2943, ditto.
40. Fleming, Lindsay, CP37, *Chichester, a selection of drawings by John Broughton*, Chichester City Council, 1963.
41. WSRO, Add MS 2128. Fleming, Lindsay, 'Pedigree of the Gruggen Family' (u/p).
42. WSRO, Add MS 2123. Apprenticeship Indenture, John Price Gruggen to William Gruggen.
43. WSRO, Add MS 2125. Articles of Agreement, William Gruggen to John Price Gruggen.
44. Chichester City Council. Mayoral boards in the Council Chamber.
45. WSRO, Add MS 2921, *op. cit.*
46. WSRO, Raper M.1.
47. WSRO, Add MS 9008. A measurement of Dearling's land made in 1815 which includes named lands of Mount Noddy, Ratham, Lyewood etc.
48. Sparrow, Giles, *op. cit.*
49. WSRO, Par 42/1/1/4. St Pancras Parish Records.
50. WSRO, Add MS 19794. Deeds to Friary Close.

51. WSRO, Add MS 47457. An attested copy of John Dearling's will.
52. WSRO, Add MS 19796 & 19797. Deeds to Friary Close.
53. WSRO Cutten E3/3. A photograph taken in the garden in 1910 carries the name 'Ivy Bank'.
54. WSRO, Par 42/13/4. The agreement is hand-written and signed by all the parties.
55. WSRO, C/3, *Chichester Common Council Minute Book 1783-1826*.
56. Saunders, Pat, 'Brewers and Malthouses of Chichester' (u/p).
57. *ibid*.
58. Chichester City Council – listing of the coffin plates found in the vaults of Eastgate Hall, March 1999.

CHAPTER TWO, JOHN MARSH – A FOUNDING FARTHER, pp.24-6.
1. Journal, 12 January 1767.
2. Waterhouse, Ellis, *Dictionary of British Art Vol.II – 18th Century Painters*, Antiques Collectors' Club, 1981.
3. WSRO, Par 39/53. Calculations made of the potential income from levying pew rents (see also Chapter Seven, p.??).

CHAPTER THREE, THE ARCHITECT – JAMES ELMES, AND HIS CHICHESTER CONNECTIONS, pp.27-34.
1. Colvin, Howard, *A Biographical Dictionary of British Architects 1600-1840*, John Murray, 1978.
2. *ibid*.
3. *ibid*.
4. *ibid*.
5. WSRO, E35A/1/1. *Proceedings of the Sussex Society of the Committee of the Western Division 1811–83*.
6. McNeil, Hugh, 'Find your ancestors' Chichester Freemasons (u/p).
7. WSRO, Add MS 2936. Deeds to 7 St John's Street.
8. Nairn, Ian and Pevsner, Nikolaus, *Buildings of England – Sussex*, Penguin, 1965.
9. *ibid*.
10. Colvin, Howard, *op. cit*.
11. *ibid*.
12. WSRO, Par 39/25.
13. WSRO, I/4/5/10, Cathedral Chapter Archives.
14. *ibid*.
15. WSRO, I/4/5/12. The Cathedral Chapter Archives relating to the fabric of the cathedral refer to James Baker as 'Surveyor' in 1815.
16. Chrimes, R., Skepton, Sir A., Rennison, R.W., Cox, R.C., Ruddick, E., and Cross-Rudham, P., *Biographical Dictionary of Civil Engineers in Great Britain and Ireland – Vol.1 1500-1830*, Thomas Telford, 2002.
17. Institution of Civil Engineers Archives, 1827. CUNRGS.
18. Hadfield, Charles, *The Canals of South and South East England*, 1969.

CHAPTER FOUR, RAISING THE MONEY – RAISING THE CHAPEL, pp.35-48.
1. WSRO, Par39/64. A bound set of coloured drawings of the Chapel.
2. Steer, Francis, CP 35, *The Church of St John the Evangelist*, Chichester 1813-1963, Chichester City Council, 1963.
3. WSRO, Par39/1. Rough Minutes of Trustees' meetings.
4. WSRO, Par42/4/3. There are two copies of the Act which are catalogued under St Pancras rather than St John's.
5. WSRO, Par39/2. Trustees' Minute Book 1812-1902.
6. Copies of the *Sussex Weekly Advertiser* for 1812 are held on microfilm by West Sussex Library Service at Chichester Library.
7. *ibid*.
8. WSRO, Par 39/22.
9. WSRO, Par39/24. Report by James Elmes to the Trustees, on the completion of the Chapel.
10. Steer, Francis, CP 35, *op. cit*.
11. WSRO Par39/25. One of a bundle of letters from Elmes to the Trustees between September 1812 and January 1814.
12. *ibid*.
13. John Marsh Journals.
14. WSRO Par39/48. A surviving copy of the printed notice.
15. Steer, Francis, CP 35, *op. cit*.
16. WSRO, Par 39/47.
17. WSRO, Par 39/50.
18. WSRO Par 39/2, *op. cit*.
19. WSRO Par39/25, *op. cit*.
20. John Marsh Journals, *op. cit*.
21. Steer, Francis CP 35, *op. cit*. which was compiled from Par 39/30, building accounts 1812-1841.
22. WSRO Par39/25, *op. cit*.
23. WSRO CAP/I/4/5/10. Cathedral Chapter Archives.
24. WSRO Par 39/25, *op. cit*.

CHAPTER FIVE, THE ARCHITECTURE OFL THE CHAPEL, pp.49-61.
1. WSRO, Par39/19. Articles of Agreement between Cooper and the Trustees dated 27 July 1812 contains a specification for the bricks in the schedule.
2. WSRO, Par39/22. Brooks' final account for his works November 1813.
3. WSRO, Par39/19, *op. cit*.
4. WSRO, Par39/22, *op. cit*.
5. Churches Conservation Trust. Hassell, C., Paint analysis carried out for CCT under the direction of Seymour and Bainbridge, December 2001.

6. WSRO, Par 39/2. Trustees' Minute Book 1812-1902.
7. WSRO, Par39/22, *op. cit.*
8. *ibid.*
9. WSRO, Par39/17. Articles of Agreement between Brooks and the Trustees dated 24 July 1812 contains a specification for the joinery in the schedule.
10. WSRO, Par39/22, *op. cit.*
11. WSRO, Par39/17, *op. cit.*
12. WSRO, Par39/2, *op. cit.*
13. WSRO, Par39/22, *op. cit.*
14. WSRO, Par 39/2, *op. cit.*
15. WSRO, Par39/22, *op. cit.*
16. WSRO, Par39/67. A plan of the gallery showing the new box pews. The plan is undated but the minute book refers to the implementation of the scheme.
17. WSRO, Par39/19, *op. cit.*
18. WSRO, Par39/17, *op. cit.*

Chapter Six, Georgian St John's 1813-1830, pp.62-75.
1. WSRO, John Marsh Journals.
2. WSRO, Par39/47.
3. WSRO, Par39/22. Brooks' final account for his work.
4. WSRO, Par39/21. Cooper's final account for his work.
5. WSRO, MP2193. This is a typed compilation of *Hampshire Telegraph* reports on musical events in the area.
6. WSRO, I/17/44 (Diocesan Records).
7. WSRO, Par39/2. St John's Trustees' Minute Book 1812-1902.
8. *ibid.*
9. Steer, Francis, CP35, *The Church of St John the Evangelist, Chichester 1813-1963*, Chichester City Council, 1963.
10. *ibid.*
11. WSRO, Par42/4/2. A document relating to a dispute over the rector's pew in 1780 carries a hand-drawn plan of the Chapel (given as Fig 31 in this book).
12. Rainbow, Bernarr, *The Choral revival in the Anglican Church, 1839-1872*, Barrie & Jenkins, 1970.
13. *ibid.*
14. WSRO, Par39/2, *op. cit.*
15. John Marsh Journals, *op. cit.*
16. *ibid.*
17. WSRO, Par39/2, *op. cit.*
18. O'Neill, Hugh, 'Edited minutes of the Chichester Freemasons Lodge of Harmony' (u/p).
19. John Marsh Journals, *op. cit.*
20. WSRO, Par39/67. A large-scale (¼ inch to 1 foot) plan (u/d) of the whole gallery with pew numbers.
21. WSRO Par39/2, *op. cit.*
22. *ibid.*
23. *ibid.*
24. *ibid.*
25. WSRO, Par39/28. Counsel's opinion in the case Trustees v Elmes.
26. *ibid.*
27. WSRO, Par39/67, *op. cit.*
28. WSRO, Par39/50. Pew rental book 1813-1869.
29. *ibid.*
30. John Marsh Journals, *op. cit.*
31. WSRO, MP2123, *op. cit.*
32. WSRO, Par39/2, *op. cit.*
33. WSRO, Par 39/29. Ledger and Account Book 1811-1851.

Chapter Seven, Victorian St John's 1831-1900, pp.76-95.
1. WSRO Par39/2. Trustees' Minute Book 1811-1902.
2. *ibid.*
3. *ibid.*
4. Steer, Francis, CP35, *Church of St John the Evangelist, Chichester 1813-1963*, Chichester City Council, 1963.
5. Willis, T.G., *Records of Chichester*, 1928 cites the report.
6. Rainbow, Bernarr, *The Choral Revival in the Anglican Church, 1839-1872*, Barrie & Jenkins, 1970.
7. WSRO, Par39/2, *op. cit.*
8. *ibid.*
9. *ibid.*
10. WSRO, Par39/61. Case with opinion of Mr Frederick Merrifield, May 1868.
11. WSRO, Par39/2, *op. cit.*
12. *ibid.*
13. WSRO, Par39/52. A copy of the printed appaeal.
14. Steer, Francis, CP35, *op. cit.*
15. WSRO, Par39/75. St John's Offertory Book, 1875-1894.
16. WSRO, Par39/70. The 'Memorandum Book' contains draft minutes of various meetings, printed accounts and other useful snippets of information.
17. Steer, Francis, CP35, *op. cit.*
18. WSRO, Par39/70, *op. cit.*
19. CDM, Acc 5055/3-1. A bound copy of the *St John's Magazine* for 1880.

20. Clarke, Paul, *The Chichester and Midhurst Railway*, Turntable Publications, Sheffield, 1979.
21. CDM Acc 5055/3-1, *op. cit.*
22. *ibid.*
23. WSRO, Par39/65. A linen original and a dye-line print of the drawing.
24. WSRO, Par39/66.
25. CDM Acc 5055/3. A bound copy of the *St John's Magazine* for 1879.
26. *ibid.*
27. *ibid.*
28. CDM, Acc. 5055/3-1, *op. cit.*
29. Par 39/2, *op. cit.* A copy of the accounts has been pasted into the book.
30. WSRO, AddMS 14316. A valuer's notebook for 1879.
31. CDM, Acc 5055/3, *op. cit.*
32. WSRO, Par39/2, *op. cit.*
33. Steer, Francis, CP35, *op. cit.*
34. *ibid.*
35. WSRO, Par39/70, *op. cit.*
36. *ibid.*
37. WSRO, Par39/2, *op. cit.*
38. Tatum, Jackie, 'The Chapel of St John, Chichester', u/p manuscript (St John's Trustees).
39. WSRO, Par39/59. Conveyance of 68 North Street to the Trustees.
40. WSRO, Par39/2, *op. cit.*
41. WSRO, Par39/70, *op. cit.*
42. WSRO, Par39/2, *op. cit.*
43. *ibid.*
44. WSRO, Par39/70, *op. cit.*
45. WSRO, Par39/2, *op. cit.*
46. *ibid.*
47. Steer, Francis, CP35, *op. cit.*
48. St John's Trustees have a copy of the order of service.
49. Lees, John, 'Organists of Chichester Cathedral' a paper in *The Organs and Organists of Chichester Cathedral*, Phillimore, 1998.
50. WSRO, Par39/2. Printed copies of the accounts for some years have been pasted into the minute book.

Chapter Eight, New Century at St John's 1901-1945, pp.96-105.

1. WSRO, Par39/2. Trustees' Minute Book, 1812-1902.
2. Steer, Francis, CP35, *The Church of St John the Evangelist, Chichester, 1813-1963*, Chichester City Council, 1963.
3. *ibid.*
4. Hobbs, Mary (ed.), *Chichester Cathedral*, Phillimore, 1994, p.138.
5. St John's Trustees; Tatum, Jackie, 'The Chapel of St John, Chichester', u/p manuscript. Cites several of Monti's letters.
6. Steer, Francis, *op. cit.*
7. St John's Trustees, Minute Book 1903-1985. (This is still held by the Trustees.)
8. *ibid.*
9. WSRO, Par39/73. A copy of the specification drawn up by Osborn – there are no drawings.
10. Tatum, Jackie, *op. cit.*
11. Minute Book, *op. cit.* – carries a full transcript of the duties.
12. WSRO, Par39/44. St John's Accounts 1928-1951.
13. WSRO, Par 39/74. A copy of the whole article which was one of a series on local churches and chapels.
14. WSRO, Par39/78. St John's Service registers, 1913-1926
15. St John's Trustees – u/p manuscript.
16. Minute Book, *op. cit.*
17. *ibid.*
18. Hassell, C., 'Report into paint scrape analysis for Churches Conservation Trust', December 2001.
19. Minute Book, *op. cit.*
20. WSRO, Par39/42. Bills and Accounts 1923-1950.
21. *ibid.*
22. Price, Bernard, *Valiant Chichester*, Phillimore, 1978.
23. Mary Hill collection.
24. WSRO, AddMSS 1316 & 1317. These are copies of the timed logs compiled by the ARP.
25. WSRO, Par39/44, *op. cit.*
26. WSRO, Par39/42, *op. cit.* S.T. Clemens' invoice quotes the licence number as 92/WDO/46/622.

Chapter Nine, St John's: Struggle flor Survival, 1946-1973, pp.106-119.

1. St John's Trustees Minute Book 1903-1985.
2. *ibid.*
3. WSRO, Par39/44. St John's Accounts Book 1928-1951 has copies of some of these letters pasted into it.
4. WSRO, Par39/82. A copy of the Order of Service for Steinitz's funeral.
5. Minute Book, *op. cit.*
6. WSRO Par39/44, *op. cit.*
7. *ibid.*
8. WSRO, Par39/50. Trustees' correspondence during the 1950s.
9. Minute Book, *op. cit.*

10. WSRO, Par39/44, *op. cit.*
11. WSRO, Par39/42, Bills for repairs 1923-1950.
12. Steer, Francis, CP 35, *The Church of St John the Evangelist, Chichester 1813-1963,* Chichester City Council, 1963.
13. Minute Book, *op. cit.*
14. *ibid.*
15. *ibid.*
16. *ibid.*
17. *ibid.*
18. WSRO, Par39/80, St John's Service Book 1942-1961.
19. St John's Trustees. Tatum, Jackie, 'The Chapel of St John the Evangelist, Chichester', u/p manuscript. Contains her eyewitness account of the usage of the pulpits.
20. Minute Book, *op. cit.*
21. *ibid.* – the outcome of the meeting is recorded.
22. *ibid.*
23. *ibid.*
24. *ibid.*
25. WSRO, Par39/83. A copy of the Scheme.
26. St John's Trustees, The Accounts Book 1938-1953 has a copy of the notification from the Church Commissioners about the listing pasted into it.

Chapter Ten, Completing Newtown 1831-2000, pp.120-32.

1. CDM, The *Chichester Directories* for 1902 to 1981 list the Sisters of St Margaret as being in residence here.
2. WSRO, AddMS 19779. Friary Close Deeds.
3. WSRO, AddMS 12018. Sale Particulars for the 1896 sale of the estate of Anne Hayllar which included 8 St John's Street.
4. *ibid.*
5. WSRO, Par39/2. St John's Trustees' Minute Book 1812-1902.
6. WSRO, AddMS 7203.
7. WSRO, AddMS 7204.
8. WSRO, Raper 329, includes this conveyance.
9. WSRO, Raper 6. There are several copies of the printed sale particulars, each marked with various annotations regarding the purchasers.
10. WSRO, Ep IX.
11. Saunders, Pat, 'Brewers and Malthouses of Chichester' (u/p) which cites James Atkey's will.
12. McKechnie, Rev. John, *The story of St Pancras and St John's Churches, Chichester,* pub. privately, 2003.
13. Nairn, Ian and Pevsner, Nikolaus, *Buildings of England – Sussex,* Penguin, 1965.
14. WSRO, MP2049. Notes by Roy Morgan on the Booth Rooms cite the sale particulars (see also reference 17 below).
15. WSRO, MP1439. Letter from the County Archivist regarding 20 St John's Street.
16. *ibid.*
17. WSRO, AddMS 6155. These documents, which contained the deeds to 20 St John's Street, were withdrawn from WSRO in 1996. Photocopies of two indentures have since been returned but the remainder, including the 1862 sale particulars (see 14 above), are no longer available for inspection.
18. *ibid.*
19. WSRO, MP1493, *op. cit.*
20. WSRO, AddMS 5295, Chichester Corn Exchange Co. Directors' Minute Book 1905-1919.
21. WSRO, AddMS 2935. Will of William Gruggen Junior.
22. WSRO, AddMS 2125. Articles of Agreement dated 11 September 1841.
23. WSRO, AddMS 2128. Fleming, Lindsay, *Pedigree of the Gruggen family.*
24. Steer, Francis, CP15, *The Royal West Sussex Hospital,* Chichester City Council, 1960.
25. *Victoria County History – Sussex,* vol.ii, p.227 summarises figures for Chichester parishes.
26. CDM, *Chichester Directories, op. cit.*
27. *Chichester Directories* list this as a separate dwelling from St John's House.
28. Land Registry, abstract of the title deeds to Friary Close.
29. Down, Alec, *Chichester Excavations,* vol.2, Phillimore, 1974.
30. Listing published by Chichester District Council.

Chapter Eleven, Commercial Newtown, pp.133-47.

1. WSRO, AddMS 5293. Chichester Corn Exchange Co. Shareholders' Minute Book.
2. Colvin, Howard, *Biographical Dictionary of British Architects 1600-1840,* John Murray, 1978.
3. Nairn, Ian, and Pevsner, Nikolaus, *Buildings of England – Sussex,* Penguin, 1965.
4. Colvin, *op. cit.*
5. *ibid.*
6. WSRO, AddMS 5293, *op. cit.*
7. *ibid.*
8. WSRO, AddMS 12018. The 1831 diary of Edward Humphry who quotes from the *Hampshire Telegraph* article.
9. WSRO, AddMS 5296. Chichester Corn Exchange Co. Directors' Minute Book 1919-1933.
10. Recollections of Mrs Kathleen Stephens.
11. Steer, Francis, CP17, *Some Chichester Tradesmen,* Chichester City Council, 1960.
12. WSRO, AddMS 6155.
13. WSRO, AddMS 5293, *op. cit.*
14. WSRO, AddMS Chichester Corn Exchange Co. Directors' Minute Book 1905-1919.
15. *ibid.*

16. CDM, *Chichester Directory 1908*.
17. WSRO, AddMS 5295, *op. cit.*
18. CDM *Chichester Directory 1923/24*.
19. WSRO, MP 3115. A hand-written memoir of the Sadler business by Mr E. Faith refers to a Sadler workshop at the rear of East Pallant car park which points to this building. Mrs K. Stephens confirms this.
20. For the outline history of The Regnum Press I am indebted to Claire Holder, the Managing Director, and her father Derek Tillyer who supplied information and photographs.
21. WSRO, Par39/42. Bills for repairs etc to St John's Chapel 1923-1950 including the correspondence on this matter.
22. WSRO, AddMS 14372. A valuer's notebook. Item (f) headed, 'Mr Arnold's property, St John's St' covers all three houses.
23. Brown, Edward, *Chichester in the 1950s,* EB Publications, 1996.
24. WSRO, AddMS 35097. 'A Short History of the Chichester Ballet School' (u/p manuscript not attributed but probably by Marian Lombard).
25. St John's Trustees, Minute Book 1903-1985.
26. WSRO, AddMs 35100. The certificate is framed.
27. Wiley, J. and Sons, *Thirty years in Chichester – a celebration*, Wiley, 1997.
28. Woolley, Michael, *The Quakers in Chichester*, Religious Society of Friends, 1998.
29. Green, Kenneth, *Chichester Remembered – a pictorial past,* Ensign, 1989.
30. For information about Stride and Sons I am indebted to Nick Stride.
31. CDM, *Chichester Directories*.
32. Recollections of Chris Kimble and Ian Kimble.
33. CDM *Chichester Directories*.
34. Recollections of Chris Kimble and Ian Kimble.
35. *ibid.*
36. Chris Kimble collection.
37. Recollections of Mrs Mary Hill (née Gough), daughter of Dr J.H.H. Gough.
38. CDM, *Chichester Directories*.
39. *ibid.*
40. For information about Dr J.H.H. Gough and his Chichester associations I am indebted to his daughter Mary Hill.
41. Mary Hill collection.
42. Title deeds to 8 St John's Street.
43. *ibid.*
44. For information on Dr Barford's legacy I am indebted to Ray Oliver of St John Ambulance Brigade, Chichester.
45. WSRO, *Chichester Directories* microfiches.
46. *ibid.*
47. For information about Dr Bostock and the founding of the Langley House Practice I am indebted to Dr Martin Collins.
48. CDM, *Chichester Directories*.
49. The 1962 *Chichester Festival Theatre* programme carries advertisements for both these businesses.
50. Cited in the deeds to 8 St John's Street.

Chapter Twelve, St John's Recession and Restoration, pp.149-54.
1. St John's Trustees Minute Book 1902-1985.
2. *ibid.*
3. *ibid.*
4. *ibid.*
5. Plumley, Nicholas, *St John's Chapel, Chichester*, Churches Conservation Trust, 1994.
6. Minute Book, *op. cit.*
7. *ibid.*
8. Plumley, *op. cit.*

Appendix C, The Organ Specifications, pp.160-61.
1. Renshaw, Martin, *John Marsh, A most elegant and beautiful instrument, The Organ*, privately published, 2002. The specification for St John's organ is quoted.
2. St John's Trustees archive.

Appendix D, The Chapel Plate, p.162.
1. Pickford, Ian (ed), *Jackson's Silver and Gold Marks*, Antiques Collectors' Club, 1989.
2. Steer, Francis, CP35, *The Church of St John the Evangelist Chichester 1813-1963*, Chichester City Council, 1963.
3. WSRO, Par39/2. St John's Trustees' Minute Book 1812-1902.
4. WSRO, Par39/72. An inventory of church plate in the Deanery of Chichester, 1903.

INDEX

References to illustrations only are given in **bold**.

Act of Parliament (St John's Chapel), 9-11, **10**, 36, 41-3, 45, 53, 56, 59, 74, 81, 98, 106, 109, 112, 113, 118, 129, 155, 157, 158
Adcock's Garage, 136, 137, 141
All Saints, Chichester, 4, 9, 74, 129
Altar, *see* communion table
Angel, Mr (organist), 88
Anniversary services, 89, 99, 115
Apedale, Maria, 143, 144, **144**
Archbishop of Canterbury, 4, 10
Archdeacon of Chichester, 32, 65, 107-10, 116, 117, 155
Architecture of St John's Chapel, 49-61
Arnold, Mr, 140
Assembly Rooms, 25, 41, 63, 86
Atkey, Charles John, 91
Atkey, Fred, 87
Atkey, James, Jnr, 22, 125
Atkey, James Snr, 21, 22, 87, 91, 125
Axton, Harry, 151

Bacon, S.C. (warden), 106, 107
Baffins Lane, 135, 136
Barbut, Mrs, 87
Barbut, Rev. Stephen (minister), 15, 16, 21, 65, 68, 77, **79**, 81, 159
Barford, Dr Arthur, 145, 146
Barford House, 146
Barnham Manor, 2, 5
Batcock, John, 17
Bath, 10, 26, 49, 68, 78, 119
Beast market, nuisance from, 21
Beaumont-Thomas, Mrs Iseult, 147
Bell, Bishop George, 106, 107, 110, 111
Bell, chapel, 42, 52, 152
Bennett, Henry (organist), 80
Bennett, Thomas (organist), 64, 68-70, 74, 80, 81, 153, 154
Ben's Gas Company, 136
Binstead, Benjamin, 123, 127, 135

Bishop of Chichester, 4, 27, 35, 38, 43, 44, 62, 65, 78, 81, 91, 93, 97, 106-11, 116
Black Friars, 1, 5, 17, 120, 131
Blisset, Rev. George (minister), 83, 84, 159
Booth, George, 141
Booth Rooms, **139**, 141-2
Bostock, Dr Arthur, 146
Bowers, Nigel, 152
Box pews, 53, 54, 58-60, **58**, 67, 80, 86, **118**
Bradley, Mr (organist), 83
Brereton, Col William, 15, 19
Brighton, 37, 55, 64, 65, 80, 97, 99
Brooks, William, 39-42, 44-6, 48, 51, 58, 62, 63, 72
Browne, Rev. Harry, 124

Campanile, St John's, 52, 102
Campbell, Miss, 130
Canal, Grand Ship, 34
Canal, Portsmouth and Arundel, 5, 34
Canon Gallery, 147
Carter, James, 15, 21
Catholicism, fear of, 68, 70, 79, 96, 97, 100
Ceiling, chapel, 60, 61, 102, 152
Central Sussex Boys' School, 28, **29**, 33, 45
Chapel plate, 162, **162**
Chapel wardens, 25, 70, 71, 73, 82, 86, 90, 99, 106, 107, 118, 122, 157, 158
Chichester Ballet Club, 141
Chichester Cathedral, xiv, 25, 26, 31-3, **32**, 47, 74, 78, 115, 151, 162
Chichester Cathedral Choir, 64-6, 70, 94, 95
Chichester Chiropractors, 147
Chichester Corn Exchange Company, 128, 133, 134, 136
Chichester Festivities, 26, 112, 151-3
Chichester-Midhurst Railway, 84, 85, 89
Chichester Motor Works, 136
Child, Mollie, 141
Choir, St John's, 68, 79-81, 89, 93, 100, 103, 115, **115**; *see also* singing boys

Church Commissioners, The, 108-11, 116, 119, 149

Churches Conservation Trust, The, 26, 61, 149, 150, 152, 153, 155, 156

City Steam Sawmills, 133

Civil War, 4, 5

Clemens, S.T., 103, 105, 111, 112

Closure of St John's (1871-74), 82

Closure of St John's (winter), 117

Closure of St John's (final, 1973), 118-19

Clydesdale House School, 143, **143**

Common Prayer, Book of, 66, 70, 80, 87, 88

Communion table, 55, 56, 65, 67, 79, **104**, 114, 149

Consecration of St John's, 65

Consort of Twelve, 26, 152

Construction costs, chapel, 45

Contractual disputes, chapel, 40, 45-8, 72, 73

Convent Street, 17, 20

Cooper, Charles, 13, 14, 37, 40, 41, 44-6, 49, 63, 72, 102, 123, 125, 127, 133, 138

Cooper Street, 13, 40, 123

Corn Exchange, 120, 133-7, **137**, 141, 142

Corn Exchange Garage, 136, 137

Cowley, Rev. William (minister), 88-92, 159

Creation, The, Haydn, 63

Crosbie, Charles, 23

Crosbie, Frances, 23

Crosbie, Maj. Gen. John Gustavus, 4-7, 15, 19, 21, 23, 27, 120, 127, 133, 135, 147, *endpiece*

Cross Street, 17, 20, 132

Dally, Richard, 6, 7, 11, 126

David Paul Gallery, 147

Dean of Chichester, 4, 5, 35, 62, 85, 96, 98, 152, 155

Dean, William (organist), 88, 90

Dearling, James, 6, 22

Dearling, William, 6, 7, 9, 11, 15, 18, 19, 22, 23, 27-30, 35-9, 46, 48, 75, 121

Derby, 25

Derby, Countess of, 5

Donnington, 2, 4-6, 23, 28

Draper, George, 71-3, 133, 134

Eagle Star Insurance Co., 147

East Street, general, 8, 15, 18, 21, 22, 126, 131, 133-5, 137, 138, 147

East Street, Nos 56/56A, **127**, 141, 147

Eastgate Brewery, 21, 91

Eastgate Chapel, 6, 22, 23

East Pallant House, 15, 120

Eggar, Thomas & Sons, 142

Electric lighting, chapel, 111

Ellerslie, 7

Elliott, John, 133, 134

Elliott, Dr Robert, 124, 146

Elmes, Harvey Lonsdale, 33, 34

Elmes, James, 27-34, 28, 36-8, 40-9, 51-3, 55-7, 59, 60, 71-3, 75, 89, 109, 112, 134, 150, 154, 155, 161

Emmerson, Dr Guy, 146

England, George Pyke, 41

Evangelicalism, 66, 78-80, 84, 86, 89, 93, 96, 97, 100, 107, 108

Evans, Miss, 144, 145

Farndell, Miss, 90, 91

Farr's Depository, 147

Feast days, observance of, 68, 70, 80

Ferris, George, 19

Ferris, Susanna, 19, 121

Ferris, Rev. William (minister), 93, 159

Fielder (builder), 85

Financial problems, St John's, 75-7, 80-4, 89, 92, 93, 95, 98, 113

Fogden, Henry, 12, **13**

Font, St John's, 56

Fookes, John, 19, 121

Foundation stone, chapel, 37-40

Free seats for the poor, 53, 85

Freeland, James, 37, 45, 48

Freemasons, 17, 28, 39, 70

Freemasons' Hall, 17, 33

Friar Street, 20

Friary Lane, buildings: No1, xiii, 14, 15, 130, **131**; No2, 14, **131**; No3, 130, **131**; No4, 130, **131**; No5, 130,**131**; No6, 132; No7, 132

Friary Close, 15, 16, **16**, 19, 66, 78, 120, 121, 130

Friary Lane, general, xiii, 14, 15, 120, 124, 130

Friary Lane, link road to car park, 132

Furnell, Mr (chapel keeper), 99

Furness-Smith, Rev. George (minister), 84-8, 159

Gallery, chapel, 53, 54, 56, **58**, 58-60, 71, 73, 75, 96, 103, 115, 153

Game, Teddie, 143

Garland, Sharp, 142

Garland, Sir Sharp Archibald, 142, 143

Gas lighting, chapel, 61, **61**, 76, 91, 111

Gatehouse, George, 12, 15

Gell, Rev. Francis (minister), 84, 159

Geneva gown, 68, **69**, 99

George Street, 17, 20

Goodman, David, 141, 147
Goodwood Races, 85
Goss, Sir John, 64, 91
Goss, John Jeremiah, 64
Gough, Dr J.H.H., 144-6, **146**
Gough, Mary, 104, 105
Grey Friars, 1
Gruggen, John Price, 17, 18, 128, 129
Gruggen, Rev. George Septimus, 129
Gruggen, William Jnr., 17, 18, 70, 71, 123, 128, 129, 133
Gruggen, William Snr., 12, 17, 18, 70, 71, 76, 80, 127, 128

Hack, James & William, 6, 16
Halsted, Charles, 80
Haviland, John, 30, 45
Hayley, William, 25
Hayllar, Anne, 122
Hayllar, Charles, 84, 122, 135
Heating of chapel, 57, 85, 86, 88, 89, 112
Heckford, Dr Frank, 146
Heming, Rev. G.F., 65, 162
Heming, Samuel, 162
Henty, Douglas, 53, 85, 86, **86**, 88
Heritage Open Days, xiv, 152
Herschel, William, 49
Hoare, Clarence, 110, 113, **114**
Hoare, Miss (organist), 100
Hoare, Mrs, 113, **114**
Hoare, Victor, 100, 102
Hobbs, Henry, 15, 16, 19, 66, 78
Hogarth, William, **63**, 67, 68, **69**
Holder, Claire, 140
Holder, Henry, 102
Holy Communion, 66-8, 79, 80, 97, 114
Home Words, 87, 88
Humphrey, John, 15
Humphrey, Dr Reginald, 122, 144
Humphry, Alfred, 136
Hymnbooks, 80

Incumbents of St John's, list of, 159
Infirmary, Chichester, 71, 129, 134

Johnson, William, 90, 91, 123, 133, **133**
Johnston, Esther, Elizabeth and Mary, 126, 135

Keble, John, 79
Kerwood, James, 127, 128
Kimble, Thomas, 144
Kingsham Farm, 6, 19
Knapp, John (organist), 80, 81

Labour Party, Chichester HQ, 147
Langhorn, Dr Douglas, 146
Langley House Surgery, 146
Lansdowne, G., 146, 147
Lee, Daniel (chapel keeper), 83, 93, 99
Liberator bomber crash, xv, 104, 105, 111
Library, chapel, 87
Lightoler, Thomas, 49
Lindsay, Rev. Alan, 116, 159
Listing of Newtown buildings, 119, 132
Lombard, Marian, 141
Lombard School of Dancing, 141
London, Brighton & South Coast Religion, 80, 96
Lonsdale, James, 28, **28**, 31

McKechnie, Rev. John, 114, 116, 159
Mansion House, East Street, 1, 7, 120, 133
Market Avenue, link road to St John's St, 20, 131, 143
Marsh, Edward, 26, 73
Marsh, Elizabeth, 74
Marsh, John, Jnr (warden), 26, 70, 77
Marsh, John, Snr (warden), xiv, 11, 24-6, 35-7, 40-4, 49, 56, 57, 62-6, 68-75, 99, 129, 153-5, 160
Marshall, Rev. Jack, 110, 111, 114, **114**, 159
Martin, Edward, 14, 123
Mayor of Chichester, 6, 14, 18, 21, 37, 38, 129, 142, 155
Medical practices, Newtown, 144-7
Messiah, Handel, 63, 64
Ministers of St John's, list of, 159
Ministry of Transport, 147
Minute Books, Corn Exchange Co., 134
Minute Books, St John's Trustees, 36, 37, 62, 97, 98, **98**, 117, 122
Missionary work, St John's, 84, 88, 89
Monti, Rev. Joseph (minister), 93, 96, 97, **97**, 107, 159
Moore, J.W., 138, 140
Moore & Tillyer, 138-40, **139**, **140**
Moore & Wingham, 138
Munro, Miss, 144, 145
Murray, Richard, 6, 21
Music Meeting, St John's, 44, 62-5
Mylett, Edward, 1

Nethersole House, 24-6
New Corn Store, 136-7, **139**, 141, 142
New Town (the street), buildings: No1, 12, **14**, 143; No2, **14**, 120, 147; No3, 12, 13, **14**, 120, 147; No4, 13, 147
New Town (the street), general, 20, 120
Newton, Rev. Maurice (minister), 107, 110, 111, 159

Nieville's Garage, 136
North Street, No68, 90, 93, 98, 102, 112, 117
Northlands, 5

Oakwood, 6, 19, 28-30, **30**
Octagon Chapel, Bath, 49
Oil lighting, chapel, 57, 61, 76
Opening of St John's (1813), 62-5
Organ, chapel, 41-5, 50, 60, 62, 68, 71, 73, 81,
    84, 93-5, **94**, 96, 111, 150, 153, 154, 160,
    161, **161**
Organ, chapel, specifications for, 160, 161
Organists, chapel, 64, 65, 68, 70, 80, 81, 83,
    88, 90, 93, 100, 144
Orme, Garton, 1, 2, **3**
Osborne, Noel, 152
Oxford Movement, the, 78-80, 89, 93, 96, 153

Page, Catherine, 3
Page, Edward, 1
Page, John, 1, 2
Page, Frances, 3, 4
Page, Francis, 1
Painted panels, chapel, 24, **24**
Parish Clerk, 67
Paternoster Row, 14, 15, 20
Paull, George, 86, 88, 90
Peay, Miss, 141
Peters, Miss, 147
Population of Newtown, 130
Powell, Eliza, 98
Private pews, 42, **42**, 43, 71, 73, 75, 76, 81, 83,
    85, 111, 123, 133
Problems with chapel fabric, 71-3, 77, 89, 91,
    102, 112, 119, 150
Proprietary chapels, 9, 10, 78, 83, 97, 111, 116,
    119, 155
Pulpit, *see* Three-decker pulpit

Railings, chapel, *frontispiece*, **50**, 53, **126**
Randall, Thomas, 9, 18
Ranking, Rev. George, 125
Redundant Churches Fund *see* Churches
    Conservation Trust
Regnum Press, 138-41
Reopening (1874), 83
Re-pewing, 53-5
Restoration (2003), 55, 153, **153**, **154**
Reynolds, Charles, 13, 14
Richardson, Rev. M.A., 115
Richmond, Duke of, 5, 47, 151
Ridge, Charles, 13, 14, 75, 77, 123, 126
Ridge, William, 6, 12, 17, 35, 36, 126
Robertson-Richie, Douglas, 147

Roman Cement, 51, 52
Royal West Sussex Hospital, 145, 146

Sadler's, corn merchants, 137
St Andrew's, Chichester, 4
St Bartholomew's, Chichester, 4, 5, 134
St Clair, J. (organist), 90, 93, 100
St George's, Whyke, 96
St John Ambulance Brigade, 145, 146
St John's Chapel Group, 152
St John's House, 15, 66; *see also* Friary Close
St John's Magazine, 84, 85, 88, **89**
St John's Mews, 130
St John's School, 105, 144, **145**
St John's Street, buildings: No1, 18, 22, 125,
    127, 131, 140; No2, 18, 22, 125, **127**, 131,
    140; No3, 18, 125, **127**, 131; No4, 122,
    123, 125, 147; No5, 17, 125; No6, 17, 125;
    No7, 17, 125, 127, 128, **129**; No8, 23, 84,
    104, 120-3, **122**, **123**, 125, 135, 144-6, **146**,
    147; No9, 105, 125, 126, 131; No10, 20,
    122, 131, 142; No11, 20, **21**, 123-5, 147;
    No12, 20, **21**, 123-5; No13, 20, **21**, 123-5,
    144, 147; No14, 13, 20, **21**, 123, 124, 146,
    147; No15, 13, 143, 144; No16, 13; No17,
    12, **14**, 143, 144; No18, 17, 147; No19, 127,
    128, **128**, 135, 136; No20, 127, 128, **128**,
    135, 136, 143, 146; Blackfriars House, 18,
    131, 132; Booth Rooms, *see* New Corn Store;
    Cambridge House, *see* No4; Dominican
    House, 132, 147; Hasted House, *see* No18;
    Ivy Bank, *see* No10; Kerwood House, *see*
    No20; Martlet House, 124, 132, 147;
    New Corn Store, 136, 137, **139**, 141, 142;
    Rectory, St Pancras, *see* No9; Regnum Press,
    138-40; Roman House, *see* No8; Southdown
    House, *see* No10; Stable yard, 124; Stocklund
    House, 131, 147
St John's Street, general, 1, 8, 11, 17-22, 52, 120,
    124, 125, 131, 132
St Martin's, Chichester, 4, 130
St Olave's, Chichester, 4
St Pancras, Chichester, 4, 5, 19, 22, 66, 67, **67**,
    97, 107, 108, 110, 111, 114, 116, 125, 126,
    149-51
St Paul's, Chichester, 82
St Peter the Great, Chichester, xiv, 4, 77, 82, 85,
    129, 141
St Peter the Less, Chichester, 4
St Richard Singers, 152
Sales of Black Friars sites, 6, 7, 7, 8, **8**, 9, 11, 18,
    19, 126, 127, 131
Schoolroom, chapel, 86, 90, 95, 98, 99, 105,
    113, 149, 151

Schools in Newtown, 143-4
Scott, Miss B.M., 130
Sennicotts, 29, 30, **31**, 52
Servants' benches, 59, 60
Shareholders, St John's, 9-11, 35, 76, 77, 82, 83
Sherlock, Dean, 4
Sibly, Stephen, 63, 64
Simeon Trustees, 108
Singing boys, 60, 70, 71, 80, 81
Sisters of St Margaret, 120, 130
Smith, William, 142
Somerstown, 7, 20, 23
Spiritualist Church, 147
Staircases, chapel, 57, 58
Steer, Francis, xiv, 115
Steinitz, Rev. Charles (minister), 97-102, 105-07, 112, 128, 159
Steinitz, Paul, 112
Stride & Sons, 20, 142, 143
Stride, W.O., **142**, 143
Stuart, James, 52
Sunday School, St John's, xiii, xiv, 80, 87, 89, 102, 113, **114**
Surplices, wearing of, 68, 70, 99
Swan Inn, 6, 36, 37

Temperance, 85
Three-decker pulpit, **54**, 55, 56, 67, 80, **103**, 114, 115, 117, 153, **154**
Tillyer, Arthur, 138
Tillyer, Derek, 138, 140
Trowel, for laying chapel foundation stone, 38, **39**

Trustees, St John's, 27, 30, 31, 36, 40-2, 44, 45, 47, 48, 53, 55, 60, 65, 68, 71-5, 76-8, 80-95, 96-119, 122, 134, 139, 141, 149-51, 155
Tutte, Sarah, 2

Uniting of benefices, St John's/St Pancras, 106-14
Uniting of congregations, St John's/St Pancras, 115-19

Vick (builder), 89, 91, 98
Voke, Maurice (organist), 144

Walker, Capt., 111, **114**
War damage in Newtown, 49, 104, 105, 111
Weller (upholsterer), 55, 56, 59, 60
White-Thomas, Frances, 4, 5, 6; *see also* Crosbie, Frances
White-Thomas, George, 4
White/yellow bricks, 13, 18, 49, 128
Whitehead, Rev. Edward (minister), 78, 80-2, 159
Wiley, John & Sons, 141, 142
Wills, Richard (organist), 80
Wilmshurst, Thomas, 55
Wilson, Dr, 146
Wilson, Jane, 140, 141
Winding-up of St John's, 81
Wingham, Arthur, 138
Wolland, William, 25, 68, 70
Worthing, 49, 93, 134
Wren, Sir Christopher, 32
Wyatt, James, 43
Wyatt, Lewis, 43, 44

Portrait bust (c.1830s), probably of Lt General Sir John Gustavus Crosbie, the founder of Newtown, one of the Crosbie family memorials in Donnington Church.